Oil, Globalization, and the War for the Arctic Refuge

Oil, Globalization, and the War for the Arctic Refuge

David M. Standlea

State University of New York Press

Published by
State University of New York Press, Albany

For information, address State University of New York Press,
194 Washington Avenue, Suite 305, Albany, NY 12210-2384

Production by Mike Haggett
Marketing by Anne M. Valentine

Library of Congress Cataloging-in-Publication Data

Standlea, David M., 1956–
    Oil, globalization, and the war for the arctic refuge / David M. Standlea.
      p. cm.
    Includes bibliographical references and index.
    ISBN 0-7914-6631-0 (hardcover : alk. paper) — ISBN 0-7914-6632-9 (pbk. : alk. paper)
    1. Petroleum industry and trade—Political aspects—United States. 2. Petroleum—
Prospecting—Environmental aspects—Alaska—Arctic National Wildlife Refuge. 3. Oil well
drilling—Envrionmental aspects—Alaska—Arctic National Wildlife Refuge. 4. Petroleum
Industry and trade—Military aspects—United States. 5. Corporate state—United States.
6. Energy policy—United States. 7. United States—Politics and government—2001– 8.
United States—Foreign relations—2001– I. Title.

HD9567.A4S72 2005
338.2'7282'0973—dc22   2005006025

ISBN-13: 978-0-7914-6631-5 (hardcover : alk. paper)
ISBN-13: 978-0-7914-6632-9 (pbk. : alk. paper)

For My Parents

Contents

Preface

The study of political ecology and resource wars will intensify in the early decades of the twenty-first century. Originally a subfield of academic geography, political ecology is now positioned upon the cusp of innovative interdisciplinary research encompassing diverse approaches in the humanities and social sciences. Global resource wars, interlocking environmental, social, and cultural conflict, global warming, overpopulation, and problems of growth and consumption are all multifaceted topics addressed by the interdisciplinary field of political ecology.

One goal of this book is to explore new research dimensions in coinciding areas of critical globalization studies and political ecology. Concentrated political economic power and the ideology of American-led globalism now necessitate more than ever an application of political ecological knowledge to globalization studies. Political ecology, in essence, is the study of how concentrated political economic power affects environmental, social, and cultural change at multiple spatial levels: the global, regional, and local. It is concerned with the twin themes of ecological sustainability and socio-economic justice, and how these are manipulated and molded by top-down political power.

The following narrative is but a case study, one depiction of a resource war landscape presently enveloping the globe. Raymond L. Bryant and Sinead Bailey produced a seminal work in *Third World Political Ecology*, outlining the major actors involved with resource and development conflicts in the Third World. Bryant contends that it is necessary to place each conflict within the context of the competing actors, whether they be local, regional, national, or external agents (e.g., a transnational corporation). The latter idea is crucial in a study of globalization, for the flow of outside financial and investment capital into local arenas makes it imperative to identify the external actors wielding the financial power.

Bryant identifies the major players: transnational corporations; the multilateral economic institutions such as the International Monetary Fund and

the World Bank (as well as the regional development banks); the environmental nongovernmental organizations (ENGOs); and the indigenous rights
organizations. Bryant's framework inspired my original interest in the multilevel linkage connecting transnational corporate investments, local and
national elites, and the various "oppositional" actors such as the nongovernmental organizations and grassroots, indigenous, and local actors. The narrative of the Arctic Refuge conflict reveals this multilevel and multiactor
scenario or matrix.

Bryant's earlier "Political ecology: an emerging research agenda in third
World-studies" (1992) initially formulates his multiactor structure that becomes the basis of his later work in 1997. In this article he concentrates upon
"naming" the actors in context, especially the Third World states, the First-
Third World interstate relationships, and the all-important transnational
corporations and their complex relationships with the states. This was an
important work in political ecology, for in 1992 many of the phenomena of
the neoconservative corporate global agenda were yet to take place, such as
the free-trade agreements of 1994 and the creation of the World Trade
Organization in 1995.

Bryant foresaw many of the coming conflicts over political economy in
the local to national to global linkage of power chains. He, like other political
ecologists, claims that the field exhibits a "radical perspective on the global
capitalist system, and the futility of all attempts to render that system environmentally sustainable through reformist measures." While traditional political ecology, including Bryant's work, has focused upon the Third World,
one of the challenges in applying this theory to the example of the Arctic
Refuge was to draw parallels in the case of the Gwich'in at the local level to
indigenous and local peoples all over the world now suffering from outside
corporate intrusion, by corporations in collusion with the respective regional
and national governments, such as the state of Alaska and the oil mafia
controlling the Bush administration.

The very nature of monopolistic corporate power, illustrated in the oil
industry, transcends all borders, bearing upon and changing the lives of poor
local populations everywhere, and this growing corporate power is thus rendering "Third World" and "First World" distinctions meaningless. I argue
that the United States is now a militaristic corporate state, rapidly becoming
devoid of public institutions, public policy, public responsibility, public accountability, and public consciousness itself. This supports the notion that the
traditional division between a "democratic" United States and the undemo-
cratic Third World autocracies and dictatorships is now becoming a very
blurred division.

Political ecology has always borrowed heavily from neo-Marxist influences,
and with the argument of the entrenchment of a plutocracy (rule by wealthy

interests that control or greatly influence the government of a society) in the United States, a militaristic corporate state, Marxist theoretical contributions are looking to be quite applicable to a new global structure based on rich and poor structural divisions, transcending Third World and First World state distinctions. The thesis of the U.S. corporate state thus enables one to apply political ecological principles to the Arctic National Wildlife Refuge (ANWR) case, as distinct from using "First World" environmental political analysis, which since the 1970s in the United States focused upon environmental political reform and regulation. The corporations are rapidly dismantling these regulations in the United States, unfortunately rendering the political and environmental landscape to appear more and more like the Third World, always known for corrupt autocracies and political economic elitist cronyism.

Bryant's neo-Weberian multiactor formulation as applied to various cases only enriches the contributions of a neo-Marxist awareness of these global structural economic inequalities now becoming increasingly overt and pronounced. The framework also enables us to name and clarify the "new social movements" involved in these resource conflicts. The ANWR case provides an excellent lens through which to discuss the various defenders of social and environmental justice involved, and whether these interest groups are truly promoting larger social movement goals at a genuinely unifying level of cross-fertilization, or merely pursuing their own political ends and agendas.

This is a narrative of clashing twenty-first century ideologies, a model of global conflict now pitting alternative ideologies against a powerful corporate globalist agenda. I chose to apply a humanistic and literary method to sociopolitical topics and issues with the express intent of providing a philosophical overview of the drama, as if it were a Greek tragedy. Thus the critical narrative paradigm, or method, seemed most consistent with political ecological theory in giving voice to the various actors and their belief systems. The chapters are organized into micronarratives as a qualitative approach to best hear the stories of the actors. The narrative example in qualitative approach fits well with descriptions of multiple actors in a resource conflict.

While the ANWR case is so complicated and involved, I have tried to merely situate some of the main actors, contrasting and comparing their worldviews, values, belief systems, motivations, political tactics, and strategies. Basic interview questions were developed, which applied to all of the expert respondents. The interviews were designed to elicit values and ideas as well as political processes, and by using the same questions as a base—obviously respondents were allowed some latitude, though I abided by the questionnaire—I could later compare and contrast converging and diverging worldviews.

A generic letter of request to interview was mailed to all potential respondents, and generally the pro-oil side of the debate declined or ignored requests for interviews, including even the public offices of U.S. Senator Ted

Stevens and Alaskan Governor Frank Murkowski, as well as the primary transnational oil corporations involved. At least a British Petroleum Alaska vice president professionally responded by phone, politely declining an interview (ExxonMobil and Phillips declined by letter and e-mail, respectively). Ironically, three of the largest corporations in the world, private institutions, were far more professional in declining my requests to interview than the offices of public officials Stevens and Murkowski. United States public officials should be ethically and professionally accountable and responsible to their own citizens. The Arctic Refuge is a national energy and economic security issue and deserves to be discussed in a public forum. Stevens and Murkowski refused to speak to me, an interested citizen, apparently because they disagreed with my stated position. Stevens' Alaskan regional office director would not be interviewed, or even offer to further assist me, having declined an interview by e-mail. Murkowski's Juneau headquarters never responded at all.

The critical narrative approach fleshes out the larger global implications of the local issues through the views of the actors themselves, not from what I imposed upon them. The questions were designed to allow the respondents flexibility in their respective answers. Nevertheless, in my narrative and correlation of the responses, I use the critical paradigm, which analyzes from an advocacy perspective critical of political economic injustice and power differentials.

While I provide a running critical analysis of the various micronarratives in the grand scheme, this does not preclude taking an advocative position with the anti-development voices. To paraphrase social philosopher and activist Howard Zinn, neutrality and passivism merely amount to a collaboration with the political economic elites in power, as spurious development is usually promoted from the top down. The heated nature of the long ANWR battle for the most part precluded my ability to obtain interviews from the pro-oil side, and I was professionally obligated from the outset to explain to possible pro-oil informants that I was taking an anti-development position in my normative argument. If one from the outset designs a research proposal that advocates a position, in this case for the grassroots cause, then one will necessarily be hampered in obtaining a so-called "unbiased" or strictly balanced sample of interviews from both sides. This is primarily a story about unequal power relations, requiring the positioning of a moral stance.

My purpose is to inform my critical approach with the subtleties and complexities of views from the local level. While I am describing the political strategies and tactics, successful and unsuccessful, the ANWR is also a medium through which to view *clashing worldviews, ideas, values,* and *belief systems.* The approach is then philosophical, as well as political and economic. Indeed, if a neo-Marxist interpretation of events and ideas reduces factors merely to the material or economic domain, then ironically the neo-Marxist ideology would coincide with the corporate theology in this larger neo-Weberian scenario of multiple ideological and value systems. In effect, the alternative ideologies depicted in part 2 of this book attempt to dispute the corporate view that all values may be reduced to economic or monetary aims.

In taking the critical approach I have sought to paint a larger philosophical picture of clashing ideologies against a wide canvas of critical globalization studies. By composing a holistic and an eclectic effort, I acknowledge a sacrifice in depth and specialization within the respective chapters. This is foremost an interdisciplinary exploration into the competing ideological claims of our new era, a period of accelerating population growth, resource consumption, pollution, and deterioration in both society and nature.

METHOD AND THE MATRIX OF ACTORS

The organization of this narrative mirrors the actual matrix of participants in the conflict over the ANWR. The chapter sequence portrays the philosophical, ideological, and tactical positions of the actors in the debate. It is important to clarify that this is an extremely complex topic that easily and precariously can spin off into diverse subissues, topics, and other actors. One example is the whole issue of indigenous rights, sovereignty, and the battle for indigenous self-determination. I must from the outset admit a disclaimer. Due to the complexity and long history of the refuge debate, I chose to focus upon a certain aspect of the story: how elitist corporate-political power, in this case, oil, shapes and controls the fate of natural environments as well as the people who depend on those environments for their survival and livelihoods. It is a narrative of top-down (globalist) corporate-political power coming face-to-face with an opposition founded upon grassroots democratic practice, tactics, and strategy.

To illustrate how the various actors view the same event, the chapter organization will literally follow a sequence of "actor perspectives," all the while tying each perspective and segment into an overall linkage of analysis pertaining to the power of the corporate state in the United States and its stark contrast to grassroots democratic practice.

For organizational clarity I begin with a chapter discussing the global dimensions of the conflict, within the theoretical context of corporate globalism and the power elites.

Chapter 2 then explores the historical bases of the debate surrounding the Arctic Refuge and the history of Alaskan oil politics, the environment, and Alaskan indigenous issues against a backdrop of "Manifest Destiny."

Subsequently I include a chapter on the oil companies involved in Alaska and the North Slope, including a brief background on the oil industry. The companies involved are some of the wealthiest and most powerful transnational corporations in the world.

Due to the close relationship between the oil companies in Alaska and the state of Alaska (and the Bush-Cheney administration), chapter 4 entails the central role of the state of Alaska in the bid to open the Arctic Refuge to drilling. As my requests for interviews with the Stevens and Murkowski offices were denied and ignored, respectively, I had no choice but to rely upon published materials for discussion of their positions in this chapter. I did interview three Democratic state politicians from the state of Alaska, and their views are presented in this chapter.

For convenience of sequence, I then include a chapter, "The Culture of Corporate Spin," to exemplify the campaign of disinformation relentlessly purveyed by the lobbying group representing and funded (publicly) by the state of Alaska, "Arctic Power." The director of Arctic Power courteously consented to be interviewed, and the ninety-nine minute in-depth interview certainly provided a summation of the ideological position and worldview represented by this lobbying arm of the oil and state of Alaska pro-drilling coalition. Arctic Power was created explicitly and formally as a nongovernmental organization designed solely to lobby the U.S. Congress to open up the Arctic Refuge for drilling. The ideas, values, and tactics represented in the Arctic Power position and language are fascinating and significant as a window into the mentality and worldview of the neoconservative, oil corporate, pro-unsustainable growth mind-set.

Part 2 sequentially examines the roles and outlooks of the environmental, indigenous, and religious communities involved in the battle, from the anti-drilling perspective. The "Alaska Coalition" fighting the oil development in the Arctic Refuge is an extremely large and complex mix of organizations and interests representing an array of overlapping and diverging philosophical positions, though bound by a common denominator of political purpose and tactics.

While this organization of actors by chapter is somewhat arbitrary, it provides the least confusing way to approach this diverse and complex issue. My intent is not to echo the many books and theses written on the actual mechanics of the ANWR battle as an insular issue, an extremely popular topic for writers and academics. My purpose is to examine the elemental positions of the primary representative actors—not all, of course, since there are over 600 groups in the Alaska Coalition alone—and to view these overlapping and diverging positions within an overarching context of corporate globalism and political ecology.

Importantly, regarding methodology, this is foremost a normative argument and approach, taking the position of the clear underdog, in this case the coalition of groups fighting big oil and their political front men. Still, there are many groups and voices in this debate, from both sides, with complex and often subtle arguments that defy easy explanation. It is impossible to include the majority of them, and I admit that I have chosen only a few major voices. It is also difficult if not impossible to approach this heated issue as an impartial academic "equally" analyzing the views and perspectives. I chose this issue because it exemplifies a classic battle of democratic grassroots interests fighting some of the most powerful companies in the world, companies causing great harm to global environments and local populations of (often indigenous) economically disadvantaged peoples. It is impossible to not take a normative and moral position by the very nature of the debate and discourse. I had to walk a fine line to courteously request interviews with pro-oil actors who knew up front my position, as professional ethics and honesty were required at all times. Still, there was a catch-22 in obtaining those interviews due to the nature of my normative position, and because this issue has become so emotionalized and heated between the two sides.

Acknowledgments

I would like to express my gratitude to anthropologist Dr. Leslie E. Sponsel, who deserves special recognition for his outstanding dedication, support, and assistance over the entire tenure of this project. Without his dedication, this work would never have reached fruition. His pursuit of excellence in teaching and research continues to inspire me.

I am indebted to Dr. Manfred Steger in political science for providing valuable assistance in reviewing the manuscript and in suggesting needed revisions relevant to political economy and critical globalization studies. Dr. Peter Manicas offered key insights concerning global political economy and social movements.

I also thank the Bishop of Alaska, Mark MacDonald, for his cooperative support and positive review of the manuscript. Dr. Barbara Johnston, director of the Center for Political Ecology at the University of California, Santa Cruz, was kind enough to volunteer her time to read the manuscript and provide helpful suggestions concerning revisions.

This book would not have succeeded without the unqualified and enthusiastic cooperation of key informants in Alaska who provided a set of outstanding interviews. Alaska State Representative Sharon Cissna, Sara Chapell, Bob Childers, Kim Duke, Richard Fineberg, Scott Fisher, Andrew Keller, Alaska State Representative Beth Kertulla, retired Alaska State Congressman Jay Kertulla, Reverend Karen Lipinczyk, Bishop of Alaska Mark MacDonald, Sean McGuire, Chanda Meek, Mary Ellen Oman, and Kelly Hill Scanlon made this work possible. Project Underground in Berkeley, California, provided an insightful interview.

I thank Evon Peter and the Gwich'in Athabascan of Arctic Village, Alaska, for their invitation to visit their village: without their cooperation, the story of the Arctic Refuge is incomplete. The story of the Arctic Refuge is ultimately about Gwich'in courage and fortitude.

Finally, my thanks to Pete Rafle of the Wilderness Society for sending me outstanding environmental scientific published reports on the Arctic Refuge, and to the Wilderness Society for giving me permission to use its copyrighted map of the Alaska National Interest Lands Conservation Act. Richard A. Fineberg generously provided his chart when comparing possible Arctic Refuge oil production to U.S. oil consumption over the period 2002–2050. The United States Geological Survey was most cooperative in providing me with extensive published material involving various geological and biological scientific assessments of the Arctic Refuge.

Part 1

Oil and the Corporate State

Chapter 1

Globalism, Oil, and the Power Elites

Now to be sure, neither expansion nor conquest of nature was unknown
before the onset of the capitalist world-economy in the sixteenth century. . . .
What we mean by historical capitalism is a system in which the institutions
that were constructed made it possible for capitalist values to take priority,
such that the world-economy was set upon the path of the commodification
of everything in order that there be a ceaseless accumulation of capital for
its own sake.

—Immanuel Wallerstein, *The End of the World As We Know It*

In the coming decades the twenty-first century will increasingly become
characterized and understood as a period of stark and fundamental historic
transition. This transition will likely be characterized by escalating and often
violent resource conflicts throughout the world. These conflicts will be precipitated by an expanding human population guided by an overarching economic
growth agenda and worldview proselytized by the current economic and corporate elites primarily centered or originating in the United States of America.[1]

The battle is on for the earth's remaining natural resources, and unprecedented expansion of human population coupled with an American-style
propagation of an unlimited economic "growth paradigm" is forcing a critical
historic transition. This epochal change or transition may become portrayed
as a descent into ever-expanding violent conflict, chaos, and anarchy fueled
by ruthless competition over Earth's remaining natural resources. It is unlikely
that the current state of affairs and rate of greed and acquisition, especially
characterizing American economic consumption, will prevail at this pace
without forcing severe environmental and social conflict and chaos.

3

The term *globalization*, withstanding its plethora of interpretations, definitions, and approaches, may be understood within the context of my argument as a primarily American corporate and economic elitist view of the world that perceives the world's remaining resources—especially fossil fuels, and specifically oil and gas—as commodities for the taking by the strongest and the richest. In the worldview of American-led global capitalism, the remaining and rapidly dwindling fossil fuel resources are sources of huge profits propelled by rising prices and consumer demand at home. Wealthy elites in the oil industry, in conjunction with their political and military allies and cronies, are scouring the globe to locate, extract, and transport dwindling oil and gas resources to their increasing numbers of demanding consumers, especially American consumers.

In this book I argue on the theoretical level that globalization, for its various interpretations, is fundamentally a twenty-five-year story about the ascendance of business values and practice over the practice of public politics and government, the co-optation or takeover of democratic and representative government by business, financial, and corporate elites.[2] This is a crucial assumption, that the U.S. national government is now a corporate state, whose increasingly privatized corporate military, funded by the average American taxpayer, is enforcing corporate global strategies to secure the remaining stores of natural resources, mostly in the form of oil and gas.[3]

If the invasion and attempted colonization of Iraq is not entirely about the seizure of up to 225 billion barrels of possible oil reserves, then it certainly is a significant part of the strategy, and likely was discussed and planned during Vice President Dick Cheney's fourteen-week energy task force in the spring of 2001.[4] The foreign policy of the neoconservative oil corporate Bush administration centers upon the targeting and seizure of oil and gas resources. The U.S. federal government is an oil government, staffed by former (and future, once they leave office) oil company executives and board members.

There does not appear to be a more crucial subject at this time in history than the nexus of two issues: how multinational corporations and big money are buying and influencing politicians and affecting policy decisions—destroying the processes of good public governance—and how the energy industry, exemplified by the big oil monopolies, is fighting with all of its financial power to keep the level of power and profit to which it has become accustomed throughout the twentieth century, the "oil century."

The almost exponential expansion of oil exploration and production for profit is causing parallel dramatic escalations of conflict mostly throughout the developing world, from the Middle East to Africa to Southeast Asia to South America. Oil production is on the decline, and according to expert energy analysts, energy derived from oil and gas will soon begin to decline by

2 percent a year, causing massive direct and indirect economic and social hemorrhages to industrial society.[5] Because of this decline, oil companies are desperately searching the globe for new and economically viable production and transportation opportunities. Expanded exploration and production is in turn causing an increasing number of conflicts with local and/or indigenous populations that are "in the way" of these proposed start-ups for oil and extraction.[6] Unfortunately, given an (American) economic growth worldview applied to political decision making, these fossil fuel resource wars are only going to get worse, as the wealthy appropriate the resource profits for themselves at the expense of local populations, and ultimately the planet. Resource conflicts are endemic to the developing world, as transnational corporations, exemplified by the oil companies, take advantage of weak or nonexistent national government labor and environmental regulations—weak law—and acquire crucial influence among national, regional, and local political elites enabling access to the resources.

CORPORATE GLOBALISM AND POLITICAL ECONOMY

This book assumes that global (fossil fuel) resource wars will dramatically escalate over the upcoming decades of the twenty-first century. My argument and discussion will address two primary theoretical questions. First, *who* is causing these wars or conflicts, that is, where does the true power lie? I argue that the private corporate sector is really in power, using political elites as front men to further its profiteering interests. That is, if democracy ever did exist in the United States—and it never did for indigenous peoples or black slaves—at present it has surely denigrated into a corporate state. Big business dictates policy to political front men and uses the Pentagon as its global police force. No corporate sector better embodies this process at present than the oil industry, and a discussion of the Alaska case is used as a rather bold, clear example of how a resource war is precipitated by economic elites and their powerful political allies.

Much of my argument involves the *naming* of the top-down hierarchical power structure and cause in these conflicts, naming the private corporate powers behind the political fronts, thus describing the corporate state.[7] Second, who is fighting this development and appropriation of resources, and what are they fighting for? Thus while the first question entails the naming of the political-economic power structure and the corporate elites, the second question confronts the fundamental clash over worldviews and a discussion of why and how these values and ideologies collide. What is at stake are deeply opposed worldviews concerning how humans perceive and interact with nature and other humans, and this places local struggles over development and resource conflicts within ever-expanding spatial contexts at the regional, national, and global levels.

The "anatomy" of resource conflicts reveals a concentration of elite political-economic power motivated by private profit, in stark contrast to those visions promoting public-spirited ecological sustainability and decentralized, local forms of grassroots democratic practice. A primary goal of this book is to portray clashing twenty-first century ideologies against the wide canvas of globalization. Globalization has been variously characterized by leading theorists, covering a diversity of perspectives. The term *globalization* itself is problematic, as it poses a myriad number of definitions and approaches as there appear to be new ideas, social movements, manufactured forms of knowledge and information, and plural forms of cultural and social identities. One scholar has used the term to denote "a compression of time and space."[8] Indeed, the almost dizzying effects of meteoric technological advancement in communications and transportation, the global flow of unprecedented amounts of capital and investment, and unprecedented numbers of human beings migrating across cultural and state boundaries all culminate in a compression of time and space not seen in the 100,000-year history of human civilization.

My purpose in this book is to focus upon one defining element that has shaped and driven the process of globalization. Manfred Steger, a preeminent scholar in critical globalization studies, calls this defining force "globalism," and he crucially distinguishes it from the broader and often inchoate term *globalization*. Globalism, asserts Steger, refers to a specific political-economic ideological project manufactured and promoted by neoliberal or modern classical Anglo-American economic interests. I use the term *neoconservative* throughout this book to convey the same meaning. Steger points out that in the past three decades,

> Anglo-American proponents of the nineteenth-century market utopia have found in the concept of "globalization" a new guiding metaphor for their neoliberal message. The central tenets of neoliberalism include the primacy of economic growth; the importance of free trade to stimulate growth; individual choice; the reduction of government regulation; and the advocacy of an evolutionary model of social development anchored in the Western experience and applicable to the entire world.[9]

The "evolutionary model of social development" is akin to what I refer to as "Manifest Destiny" in later chapters, which logically extends to what Andrew Bacevich calls "Pax Americana," derived from a parallel to Roman imperialism.[10] Pax Americana consists of nothing less than an American political-economic-militarist effort to spread and enforce American liberal democratic capitalism across the globe. It is corporate-militarist globalism, securing consumer markets, by force if necessary.

Steger argues that the globalist neoliberal project is in essence one ideology of many in the constellation of globalization. The neoliberals or neoconservatives have merely harnessed a sophisticated public relations machine—propaganda, in Noam Chomsky's analyses—to convince a naïve public that laissez-faire liberal capitalist ideology is actually nothing less than an end point of history, a culmination of natural scientific process and evolution. The mistake, Steger would argue, is to confuse a political economic ideology with some kind of inevitable evolutionary process interpreted through a lens of scientific method.

Thus the Anglo-American global capitalist agenda is but one competing ideology, not a teleological culmination of historical grand design in the twenty-first century. My purpose in this book is to illuminate the presence of some important alternative ideologies to this powerful globalist agenda, as witnessed in one case study. The need to peacefully and ideologically confront and challenge the American corporate-militarist project, Pax Americana, in the upcoming years will determine for the most part the type of world succeeding generations will find themselves living within. It is this second great global force, public civil society, in Chomsky's view, that poses the greatest threat to the legitimation of the corporate-political-military power elites.[11]

Sociologist Amory Starr's theory on anti-globalist resistance movements provided initial inspiration for the development of this work. Six concepts describe Starr's understanding of global corporate economic development in the Third World, concepts that apply to indigenous societies in the First World as well: growth, enclosure, dependency, colonialism, anti-democracy, and consumption.

In summary, economic growth threatens to destroy global ecological systems as the South attempts to industrialize at accelerated rates to match the North, and as northern transnational corporations work to exploit natural and human resources in the Third World. China is a perfect example of this phenomenon, especially in its meteoric rise in oil use, thus contributing to global warming at accelerating rates.

Global corporations either purchase local land or work with local allies in these countries, displacing indigenous farmers or forest peoples, "enclosing" the natural resources for the benefit of exports and consumers in developed countries. The ANWR case fits this model, but it may be narrowed to the analysis of political-economic control over nonrenewable fossil fuel resources in indigenous lands, a phenomenon taking place all over the world.

In the dependency concept of the model, indigenous populations become dependent upon introduced monied economies, providing cheap labor for foreign corporations, and this economic colonialism thus becomes anti-democratic. In

Starr's model, consumption accompanies economic growth as an ideology, a cultural form of consciousness, destroying—subtly—indigenous or local traditions and legacies, often spiritual and religious, in the face of homogenous consumer acculturation and the commodification of human beings. These factors all apply in varying degrees to the ANWR story, to the "corporate and anti-corporate natives." This model is relevant to tying corporate activity to the direct and often indirect economic abuses of indigenous or local peoples and cultures throughout the world.

THE TWENTY-FIRST CENTURY POWER ELITES

Starr's economic growth and enclosure concepts align with current and future goals of the Anglo-American oil-military power complex. The major oil corporations are utilizing military power to forcibly take oil and gas fields throughout the world, relying upon outright force once peaceful economic enclosure becomes impossible. Iraq is the prime example, however, U.S. military force is supporting oil company aims on all continents—U.S. military bases, advisors, and private military firms are guarding oil sites and pipelines in Columbia, the Caspian region, Africa, the Balkans, and the Middle East. In Burma, Unocal just hires the local military dictatorship to take care of "security."[12]

Throughout this book I refer to the U.S. "oil-military complex." It is a twenty-first century force of unprecedented economic and technological power. Perhaps no theoretical work better predicted this monopoly of political-economic power than C. Wright Mills' *The Power Elite*, first published in 1956. In Mills' analysis of the American elite decision makers, a triad of power largely inaccessible to the middle and lower levels of society is outlined. This elite of corporate executives and lawyers, military generals, and politicians in the executive branch forms an interlocking directorate overseeing vastly enlarged and centralized economic, military, and political hierarchies. These institutional domains are structural in the sense that individuals are for the most part absorbed into their respective yet overlapping value systems.

At mid-twentieth century, Mills was actually writing about the U.S. corporate-military globalism of the twenty-first century. The corporate-military-political executive directorate encapsulates U.S. domestic and foreign policy alike, driving corporate globalism. The "higher circles" of these three institutional hierarchies are for the most part fluid and interchangeable, as corporate executives, generals, and politicians in the executive branch work in a revolving door, moving freely among the three domains. In 1956, Mills was careful to avoid characterizing this triad of elite decision making as being perfectly conspiratorial or always unified in its goals, values, and policy making.

However, the corporate monopolization of economic power of the late 1990s and the early twenty-first century dwarfed anything seen at the time of Mills' writing. Many of the top corporations at the time merged in the late 1990s, and some of the prominent ones are the subjects in this book. These oil companies now wield enormous political-economic power and are more closely allied with the military elites and political front men in Washington, D.C., than ever before. In this sense, Mills foresaw the future.

Mills' theory of the elite triad is relevant for any study of the oil-military complex today and the upcoming decades, as the key lies in the relative power of each domain relative to the other two. Corporate monopolization and control over the political domain is not new to the neoliberal globalist project of the past thirty years since the late 1970s, for corporations exerted great control in the United States from circa 1890 until the early 1930s and the New Deal. And contrary to other analyses, Mills did not believe that the political domain of the New Deal era clearly reestablished control over the corporate domain but merely equalized relations, infusing a balance of interests such as labor into the political mix.

With the advent of World War II, and the succeeding Cold War until 1989, the U.S. military rose to unparalleled levels of power, and in the globalist era it has come to dominate the international arena. Through the progression of American history, as noted by Mills, the political domain has diminished in power relative to the corporate and military sectors: "Insofar as the structural clue to the power elite today lies in the political order, that clue is the decline of politics as genuine and public debate of alternative decisions."[13] Mills believed that since 1939, the attention of the power elite directorate shifted from domestic toward international affairs, and that "Since the governing apparatus of the United States has by long historic usage been adapted to and shaped by domestic clash and balance, it has not, from any angle, had suitable agencies and traditions for the handling of international problems."[14] In Mills' diagram of the power triad, then, the U.S. military filled that political vacuum to essentially take a dominant role in international affairs and U.S. foreign policymaking, along with the corporate "chieftains." Thus today we see the corporate oil-military complex as the primary driver of policy in the political executive branch. Mills' corporate chieftains and "warlords" wield the political power. Chalmers Johnson and Bacevich refer to these military warlords as the new Roman "proconsuls," exerting enormous political decision-making ability in global affairs.[15]

We may view the corporate oil-military complex in light of Mills' concept of the American "permanent-war economy and a private-corporation economy":

American capitalism is now in considerable part a military capitalism, and the most important relation of the big corporation to the state rests on the coincidence of interests between military and corporate needs, as defined by the warlords and the corporate rich. Within the elite as a whole, this coincidence of interest between the high military and the corporate chieftains strengthens both of them and further subordinates the role of the merely political men. Not politicians but corporate executives sit with the military and plan the organization of the war effort.[16]

In this view the military capitalism of private corporations exists within a weakened and merely formal democratic system "containing a military order already quite political in outlook and demeanor":

> Accordingly, at the top of this structure, the power elite has been shaped by the coincidence of interest between those who control the major means of production and those who control the newly enlarged means of violence; from the decline of the professional politician and the rise to explicit political command of the corporate chieftains and the professional warlords; from the absence of any genuine civil service of skill and integrity, independent of vested interests.[17]

Eerily, this describes the American political-economic landscape today, sixty years after its writing. The corporate-military elites become more unified in dramatic fashion, for example, in dominating the world for the last fossil fuel reserves, while mid-level political interest groups and politicians battle each other to perpetual stalemates, and the lower-level masses remain fragmented and oblivious to a sophisticated propaganda machine designed to draw attention away from the secret decisions made by the elites. This is a theory of American political-economic power, and as such it is highly relevant to any discussion of twenty-first century corporate oil-military globalism, as well as the competing ideologies challenging such a liberal capitalist global order, the Manifest Destiny of Pax Americana. This "American Peace" is already precipitating violent resource wars across the globe, conflicts eliciting deep-seated ideological, political-economic, and cultural clashes.

SCALE AND SIGNIFICANCE OF THE ARCTIC REFUGE

This book focuses upon one of those wars, perhaps the most widely recognized and prominent resource conflict in the United States over the past thirty-five years. It has certainly intensified over the past decade to reach a level of white-hot polarization of values, ideas, emotions, and political strategies and tactics, all culminating in what I argue is a conflict representative of a fundamental clash of the German *weltanschauung,* the term for world outlook, or worldview.[18]

The battle or resource war over the ANWR is far more significant both on a global level and on a historic level—in spatial and temporal scope— than is typically portrayed as the fight to protect public, federal, and wilderness lands against development interests in industry and politics. Indeed, it is comprised of the uniquely American environmental battle to protect wild public lands from development, however, it symbolizes much more. It is far more representative of this critical juncture in our historical period, the "transition point" as it were between two roads: the choosing of hopeful values and socially and ecologically sound visions for our future relationships to other human beings and the natural world, along with just political-economic policies to implement these values, versus the current values and policies instilled by economic elites to garner greed and profit at the expense of the human poor and disadvantaged, as well as the destruction of the natural world, including nonhuman species of life.[19]

The Arctic Refuge "war" takes on real and symbolic value of historic and global significance and needs to be understood in context of global (spatial) and historical (temporal) scales for its value as a precursor for events to come. The war of values and ideas over the refuge, and the political tactics stemming from those contrasting ideologies, is a model or blueprint for resource conflicts in the era of corporate globalization, where wealthy and powerful economic elites use their political "front men" to pursue and obtain favorable political policy decisions and corporate subsidies—paid by the public—favoring business elites. No example is clearer or more apropos at present than in viewing the relationships between oil companies and national politicians in the United States.

It may be, and it has been argued, that Third World political ecology, or the study of how powerful transnational political-economic elites exploit and degrade natural environments as well as the poor peoples who live in those environments, cannot be applied to a conflict in the developed world, such as the United States.[20] I argue that it may certainly be applied, for the plight of the Gwich'in Athabascan indigenous people at the heart of the conflict in the refuge is little different than that of any materially disadvantaged, locally based community around the globe currently targeted by oil and gas development.

The Arctic Refuge has not entailed overt violent conflict—yet. Its remarkable and unique characteristic among global "resource wars" is precisely because the vast coalition defending the refuge and the indigenous people fighting oil development in that area has been so successful to this day. The success story of the anti-development alignment of environmental, indigenous, religious, labor, investment, and national political congressional actors makes the apparently nonviolent refuge conflict a special model in the study of resource conflicts, by virtue of its popular and grassroots democratic action and mobilization network and appeal to the legal and political process at the national level. Activists long involved in the issue emphasize that the battle to deter oil development in the refuge has been nothing short of a "miracle" in the face of incredible political-economic power, some of the most powerful and richest forces in the world.

ASSAULT ON THE DEMOCRATIC PROCESS BY WEALTHY ELITES

Still, the refuge may be developed at any time in the relative near future, given the change in just one or two votes of a neoconservative-controlled Congress, specifically the Senate, where the proposals to drill have been stopped time and again. Thus the future of the refuge, like any pristine natural area in the world inhabited by indigenous peoples affected by oil development, is tenuous at best, given the profit-crazed agenda by the federal oil administration now in control. The only reason the Arctic Refuge has remained unscathed to date is due to an amazing and a dedicated phalanx of diverse nongovernmental organizations that have labored long and tirelessly to lobby congressional members and to educate the general public all over the country as to the long-term significance of saving a natural area, its wildlife, and the entire culture of an indigenous people whose very way of life personifies the principles of sustainability and subsistence in contrast to short-term economic greed and growth.

A political ecological approach to resource conflict in the United States is applicable at this point in history, precisely because democratic processes and honest representative government have been severely weakened and continue to be weakened by the power of big money corrupting the political process, just as in the traditional developing or "Third World." Concerning political corruption, I argue that the United States is rapidly coming to demonstrate political qualities that have always characterized developing countries, exhibiting the same patterns of an utter disregard for democratic process and the respect for a fair and an uncorrupted legal system. In the terms of one activist, the "violence of money"[21] is thoroughly corrupting a relatively sound constitutional structure. The financial interests and obligations of elected and appointed public officials are quickly dismantling any respect for representative government and accountability to those politicians' constituents.

For example, three weeks prior to the 2004 presidential election, the U.S. Senate, by a bipartisan vote of 69 to 17, voted for a $136 billion reduction in corporate taxes. Heavily lobbied by business, the Senate replaced a $50 billion export tax subsidy for corporations such as Boeing, Microsoft, and Caterpillar with an across-the-board $77 billion corporate tax cut for manufacturers and a

$43 billion cut for companies operating overseas.[22] In response to complaints by the European Union regarding the export tax subsidy extended to benefit U.S. corporations such as Boeing and Microsoft, the World Trade Organization ruled against the subsidies. In turn, the U.S. Senate and House of Representatives cut the $50 billion subsidy, replacing it with the $77 billion and $43 billion tax cuts. The tax cuts for the overseas operators will greatly benefit the energy companies and the military corporate contractors, further enriching the power elites at the expense of the public. General Electric alone will benefit from an $8 billion tax cut over ten years. The U.S. Congress, with a strong bipartisan vote, demonstrated that its members have degenerated into mere corporate salesmen, contradicting any notion that public representative government still exists. Unfortunately, many of these "public officials" are part of a revolving door, moving freely back and forth between their public and private corporate positions.

With the state of the current U.S. government and political economy, we are witnessing an unprecedented abuse of public power for private interests. The contemporary account of American corporate globalism, as well as that of the Arctic Refuge as one example here "at home," is the sophisticated and devious use by economic elites of front individuals, groups, organizations, and politicians to shift attention away from (secretive) corporate activities, to remain anonymous and unnoticed in the face of civil and public scrutiny. The secretive strategies and tactics displayed by the pro-energy Bush-Cheney administration are unprecedented in conservative or Republican American politics, simply because the "public" federal government is operating exactly as private corporations and business have always operated, in secret, unaccountable to public view, working overtime to circumvent public laws.[23]

Importantly, this subversion of the public democratic process bears greatly upon a discussion of the Arctic Refuge as a case study of political economic power exerting its will to change a physical environment and adversely affect a 30,000 year-old indigenous culture purely for an immediate profit for a current generation of people, and a few people at the top, to be specific. Any political ecological analysis of a resource conflict must take into account, above all, the top-down nature of the conflict and the resistance from "below" to elitist money power propelling the unsustainable development. It involves the essential battle between authoritarian and centralized power versus the horizontal democratic process, two fundamentally different sets of values and subsequent political tactics to achieve those values.

FUNDAMENTAL CLASH OF WORLDVIEWS, IDEAS, AND VALUES

The battle over the Arctic Refuge has portrayed the supreme war over public relations, using words and ideas in lieu of guns as weapons, with the pro-oil development and anti-development sides passionately arguing their respective positions. On its face, the Arctic Refuge represents a classic pitched battle between economic growth and environmental conservation. This is indicative of a general polarized split that we have seen in environmental politics in the United States ever since the early 1970s, when environmental regulation, whether in the form of pollution control (e.g., the Clean Air and Water acts) or public lands and wilderness protection, received great levels of support in Congress and the executive administrations, especially the Carter administration. The argument concerning development and environmental politics in the United States has usually been one framed by an either/or debate, as in allowing one of two options, either blatant unsustainable economic growth, or the opposite, protecting wild lands set aside from human and industrial intrusion, that is, preservationism.

We can still see this either/or "particularly American" mentality in the Arctic Refuge war of ideas, coming from the traditional pro-growth (in this case, oil) position and the traditional environmental community's stand on wilderness and wildlife protection. However, this is where the significance of the Arctic Refuge case becomes much more complex and murky given present and future realities of issues, including indigenous rights, human rights, and social justice, more generally, as well as what it means to live in ecologically sustainable local habitats and communities, both in rural and suburban and urban areas.

If we probe the basic, deeper values—worldviews— of the actors and participants in the Arctic Refuge debate, we come up with much more complex and subtle revelations concerning the nature and purpose of development and the very relationship at stake between humans and the nonhuman natural world. The Gwich'in Athabascan presence in the matrix of actors in the Arctic Refuge truly gives the case a different quality than would be present if this were just about developing oil or saving wildlife and what traditional American environmentalists view as separate "wilderness," the latter being viewed as some primitive as yet uncivilized area still protected from the groping hands of an American unlimited growth worldview depicted in the notion of "Manifest Destiny."

The unlimited growth paradigm of development ideas, personified in the pro-oil actors in this story, is the polar opposite of the pro-wilderness view, however, it could be argued that both are products of a distinctly Euro-American industrial and Christian dominion worldview that sees "nature" as something entirely separate from human society, whether it be conquered and "tamed" (pro-economic growth) or put aside from human intrusion. The interesting and subtle aspect of the refuge debate brings in the indigenous piece of the puzzle, and what that piece signifies not only to the other actors in the issue but to the overarching significance of the debate in temporal and spatial terms, or "future history" and global meanings.

The whole issue of ecological sustainability, whether in rural or urban settings, involves the traditional idea of humans living in some kind of inseparable balance with their natural surroundings, with balance and relative equilibrium being the key concepts. In this sense, the indigenous voice in the Arctic Refuge debate represents far more than just asking congressional officials to save the caribou, which the Gwich'in have subsisted upon for hundreds of generations. The Gwich'in, I learned in my brief visit to their village above the Arctic Circle, represent and signify a most profound message for our future global world, and this concerns what it means to be sustainable in all of the forms inherent to that term, as well as locally self-sufficient and self-determined socially and politically. Both of these aspects, sustainability and local self-determination, stand powerfully as representations flying in the face of a global capitalist agenda engineered by American economic elites.

Physically, and on the face, the battle for the refuge appears to be another traditional fight between American neoconservative Republicans pushing a pro-growth economic agenda and traditional American environmentalists seeking wilderness protection. However, what is at stake in this representative battle is a model of ideas and proposals for the future, proposals for living in sustainable balance with our differing natural geographical environments as well as instructing us how to live locally politically and socially (relatively to be realistic) self-reliant lives actually demonstrative of democratic process. The Gwich'in set of values starkly contradicts everything representative about American global capitalism and the latter's control of distant, local communities through the use of centralized networks of political-economic power.

The case of the Arctic Refuge and its stage of actors is an excellent lens through which to view our future history and the coming conflicts between competing worldviews and values that truly cut to the core of diverging and converging human psychosocial belief systems. The incredible political polarization of the debate, and the heated emotions involved, which I experienced firsthand in my two visits to Alaska over two summers, has to point to something far deeper at stake in the psyches of the actors, of global and future historical dimension. It is important to see the amazing local, regional, and national political and information battle over a remote area of land on the Arctic coast as nothing less than a battle against global capitalism, with historical importance.

What is at stake is not merely how many barrels of oil might be pumped out of the refuge to fill up gas tanks in Southern California, or whether the refuge might be developed with a minimal "human footprint" as the pro-drilling adherents argue. They do not get the big picture, for they are still ensconced within that very American belief system comfortable with the unconscious conviction in one's inexorable right to exploit and dominate nature for economic profit. The symbol of the Iroquois nation belief of "seven generations" is really what is at stake: future sustainability for future generations of children and their descendents. What is the growth paradigm leaving to those future generations? At present rates of climate change, environmental devastation, and unmitigated consumption of the diverse natural resource base globally, the "tragedy of the commons" appears to be the fate of the future planet as a whole: too many people swallowing the propaganda of economic elites preaching unlimited growth, rapidly destroying resources and creating chaos with Earth's climatic ecosystem.

POLITICAL STRATEGIES AND TACTICS

If the war of ideas, values, and worldviews over the Arctic Refuge has illustrated an almost perfect example of polarized visions between neoconservatives and progressives in the American political landscape, then the values of the neoconservative and progressive worldviews absolutely extend to dictate the types of political tactics used by the respective belief systems.

The pro-oil big business, Republican-led, neoconservative attempt to develop the Arctic Refuge has become increasingly characterized as a type of "take no prisoners" ideological war, led by the politicians of the Alaska State delegation, in conjunction with its extreme right political allies in the Bush-Cheney administration. Through research and live interviews with various actors in the refuge debate, it became readily apparent that I was not dealing with an ordinary issue or contest guided by fair and reasonable guidelines for dialogue and discussion. The situation was and continues to be extremely emotional, defying the rules of civil debate and the public responsibility of elected government officials. I made every effort to professionally contact and request interviews with the pro-drilling actors in the issue, and if not entirely ignored, such as by Governor Frank Murkowski's office in Juneau, Alaska, then I received outright refusals to interview, as with Senator Ted Stevens in the Anchorage, Alaska, office. This is not to suggest that all parties from the anti-drilling side responded to my letter, phone, or e-mail solicitations, as some did not even do so.

What became obvious was the overall difference of the two sides in tone and approach in tactics. The pro-drilling actors are some of the wealthiest and most powerful people in the world, which makes the Arctic Refuge a crystalline symbol of global wealth-power disparity once this power is starkly contrasted with the villages of Venetie and Arctic Village, the two Gwich'in villages 200 miles north of Fairbanks that have single dirt roads running down materially poor villages of some 200 people each. The glaring difference between political economic power and wealth contrasted with people just struggling to survive and be left alone carries over into political tactics as well.

The pro-drilling right in Alaska mirrors the extremist neoconservative right at the national level in the Bush-Cheney administration and seems to demonstrate the same disregard for civil discourse, relying upon secrecy, the propagation of disinformation, an utter disregard or manipulation for scientific evidence, and what I refer to as a "bunker mentality" in approaching and dealing with anti-drilling forces. I will explore the tactics of disinformation in a later chapter, illustrating this through my interview with Arctic Power, the primary lobbying "front" organization for the state of Alaska, the Alaska congressional delegation, and the oil industry (British Petroleum, as I will explain later, has pulled out of publicly supporting Arctic Power).

The war over the refuge has, for the pro-drilling side, become a war of propaganda, paralleling the constant misuse of information by the neoconservative Republican administration now in Washington, D.C. This war of disinformation is frightening for its underlying dismissal and contempt for truth, scientific evidence and knowledge, intolerance of differing viewpoints and values, and in general a basic unwillingness to participate in reasonable civil dialogue, the backbone of democratic practice. As Alaska State Representative Sharon Cissna substantiated in an interview with me in Anchorage, the Republicans in Alaska and the federal government have "morphed" into something quite different than previously experienced, even in the Reagan and first Bush administrations.

Whether it is the bullying, or the take no prisoners mentality, or the secrecy, or the disinformation campaign, I was fascinated with the underlying reasons *why* the extreme right has taken on these tendencies thus characterizing its tactics indicative of a dismissal of democratic process. For the Arctic Refuge, nonviolent "war" over development has devolved into very real hatreds and fears, becoming something much more significant than the extraction of zero to 7 billion barrels of oil, or the preservation of 120,000 caribou and many other forms of wildlife. As the astute and philosophical episcopal bishop of Alaska alluded to in an interview in Fairbanks, these deep-seated emotions, hatreds, and fears are representative of some truly epoch-changing crossroads now hanging in the balance for our future history, and on a global level.[24]

The recent social Darwinistic attitude of the radical corporate/Republican right—the belief in the survival of the richest, and a "you are either with us or against us" mentality—might be understood in broader historical terms, as a kind of Hegelian "antithesis" reacting to the rise of ecological and environmental consciousness and political activism.[25]

The reaction and hatred are likely indicative of a deep-seated knowledge—both conscious and unconscious—that the industrial age, fueled by oil, *is already* at its end, its deathbed. The severe reaction by the radical right at this point in time points to a rich and spoiled minority unwilling to give up its wealth and power, knowing full well that the growth paradigm driven by fossil fuel energy must give way to an ecologically sustainable form of paradigm for the upcoming century and beyond. There is obviously nothing new about rich (industrial) elites pulling up their drawbridges, protected by their moats. However, at this critical time in the world, massive human overpopulation is combining synergistically with the outdated "economic growth is progress" worldview to create dangerous ecological instability at the global level. Those elites know this, that the oil age is finished, primarily because of global warming and climate change.[26]

The bellicose reaction at this historical time, and I think what is really characterizing the tone and nature of the debate over the Arctic Refuge, is the refusal to relinquish power to those new visionaries who accept the death of an age and embrace the challenge of facing a difficult transitional point in history. It is all about money, and as we see all around the world, from the isolation of the Arctic Refuge to the chaos of Iraq, the oil era is about the violence of money.

Chapter 2

Background to Battle:
The Thirty Years' War

I don't believe there has ever been an issue so contentious in the U.S. Congress that involved more powerful interests marshaled against one another.

—President Jimmy Carter, Anchorage, Alaska, 2000

While the high-profile fight over U.S. congressional votes on whether or not to open the Arctic National Wildlife Refuge (ANWR) to oil drilling really started at the end of the 1980s, continuing into the 1990s until the present moment, the history of this clash of worldviews and political ideologies dates particularly to the inception of Alaska as a U.S. state in 1959, and even more generally to its inclusion as a U.S. territory in 1867.

Russia sold its Alaskan colony to the United States in 1867, as the czar's treasury had become depleted as a result of war with Britain. The indigenous peoples of Alaska, having endured 100 years of Russian occupation, braced for a new colonizer. From the 1867 sale until the present day, Alaska has been torn by the clash over white settlers intent on becoming rich from the extraction of natural resources and Alaska native tribes seeking to sustain a subsistence-based way of life as well as tribal self-determination. In one sense, the Arctic Refuge represents a culmination of this historical clash of fundamentally different ways of seeing life and nature.

From its origin as a U.S. territory in the nineteenth century, Alaska has been perceived by Anglo-American newcomers as a vast repository of natural wealth, a source for economic development, whether those resources came in the form of gold, timber, fisheries, or oil and gas. After it became a federal territory, it was hailed as "the last frontier." Interestingly, the American notion

of "frontier" entails that of an "uncivilized," naturally pristine landscape begging
for economic development, the latter equated with progress and civilization.
This comprises the worldview of Manifest Destiny, where lands and resources
are actually believed to be there for the taking and development by an assumed morally and technologically superior Anglo-American settler or colonizer. Once these settlers developed and "civilized" the American West, they
simply took the Western frontier mentality northward to Alaska, where
Manifest Destiny came to clash with indigenous civilizations that anthropologists now believe may have actually existed in the area for 30,000 years
(Athabascan Indian tribes that is, Eskimos tribes much later).

The current clash over the Arctic Refuge is not an isolated, discon-
nected "issue" or incident in time, confined to lobbying for congressional
votes in Washington, D.C., in the latter twentieth and early twenty-first
centuries. It is a lens through which we may view deep ideological and
axiological divisions over how we humans decide that we will live with
"nature" and other humans.[1] The refuge battle is a culmination of deep
resentments and hatreds that have been developing since Alaska became a
territory. The Anglo-Americans sought wealth and economic fortune in
Alaska and did not care who stood in their way, a mind-set continued from
the takeover of the American West. Importantly, the debate over the Arctic
Refuge is not confined to a current temporal generation; it is merely the
apex of simmering, conflicting values over nothing less than a customary,
unsustainable economic growth paradigm, personified by the white Anglo-
American incursion into an incredibly rich landscape of natural, biological,
and indigenous cultural diversity.

Alaska is a model example by which to view the classic historic clash of
the economic development (through resource extraction) and conservation-
sustainability paradigms. From the outset in the 1867 acquisition of Alaska
from Russia, through the enactment of Alaskan statehood in 1959 almost 100
years later, the battle over land and natural resources—and the philosophy of
land use—took center stage in the conflict and competition between federal,
state, and native land claims.

THE DRIVE TO STATEHOOD

While Alaska had always been a target for resource extraction in the eyes
of many white settlers since the nineteenth century, not until World War II
did the territory become recognized by the federal government for its key
strategic geographic importance. Following the bombing of Pearl Harbor in
1941, the Japanese attacked the Aleutian Islands as part of its North Pacific
campaign. In swift response, the U.S. military moved forces into Adak, Dutch
Harbor, and Cold Bay, engaging the Japanese on the outer islands. The war

effort prompted the rapid completion of the Alaska-Canada ("The ALCAN") highway in an effort to connect Alaska to the "lower 48," and it was used as a supply route for the war in the Aleutians, as well as opening up access to the interior of Alaska through its terminus in Fairbanks.

The incursion of the U.S. military bases into Alaska forever changed the demographic nature of the state. According to one interviewee, an indigenous cultural and political activist, the arrival of U.S. military personnel during and following the war marked the first time in Alaskan history that the non-native population outnumbered the Alaskan native population. During the 1940s the non-native population grew by 77 percent to 128,643 residents, and most of this increase was due to military presence. By 1959, when Alaska became a state, the population had again almost doubled through the previous decade.[2] This was a crucial turning point in the history of the territory for parallel implications of economic development. Indeed, Alaska has not only been defined as an "oil state," since the Prudhoe Bay find in 1968, but as a "military state." In the aftermath of World War II, the escalation of the Cold War with the Soviet Union brought strategic air command bases into Alaska because of its geopolitical importance in the Arctic.

Because of this unique coupling of military and oil interests in one American state since 1941, Alaska is a perfect "petri dish" through which to observe the presence and values of the military-industrial complex. It provides an interesting parallel to the national agenda of the current federal administration that is firmly committed to furthering the interests of both the oil companies and the new privatized military, the new corporate military.[3] In one sense, Alaska provides a mirror into the past, into the old industrial economy, a dinosaur where oil energy propelled—and still does with the Bush-Cheney-Rove platform—a global military machine. The state symbolizes a national and even global crossroads of values between backward-thinking oil industrial economic types and forward-thinking people (albeit a marked minority in Alaska) envisioning an ecologically sustainable future founded upon principles of nature conservation and sociopolitical democratic practice.

ALASKA'S TRADITIONAL BIPOLAR PERSONALITY OF VALUES

If Alaskan U.S. territorial and subsequent statehood history has been characterized by the greed of rampant resource development and extraction, by the lure of Anglo-American adventurers from the "lower 48" looking for fast money and personal freedom from social legal restraints, it has conversely and in bright contrast been the object of a revered conservationist ethic at the local, regional, and national levels. In postwar Alaska, development interests shot forward at an accelerated pace, with widespread fishing, oil development on the Kenai Peninsula, and logging in the Tongass National Forest. These postwar forms of resource exploitation followed earlier territorial pursuits of gold extraction and fur trapping.[4]

On the other extreme, however, Alaska from the nineteenth century had been recognized by conservationists as a world-class model of wilderness values. With the Harriman Expedition of 1899, naturalists such as John Muir, John Burroughs, and Louis Agassiz Fuertes portrayed Alaska's unique wild character in chronicles, journals, and artistic depictions. A wide range of scientists and explorers documented Alaska's geography and wildlife from 1870 to 1895, including the U.S. Army Signal Service's compilation of surveys and reports from 1885 to 1887.

These early efforts all supported a federal conservationist agenda leading to legal protections of federally "owned" wild lands. As early as 1892, President Benjamin Harrison created a forest reserve and fish culture station on Afognak Island. President Teddy Roosevelt, in 1907 and 1908, established the Tongass and Chugach national forests, and in 1909, he issued seven executive orders setting aside national bird and mammal reservations, the forerunners of national wildlife refuges. In 1912 and 1913, President Taft issued executive orders to protect more than 3.5 million acres of land, most of it on the Aleutian Island chain. Congress established Mt. McKinley National Park in 1917, and in 1918, President Woodrow Wilson created Katmai National Monument under the Antiquities Act of 1906.[5] In 1925, President Calvin Coolidge employed the Antiquities Act to designate Glacier Bay National Monument. President Franklin Roosevelt expanded the area of Glacier Bay in 1939 and created the Kodiak National Wildlife Refuge and the Kenai National Moose range by presidential order in 1941.

We see that an environmental ethic guided thinking at the national and federal government levels as far back as 1909. In this light, the issue over the Arctic Refuge has been contested for over 100 years, with conservationism at odds with overt resource exploitation. Importantly, this polarity parallels and signifies a fundamental difference between private and public values, the very split at stake in the process of "globalization," the constant erosion and dismantling of public process, policy, and institutions by private wealthy individual and corporate interests.

The bitter fight between the pro-development state of Alaska, the big three oil companies, and the opposing conservationist-minded coalition actually has a long history dating to the previous century, where the very meaning of "nature" and the human relationship to nature is squeezed between two colliding worldviews. This is not only a collision between development and conservationism in the overt traditional sense but one between private interest and public governmental protection.

The "state" of Alaska, as we shall see, has not practiced ecological stewardship in any fashion since its inception in 1959, compared to the protections promoted and enforced by the federal government. The state of Alaska is really a public institutional front for powerful private corporate interests. We are seeing this phenomenon more and more in the present United States, where business interests attempt to remain anonymous and secretive while they use their (formally) public political front people to take the heat from civil society. Any public form of government that takes 80 percent of its entire budget from oil company revenue is hardly a public institution, or at least in name only.

THE NEW STATE AND THE BIG LAND GRAB: GREED AND BLACK GOLD

The early federal efforts to conserve parts of wild Alaska continually met with discontent and friction among the Anglo-American settlers intent upon immediate resource exploitation. Caught between these two major elements were the indigenous native Alaskans, who only wanted to preserve their lifestyle and ethnic identity. The competition subsequently, and to this day, has been borne out in the fight over land claims, reflective of competing visions over how natural resources are to be understood and used.

The division between the federal government and the non-native settlers deepened in the territory through the postwar period and resulted in a push for statehood. "Largely as a result of dissatisfaction with the federal government's management of fisheries in Alaska, residents of the Alaska Territory fought for and won statehood in 1959. The prize was huge. Congress granted the new State of Alaska 105 million acres of public lands, an amount equal to one-third of the total acreage granted to all of the 50 states over the course of the nation's history. And for the first time ever, a state was allowed to select its statehood grant from any vacant, unreserved federal lands. This major benefit for the state quickly led to conflict with long-standing Native land claims."[6]

The Alaska Statehood Act included two important provisions that would set the tone for the upcoming decades and how the new state would define itself. Statehood proponents urged Congress to write special provisions that would offer special sources of revenue to the Alaska State government. One provision required the Bureau of Land Management (BLM), the Interior Department agency that manages unreserved federal lands, to pay the new state 90 percent of the revenue taken from oil and mineral exploration and development leases on federal land in Alaska. The second provision conveyed the legal title of 105 million acres of federal land to state ownership.

Bill Egan served as governor of Alaska for the first two terms, through 1967. He immediately set out to base state government budgets and expenditures on monies derived from oil leases on the new state lands, lands transferred from BLM stewardship. From the outset, the new state "banked" its future upon oil exploration and development.

As early as 1902, oil had been discovered in Alaska, near the mouth of the Katalla River, which empties into the southeastern corner of Prince William Sound, ironically not far from Exxon's great oil spill of 1989. There were sixteen wells at Katalla by 1929. This was a small enterprise, however, and in 1953, six years before statehood, a major oil field was under exploration on the Kenai Peninsula south of Anchorage. Richfield Oil, the precursor to Atlantic Richfield Company (ARCO), struck oil at Swanson River inside the Kenai National Moose Range.

When Alaska became part of the United States in 1959, the Richfield discovery well was producing 500 barrels a day and a nearby second well 300 to 500 barrels. These numbers themselves signified nothing, however, the discovery on the Kenai precipitated a flurry of speculation in keeping with the type of mentality that had moved into Alaska with the earlier gold rushes.

Since the discovery in 1953, the BLM had received hundreds of applications for noncompetitive oil leases, all from "prospective" John D. Rockefellers. In 1953, the BLM charged a paltry twenty-five (later fifty) cents an acre rent for these oil leases on federal land. The leaseholders waited impatiently to see whether oil companies would offer to drill on one's land. During the eighteen months following the Kenai discovery, 6,894 leases were issued by the BLM![7] In essence, the new gold rush was on, but this time in black gold: oil. To this day, Alaska has staked its future on the stuff (see Figure 2.1 for a striking overall view of the amount of Alaskan land currently under proposal for oil leasing).

As stipulated in the Alaska Statehood Act, the new state received 90 percent of the annual rent received from oil leases by the BLM, and this accounted for over 30 percent of the 1959 first state legislature's spending budget. According to the new Alaska Secretary of State, Hugh Wade, "In looking ahead, it would be my disposition to be grateful for what we have and hopeful that discovery and production will lead to further exploration and a firmly founded oil industry which for years to come will assist state financing both through leasing income and production royalties."[8]

Wade's dream came true, and Egan instructed his Alaska Department of Natural Resources (DNR) to lease competitively the right to explore for oil on state land under the waters of Cook Inlet offshore the Kenai Peninsula location of the 1953 oil strike. Along with the 105 million acres of land that the federal government had so generously donated to the new state, the Statehood Act also granted the state legal title to all federal land under coastal waters seaward to the three-mile limit. Over the period of Egan's first term in office, the DNR offered nine competitive lease sales for

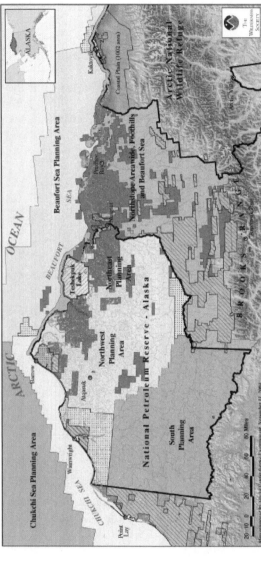

Existing Federal and State leases

Active Federal Lease Plan Area

Proposed Federal Lease Plan Area

1999 Teshekpuk Lake Area deleted from leasing. June 2004 BLM releases a new plan to lease the area.

State Lease Areas

ASRC Surface and/or subsurface lands

Barrow Native Lands

National Petroleum Reserve—Alaska (Federal BLM)

*Northeast Planning Area
4.6 million acres—87% opened to lease 1998
Next lease sale June 2005

*Northwest Planning Area
8.8 million acres—100% opened to lease 2004
Open to exploration but deferred from development until 2014
Next lease sale June 2005

*South Planning Area
9.2 million acres
Scoping starts January 2005

Arctic Ocean (Federal MMS)

*Beaufort Sea Planning Area
9.4 million acres—87% opened to lease 1998
Lease sale 186 offered 97% September 2003
Next lease sale (195) March 2005
Barrow and Kaktovik Whaling Deferrals

*Chukchi Sea Planning Area
33.8 million acres
Call for Industry Nominations April 2004

State

*Northslope Areawide, Foothills and Beaufort Sea
14.4 million acres in active lease plan areas
4.0 million acres in existing leases
Next lease sale October 2005

FIGURE 2.1 Current and Proposed Oil and Gas Leases on Alaska's North Slope
Source: Conservation GIS Center a project of Alaska Center for the Environment

oil exploration, all but two surrounding the Cook Inlet area. These nine sales garnered $42.6 million for the state in its first four years. To give some perspective, in 1959, the first Alaskan legislature required almost $27 million to operate for its first year. Even before Prudhoe Bay was discovered by ARCO in 1968, the state was betting its entire future on oil discovery, in one big lottery. The exploration leases alone prior to 1968 secured the state's fat revenues.

During Bill Egan's second term his DNR conducted seven more lease sales, five more in the Cook Inlet area, and these totaled $30.7 million. Thus the state conducted sixteen lease sales in its first eight years of existence, totaling some $72.7 million, even before the Prudhoe Bay field was discovered.

From its inception, the state of Alaska went out of its way to lure and entice oil companies to drill on its new lands. In 1959, the Alaska DNR filed its first application for the 105 million acres donated under the Statehood Act. By 1960, the DNR Division of Lands had implemented its plan to select 4 million acres of federal land each year for the next twenty-five years. The new state was receiving 90 percent of all revenues collected from resource rents on federal lands, and 100 percent of all revenues on its own lands, from oil exploration and timber sales (the federal government had given the state legal title to 400,000 acres of timber in the Tongass and Chugach National Forests), among the most prominent forms of resource extraction. From its birth, the regional government depended wholly upon expedient resource extraction for its existence and became used to fast profits derived therein.

PRUDHOE BAY AND THE ALASKA NATIVE CLAIMS SETTLEMENT ACT

The current conflict over the Arctic Refuge is a continuation of events that heated up in the 1960s, as the new state anxiously attempted to appropriate its share of federally granted lands for resource development. The fight that began in earnest in the 1960s over land claims accelerated into the 1970s. It became one of the classic battles ever waged in the United States, pitting resource development against environmental protection. However, it was not only to become a fight between regional governmental interests allied to the oil industry and federal interests protecting public wild lands but also one involving Alaskan native land claims.

Alaskan natives had carefully watched and grown nervous over the state of Alaska's selection of federal lands, selections targeted especially for oil development. Alaskan indigenous peoples were accurately worried about preserving their subsistence ways of life in the face of this development juggernaut. While they had lived for thousands of years—in the Athabascan case tens of thousands—on a subsistence relationship to nature, with the passage of statehood the new regional government was risking its financial future on oil development. By 1965, the clash over land claims was already in full force, and native representatives had stalled the state's land selection program through protests to federal authorities. A native political movement advocating aboriginal land rights voiced its concerns in Washington, D.C. In 1966, Alaskan native political activists persuaded Interior Secretary Stewart Udall to order the BLM to curtail the issuance of noncompetitive oil leases (and mining claims, homestead, among other applications) for use on, or conveyance of title to, federal land.

Importantly, Alaskan native activists almost blocked the state's Prudhoe Bay land selection applications to the BLM. After oil was discovered in Prudhoe Bay in 1968 by ARCO on state-selected land, by 1970 five native villages located along the right-of-way of the newly proposed trans-Alaskan pipeline convinced a U.S. district court to prohibit the interior secretary from giving the go-ahead for construction of the pipeline. Native leaders demanded that indigenous land claims be resolved before oil development on the North Slope of Alaska, and an oil transportation system to deliver that oil could irreparably damage native cultures and subsistence ways of life.

Conversely, the state of Alaska and its friends in the oil industry were, to say the least, ecstatic at finding the largest oil field to date on the North American land mass. The state had bet everything on finding oil, and it hit the jackpot, assuring its state wealth for the next forty years. The trick now, for the state and the oil companies, was how to placate the Alaska natives and take the aboriginal land claims factor out of the development issue.

It is ironic, or maybe it is not, that one of the most powerful players in the entire Arctic Refuge debate, Alaskan Senator Ted Stevens, currently one of the most powerful men in Washington, D.C., and the head of the Republican Senate's Appropriations Committee, originally came up with the brilliant idea of how to silence the natives' calls for land claims that were interfering with oil development. Before he became a politician, Stevens worked as a young lawyer with the Interior Department. He actually proposed the idea, which became the Alaska Native Claims Settlement Act (ANCSA) in 1971. The ANCSA of 1971, which by the way is presently severely criticized by Alaskan native sovereignty movement alliances in Alaska, gave $1 billion and 44 million acres, including subsurface rights, to twelve regional and over 200 village native corporations. While the act has been glamorized by its proponents over the past thirty years, the fact is it was a calculated effort to get the natives "out of the way" of oil development.

The very act of conferring upon land or local resource-dependent indigenous people the enactment of regional and village corporations may be viewed as a not so subtle form of cultural imperialism. It was an effort to assimilate the "natives" into the dominant Anglo-American worldview, and quite simply to buy them off with money and land to keep them quiet. At the time, archly conservative Alaskan U.S. Senator Mike Gravel proposed giving the natives only the $1 billion, however, Stevens countered this idea by adding the land allotment to the monetary buyout. Billions of dollars would be profited from the Prudhoe Bay fields for decades after the ANCSA so a $1 billion buyout would not be much comparatively. Most importantly, the villages that chose to take the money and incorporate gave up future aboriginal claims to land. This was key.

This is not abstruse history unrelated to the story of the Arctic Refuge. The Gwich'in Athabascan of Arctic Village and Venetie were the only two villages in Alaska to not accept the terms of the ANCSA, and these Indians are at the center of the Arctic Refuge debate that involves the same protests over the rights to subsistence, the same protests that took place in Washington, D.C., in the 1960s as the state of Alaska was trying to swallow up land for rapid development and resource rents. These two Gwich'in villages have held out all these years, refusing to be "incorporated" and assimilated into the dominant economic worldview, where nature is but understood as a source of profit, not livelihood or balanced sustainability. The Gwich'in from these two villages refused to give up their aboriginal land rights, proudly standing up against the state of Alaska and the most powerful oil companies in the world.

Young Alaskan natives are now asking their elders why they agreed to the ANCSA, and many of these young people are going to law school to fight for their tribal rights. On the other hand, I have heard typical white Alaskans in Anchorage scoff at the very idea of giving the natives land and money. The average white Alaskan would rather not even think about the Alaskan natives. They are best ignored.

Racism is deep in Alaska, as it exemplifies the frontier mentality of the American West.[9] It is a very different mind-set than that found in Canada, for example, where indigenous peoples are consulted and respected as sovereign tribes, political entities. The tension between white Alaska and indigenous Alaska is palpable, and it just may be the indigenous piece of the puzzle, which makes the Arctic Refuge controversy so bitter, eliciting deep emotion and hatred. It is not merely the issue of saving the wildlife, or that of a classic conservation issue, but one that brings indigenous human rights to the fore. It involves racism and ethnocentrism as well.

ALASKA NATIONAL INTEREST LANDS CONSERVATION ACT

The contested themes of the Arctic Refuge may be traced to the ANCSA and even more fundamentally to the Alaska National Interest Lands Conservation Act (ANILCA).

The ANCSA did not include provisions for native subsistence rights, but Congress promised to address the issue at a later period. The ANCSA also provided a second, very important, stipulation in Section 17(d)(2) that would carry enormous significance over the meaning of public lands and development into the twenty-first century. That section directed the interior secretary to withdraw "from other uses" up to 80 million acres of federal lands that the secretary interpreted as being appropriate for study as possible new national parks, wildlife refuges, forests, wild and scenic rivers, or additions to such protected areas. In other words, the ANCSA was the precursor to what would become the largest legal protection of federal wilderness in the history of the United States.

The questions of subsistence and unprotected federal lands included in the ANCSA provoked a furious battle through the 1970s, practically an entire decade of debate, which ultimately ended with the passage of the ANILCA. This debate was raging just as the trans-Alaska pipeline was being built from 1973 to 1976. Prudhoe Bay would start pumping oil through the pipeline on its way to Valdez in 1977. The decade-long debate over the studies for new designations of protected federal lands brought together the main protagonists, which to this day comprise a conflict of global dimension in its significance.

The 1970s marked a turbulent period as opponents mobilized over the land and resource debate in Alaska initiated by the ANCSA's call for federal lands studies. These studies stalled the state of Alaska's land selection program, and the Alaskan delegation would bitterly fight the implementation of the ANILCA and its protection of federal wilderness areas. Senators Ted Stevens and Mike Gravel would battle the proposed legislation all the way until its passage in 1980. Allied with the delegation were industrial development interests—especially oil—anxious to exploit Alaska's resources.

In opposition to this alliance, one of the most powerful anti-development coalitions ever formed in the United States entered the stage. The Alaska Coalition, presently spearheading the drive to protect the Arctic Refuge as designated wilderness, was originally founded as an organization of conservation groups allied with native groups to protect native societies and the wild areas providing habitat for the wildlife populations upon which their subsistence depended. The Alaska Coalition today is one of the most influential alliances of conservation and indigenous groups in the country. The story of this alliance is a remarkable one, and in the 1970s it stood up against the powerful interests of the state of Alaska and oil, mining, and timber companies. It's goals, views, and tactics will be addressed in the second part of this book.

In 1972, Interior Secretary Rogers Morton submitted his recommendations to President Richard Nixon by calling for the inclusion of 83 million acres in new wildlife refuge, national park, national forest, and BLM areas.

The recommendations were forwarded to Congress in late 1973, and as specified under sections of the ANCSA, a series of wilderness studies was subsequently undertaken over a five-year period by a joint federal-state land use planning commission. These studies included analyses, research, maps, and public comments on diverse aspects of Alaska's natural and cultural resources and histories. Federal management agencies also issued land protection proposals, reports, studies, and environmental impact statements, including public comments on protection proposals for the Alaskan lands in question. These detailed and diverse studies comprised an involved body of scientific work that would later constitute the basis of the legislation to create permanent protection for federal wild lands in Alaska.

The fight for the ANILCA heated up once Jimmy Carter took office as president in 1977. Carter has to this day remained the political champion of the anti-development groups formed by the Alaska Coalition. This passage evokes the intellect and dedication of possibly the United States' greatest conservation-minded president and his commitment to passing the ANILCA:

> I don't believe there has ever been an issue so contentious in the U.S. Congress that involved more powerful interests marshaled against one another. The debate really began as soon as Alaska became a state. How would it be possible to treat the State of Alaska with respect and to allot to the state a substantial portion of the land that belonged to the American people? How would it be possible to honor the Natives who had been here since time immemorial and treat them fairly? How would it be possible to protect the incredible and unmatched beauty of Alaska? And how would it be possible to protect the interests of the rest of the country?[10]

When Carter took office, another hero of the conservationist groups, Morris Udall, from Arizona, took over as chairman of the House of Representatives Interior Committee. Udall would face off with the Alaskan delegation until the ANILCA was passed in 1980.

Udall introduced the bill H.R. 39 to protect 140 million acres of federal lands in Alaska as national parks, wildlife refuges, wilderness, and wild and scenic rivers. The bill proposal sparked public hearings in Washington, D.C., and Alaska, which led to further refinements that were passed in the House in 1978. However, in the Senate, Alaskan Senator Mike Gravel blocked the passage of the bill.

The Alaskan delegation was hoping to stall the passage of the bill until the five-year limit expired: Section 17(d)(2) of the ANCSA required that Congress would have five years to pass a bill based on the body of research conducted by the various agencies involved. However, the new Interior Secretary, Cecil Andrus, close to Carter, countered Gravel's stall tactic, and just as the previous Interior Secretary Morton's recommendations were about to expire in late 1978, Andrus withdrew more than 110 million acres under the emergency powers of the Federal Land Policy and Management Act of 1976. At the same time, Carter utilized the Antiquities Act to designate 56 million acres of new national monuments. This was a critical move, for the pro-conservationist executive branch at the time played checkmate with the tactics of the Alaskan delegation in the Senate. These emergency moves gave "national interest lands" in Alaska temporary protection until the ANILCA could be passed two years later.

The state of Alaska and its friends in industry quickly sought to stop these land withdrawals in "their state" by challenging these protections in court. The U.S. District Court of Alaska, however, found that the president and the interior secretary had acted within their legal bounds of authority.

Following Carter's protections for national monuments, hard-fought negotiations ensued with House and Senate bills H.R. 39 and S. 9, respectively. The House passed a Udall cosponsored bill in May 1979, and the Senate Energy and Natural Resources Committee approved Paul Tsongas's Senate version in the summer of 1980. The final Senate version reduced Udall's protection of 130 million acres to 104 million (Figure 2.2 illustrates the breakdown of federal management units under the ANILCA).

The passage of the ANILCA not only set aside 104 million acres of federal land for protection from development but specified directions for management of these lands. The act was unprecedented in scope: it created thirteen national parks, sixteen wildlife refuges, two BLM conservation areas, two national forests, and twenty-six wild and scenic rivers. sixty percent of Alaska is federal land, while 23 percent is in state hands. Of that 60 percent, 26 percent is composed of wildlife refuges, of which the contested Arctic Refuge is but one of sixteen; 15.5 percent is in the national park system, 15.5 percent is in the preservation system, and 6 percent are national forests.[11]

Carter and Udall had led the charge to protect more wild land than any other bill in the history of the United States. Unfortunately, the bill was just signed in 1980, when national elections marked a dramatic shift in power toward Republican and pro-development interests. Ronald Reagan took over as president, and James Watt became the interior secretary. According to Jimmy Carter: "After I was out of office, and even during the campaign in 1980, Ronald Reagan looked upon this as a land grab. He carefully chose his Secretary of Interior to subvert and to repeal, if possible, the historic legislation. James Watt represented the views of those who had opposed this legislation since it was first introduced. The struggle to subvert the basic elements of ANILCA is still going on, led by members of the Alaskan Congressional delegation."[12]

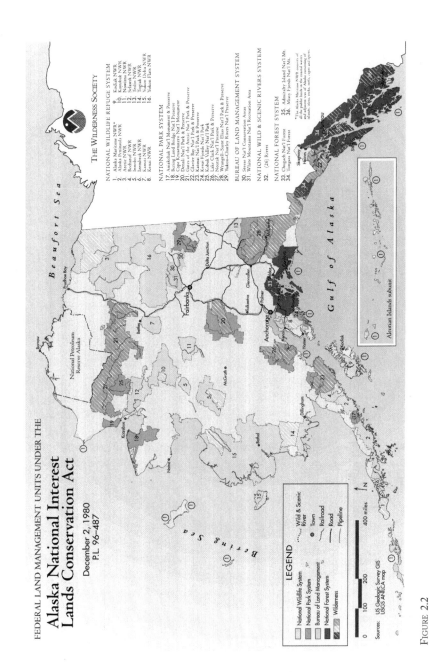

Figure 2.2

Sources: Wilderness Society (copyright) U.S. Geologic Survey GIS USGS ANILCA map

During his tenure, Watt ordered the BLM to curtail any further studies for possible wilderness protections on BLM lands. His order still stands some thirty years later. The Reagan era ushered in the era of "globalization," the corporate privatization and deregulation of public governance, oversight, and laws. The battle over federal land designations in Alaska, culminating in the ANILCA in 1980 as Carter left office, signified a face-off between clear opponents, with future definitions of development at stake.

Once Reagan took office, the very pro-development people who fought the ANILCA tooth and nail suddenly became its stewards over the next twelve years. An onslaught of attacks on the legislation came in the form of weak agency regulations and management directives for implementing the act's conservation provisions as well as new legislative efforts to destroy the act.

After the 1994 elections, Alaska's three Republican congressional delegates took control of influential congressional committees. Representative Don Young became chairman of the House Resources Committee, and Senator Frank Murkowski (now governor of Alaska) became chairman of the Senate Energy and Natural Resources Committee. Two of the strongest proponents of resource extraction and exploitation, opponents of the ANILCA fourteen years earlier, were now in charge of overseeing all federal lands! To further ensconce the power of the Alaskan delegation at the federal level, Senator Ted Stevens, the most powerful of the three, became chair of the Senate Appropriations Committee. Stevens is an ardent Bush-Cheney ally and has overseen his committee's approval of massive funds, tens of billions of public dollars, allocated to military corporate contractors and the Pentagon for the invasion and subsequent occupation of Iraq. I discuss Stevens's views and relationships to the big oil companies in chapters 3 and 4.

The Alaskan delegation has spearheaded opposition to the ANILCA all along, for decades, and since 1995 has led the charge to amend the act and weaken its regulatory protections. It is unlikely that there is a more traditional pro-growth resource development mentality in the United States than in the Alaskan state delegation.

The political battles over the ANCSA and the ANILCA provided historical backdrops to the continuing philosophical struggle between fundamentally different worldviews, and these are still played out in Alaska and Washington, D.C., over the perceived value of the Arctic Refuge. The clash is about short-term profit versus long-term visions of how to live ecologically sustainably within the finite bounds of our natural world, and it is politically about the battle to ensure democratic practice and grassroots participation versus continuing and growing efforts by big business to monopolize public institutions and processes for their own narrow profit-making purposes. One long-term Arctic Refuge environmental activist explained to me that the history of public land protection in the United States represents nothing less than the protection of democratic process. The battle is that of David versus Goliath, democratic activists pitted against an elite political economic machine.

The issue raises elemental questions about global capitalism and its insatiable greed: How much money is enough? Are ancient cultures worth saving or not? Should those cultures merely be absorbed and sacrificed into the modernized engine of material progress (for a few)? If we destroy places represented by the Arctic Refuge, step by insidious step for immediate profits, are we not destroying ourselves as well, and future generations, by ensuring the tragedy of the commons?

On the basis of this brief historical background of the contest over the ANWR, I proceed to respective analyses and portrayals of the main actors themselves in the conflict. First I turn to the pro-oil development forces in the debate. The oil companies involved are some of the largest and most powerful corporations in the world.

Chapter 3

The Oil Companies:
A Legacy of Global Power

Energy has become the currency of political and economic power, the determinant of the hierarchy of nations, a new marker, even, for success and material advancement. Access to energy has thus emerged as the overriding imperative of the twenty-first century.

—Paul Roberts, *The End of Oil: On the Edge of a Perilous New World*

The major transnational oil corporations are presently exploring for oil and gas all over the world, at a fevered pace. Oil production, according to a wide variety of energy experts, including geophysicists who have worked within the industry for decades, is predicted to begin a permanent decline in global production rates in this first decade of the twenty-first century. Oil production in the United States reached its zenith in the late 1970s, coinciding with the peak of Alaska's production on the North Slope.

The U.S. peak of oil production in the late 1970s preceded the rise of "globalization" in the 1980s and beyond, ushered in by the neoconservative governments of Ronald Reagan and Margaret Thatcher. Corporate globalization after 1980 paralleled the ever-escalating search by large oil companies to obtain oil outside of the United States, as the United States had already passed its production peak. The majority of oil reserves in the world lie in the Middle East, primarily in Saudi Arabia (262 billion barrels, 25 percent of the world's proven reserves), and secondly in Iraq. Iraq has known reserves of 112 billion barrels of oil, and industry experts believe that the country may hold 270 to 300 billion barrels, rivaling Saudi reserves.[1]

For perspective on this amount of oil, Alaska's North Slope Prudhoe Bay fields have operated since 1976 and will keep producing for another fifty

years, according to British Petroleum reports.[2] Those fields originally held
approximately 15 billion barrels. The ANWR, according to Richard Fineberg,
a former oil analyst and advisor to the governor in the state of Alaska, holds
anywhere between zero and 7 billion barrels. Even if a mean of 3.5 billion
barrels were produced, exploration and production in the refuge would likely
yield approximately six months of gasoline for U.S. automobile consumers,
since the United States presently consumes 21 million barrels of oil each day,
with this expected to rise to 25 million barrels (the pronounced disparity
between current and future U.S. oil consumption and the projected production of the Arctic Refuge is delineated in Figure 3.1).[3]

The point of these numbers is that the United States consumes up to
one-third of the world's oil and gas reserves, and its growing population is
demanding more fossil fuel energy every year. The rising demand, coupled
with a soon-to-be global oil production peak and decline, is driving the oil
companies to push for expanded exploration opportunities all over the world,
including the remaining small reserves left in the United States.

Oil industry experts, scientists, and executives advised the Bush-Cheney
administration during the series of secret meetings over the spring of 2001
in Cheney's "Energy Task Force" and educated the administration as to the
reality of "Hubbert's peak," the theory originally formulated by oil geophysicist M. King Hubbert,[4] who predicted the peak and decline of oil
production in the United States. The theory was extended to try to predict
the peak of global production, and experts now believe that ceiling to be
reached possibly between 2003 and 2008. Bush and Cheney were advised
concerning the peak and decline in oil production, and the new energy
policy is based on that information, allowing the companies to explore for

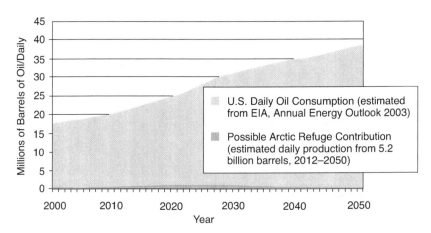

FIGURE 3.1 U.S. Daily Oil Consumption vs. Possible Arctic Refuge Production, 2000–2050
Source: Richard Fineberg

smaller finds at an accelerated rate to keep up with rising demand. The physical peak and decline of global oil production, coupled with skyrocketing human population rates, in turn guided by an elitist business economic growth worldview, spells big trouble for poor populations around the world that live in the way of oil and gas exploration. Local populations, including indigenous peoples, are now fighting for their physical and cultural survival as they live on lands targeted by large corporations allied with the national, regional, and local governments that hold jurisdiction over those local populations.

Much is now written on "resource wars," or global conflicts generated by contestation over a finite resource, whether oil, gas, water, diamonds, or gold, for example. My concern here is oil conflict, for apart from water, competition to acquire the remaining stores of oil and gas around the world is causing horrific social conflict and environmental damage. The contest over the Arctic Refuge is a "First World" conflict, and though it is thus far nonviolent as opposed to oil and gas wars taking place from the Middle East to Central and Southeast Asia to South America to Africa, it is relevant to see that the conflict in Alaska has much in common with these "developing world" resource wars. Primarily, it involves two of the same actors involved in all of these conflicts: major transnational oil companies, and indigenous people fighting for their physical and cultural survival. This makes the Arctic Refuge battle a global one verified by the fact that the Gwich'in involved in this are aligning and cooperating with anti-oil development organizations and individuals all over the world, cutting across national boundaries of developed and undeveloped countries.

Though the Gwich'in have lobbied hard in Washington, D.C., along with their powerful environmental allies, to barely garner enough votes each time in the U.S. Senate to stave off the oil companies and their political front men in the Alaska delegation (and since the 2000 election in the federal administration as well) from drilling exploration in the Arctic Refuge, the reliance on the votes in the U.S. Senate is tenuous for the immediate future. The Gwich'in are up against some of the richest corporations in the world, one of which—ExxonMobil—is the second richest in the world. While Wal-Mart actually posted a higher sales volume in 2003, ExxonMobil beat it out as the company posting the largest share of profits in the world that year. ChevronTexaco became the sixth largest company in the world in 2003, and ConocoPhillips the seventh.

THE OIL CENTURY AND PLAYERS IN RETROSPECT

Oil was first discovered in Pennsylvania in the United States in 1859, two years before the American Civil War. The industry exploded on the scene right after the war, ushering in the next 140 years of global economics powered by oil energy. John D. Rockefeller, the "father of the oil era," bought his first refinery at age twenty-six, and he became a billionaire within fifteen years through transporting and refining oil. He learned, from the beginning, as we will see with British Petroleum, ConocoPhillips, and ExxonMobil with the trans-Alaska pipeline, that the real money in oil is made by controlling its transportation.

Rockefeller founded Standard Oil, the American giant whose successors are, over 100 years later, prominent in the conflict over the Arctic Refuge. By the early twentieth century, Rockefeller's infamous ruthless business tactics and near monopolization of the U.S. oil industry prompted a federal government anti-trust suit. A 1911 decision by the Supreme Court forced the breakup of Standard Oil Company into smaller companies that are now part of the Alaskan oil monopoly. Standard Oil broke up into Standard Oil of New Jersey (which later became Exxon), Standard Oil of New York (Mobil), Standard Oil of California (Chevron), Standard Oil of Ohio (Sohio, later acquired by BP), Standard Oil of Indiana (Amoco, now BP), Continental Oil (Conoco, now merged with Phillips from Oklahoma), and Atlantic, subsequently Atlantic Richfield (then ARCO, then Sun, now BP).[5]

Three of the original Standards were bought up by BP, one of the three big companies dominating Alaskan oil and involved with the Arctic Refuge. ExxonMobil is another one of these three in Alaska, and it traces its roots to Standard of New Jersey and New York. ExxonMobil, according to Sara Chapell, an oil and gas researcher in the Alaska Sierra Club office, leases subsurface rights to the Arctic Refuge and has the most to gain from drilling in the Arctic Refuge.[6] The other big player in Alaska, with an aggressive interest in opening up the refuge, is Conoco-Phillips. ChevronTexaco also has a major stake in the North Slope and the Arctic Refuge and leases subsurface rights from the state of Alaska to the immediate west of the refuge boundaries. ChevronTexaco drilled the only exploratory well in the refuge, and the results to this day have been kept absolutely secret, outside of Chevron.

New oil discoveries in the United States, in Texas, Oklahoma, and California, after the turn of the twentieth century, would make the United States the primary oil-producing and oil-exporting nation in the world for the first half of the century. Texaco and Gulf Oil were among the new companies created during the 1930s, when new discoveries led to dramatic overproduction and cheap prices (oil was as low as four cents a barrel).

For the rest of the twentieth century, the "Seven Sisters"[7]—Exxon, Mobil, Chevron, Gulf, Texaco, BP, and Shell—owned "four-fifths of the known reserves outside of the US and the USSR and controlled nine-tenths of the production, three quarters of the refining capacity, two-thirds of the tanker fleet, and virtually all of the pipelines."[8] It is interesting to note that of the

Seven Sisters' monopoly, those seven have been reduced to four, and three of those, with the exception of Phillips, are primary players in Alaska and in the center of the Arctic Refuge debate.

During the second half of the twentieth century, U.S. domestic production, as mentioned previously, declined, as the Middle East soared in production. Furthermore, the Organization of Petroleum Exporting Countries (OPEC), spearheaded by Saudi Arabia, came to control global oil production, and most importantly, pricing. According to Daniel Yergin:

> The international order had been turned upside down. OPEC's members were courted, flattered, railed against, and denounced. Oil prices were at the heart of world commerce, and those who seemed to control prices were regarded as the new masters of the global economy. OPEC's membership in the mid-1970's was virtually synonymous with all the world's petroleum exporters, excepting the Soviet Union. And OPEC's members would determine if there was to be inflation or recession. They would be the world's new bankers. They would seek to ordain a new international economic order, which would go beyond the redistribution of rents from consumers to producers, to one that established a wholesale redistribution of both economic and political power. . . . The member countries of OPEC would have a significant say over the foreign policies and even the autonomy of some of the most powerful countries in the world.

Yergin's last sentence may correctly hold the key to the U.S. invasion of Iraq, as part of the U.S. oil companies'—and their political allies in the U.S. neoconservative administration— grand energy plan to take control of the world's remaining oil fields.[10] The U.S. oil companies and their political allies were certainly frustrated with this history of the Arab-led OPEC controlling oil prices and production flows to the West and the United States. Couple this with an inside knowledge of the coming peak and decline of finite oil resources around the world, and the result was the choice to pursue an aggressive policy to take over these resources militarily.[11] This strategy was developed to hedge against future unpredictability regarding Middle East oil, particularly Saudi Arabia, the oil giant.

Saudi Arabia is suffering from internal tension and may descend into chaos due to several reasons: "These governments (oil-rich Arab nations) are clearly now under greater internal stress than at any time in the past few decades. The Saudi royal family appears divided as to the line of succession from King Fahd, who cannot be expected to live much longer. Moreover, most of the citizens of Saudi Arabia subsist largely on state subsidies derived from oil revenues, which have been falling due to population expansion. This fall in payments to the young is one of the causes of tensions within that country. Thus, Saudi Arabia may be headed toward turmoil, which could lead the U.S. to intervene to seize the oil fields in the eastern part of the country."[12]

Due to Saudi Arabia's complex involvement with Osama Bin Laden and the attack on the World Trade Center in 2001, as well as its future political and social instability, the invasion of Iraq to obtain a minimum of 112 and up to 300 billion barrels of oil by a U.S. corporate oil military machine appears to be central to the policy of the Bush-Cheney oil administration. According to Renner:

> The impact on the world markets is hard to overstate. Saudi Arabia would no longer be the sole dominant producer, able to influence oil markets single-handedly. U.S.-Saudi relations cooled substantially in the wake of the September 11, 2001, terrorist attacks. . . . An unnamed U.S. diplomat confided to Scotlands *Sunday Herald* that a rehabilitated Iraq is the only sound long-term strategic alternative to Saudi Arabia. It's not just a case of swapping horses in mid-stream, the impending U.S. regime change in Baghdad is a strategic necessity.[13]

In an April 2003 article in The Ecologist, Lutz C. Kleveman states:

> War on Iraq is about a lot more than boosting oil companies' profits. It's the latest battle in the ongoing war over who gets to control the earth's remaining energy reserves. Few people have an idea just how momentous a strategic struggle is being waged behind the rhetoric of weapons inspections and human rights. What is at stake is nothing less than who controls the earth's remaining energy reserves. This new "Great Game" (a modern variant of the imperial rivalry between Great Britain and Tsarist Russia in the 19th century) over oil is about to enter a crucial stage. However vehement the denials by the Bush administration, Washington's true intention is to turn Iraq into an alternative to Saudi Arabia: a strategic oil supplier for its economy and a key US ally in the Middle East.[14]

This is not to divert attention or focus from the issue of oil on Alaska's North Slope but merely to expose the larger dimensions of the U.S. domestic debate over "oil security"—a primary term and issue inaccurately used by the Alaskan political delegation and its allies in the Bush administration while arguing to open the Arctic Refuge—to see it in global oil terms. It is imperative to understand that in the era of corporate globalization, giant energy companies from different "nations" are not only competing with each other but are forming consortiums with regional and local governmental elites to gain access to the world's 1,033 billion barrels of proven oil reserves.[15] Of course, these consortiums are now comprised by a few megacorporations, and the biggest is ExxonMobil, as well as the most infamous and secretive. Another is BP-Amoco, which swallowed up Arco in 2000. Add to this list ChevronTexaco, and you have companies involved in multibillion-dollar operations from Africa to Iraq to the Caspian Sea to Southeast Asia, Latin America, and Alaska's North Slope.

Most analyses of the forty-year debate over the nature and future of public lands in Alaska, conservation, and oil development have not dealt with the broader picture of oil globalization. My point here is to first provide the larger temporal and spatial scales of the oil industry and to place the oil actors in the Arctic Refuge debate within these scales, to especially illustrate the massive breadth of their economic and political power. They are aggressively pursuing oil and gas internationally, and this is critical to then understand why they are taking certain tactical positions in the Arctic Refuge political campaign, on U.S. ground, as of now taking "silent" positions for purposes of public relations.

We have witnessed, at the end of the twentieth century, oil mergers that have severely damaged the spirit of competition in the industry. In December 1999, Exxon merged with Mobil for $81 billion, and the two former Standard Oil companies, the largest at the time in the United States, sported combined revenues of $146 billion just for 1998, second only to two other fossil fuel giants, General Motors and Daimler Chrysler.[16] This merger precipitated the takeover of Arco by BP shortly thereafter. Along with the giant ChevronTexaco, these oil powers are now attempting to dominate the global oil market, and they are using the U.S. *corporate* military to do it, to control production, pricing, and transportation to meet the rising petroleum needs of a rapidly expanding U.S. population.

In a global context over the seizure and security of oil, three of the four large companies involved in Alaska and the Arctic Refuge—BP, Conoco Phillips, and ChevronTexaco—are all involved in the escalating sociopolitical crisis in Iraq. According to an August 2003 article by Corporate Watch:

> Shell, along with ChevronTexaco, BP, and seven other oil giants have won contracts to buy Iraq's new oil production of Basra Light crude. The contracts cover production from the Mina Al-Bakr port in southern Iraq from August to December of 2003. Under the deal, Iraq will supply 645,000 barrels per day (bpd) for export, an increase on the 450,000 bpd produced in July but still a third of prewar levels. BP and Shell will each send one very large tanker every month to Iraq to pick up their two million barrels. Among the other companies that have signed deals to buy the oil are Conoco Phillips, Valero Energy and Marathon Oil, Total of France, Sinochem of China, and a company from the Mitsubishi group.[17]

This knowledge is important in understanding how and why the most powerful forces in the Arctic Refuge debate, the oil companies, present themselves strategically and tactically. BP, Phillips, and ExxonMobil all are indeed making money on the Alaskan North Slope, however, they are all looking overseas to reap far greater profits. Production in the United States, exemplified by the North Slope, is in decline, as has been mentioned. The profits lie overseas, where these companies do not have to fight public relations battles as with the Arctic Refuge. For them it is a headache to constantly pour money into a PR battle to explore for what Richard Fineberg, basing his analyses on U.S. Geological Survey data, argues are only 0–7 billion economically (not technically, a critical distinction) recoverable barrels of oil in the Arctic Refuge. In one report, Fineberg shows that the U.S. Interior Department itself, through the U.S. Geological Survey, has admitted that because of far different geological conditions from that of Prudhoe Bay, the refuge rock formations may preclude economically sustainable extraction, even if, for example, a mean of 3.5 billion barrels is discovered. Compare this to over 1 trillion *proven* barrels of oil in the world.

In this context, the ANWR is seen for its economic value only to the oil companies, and that value is a fraction of the profit pie that they are reaping currently and in the future overseas. Importantly, the refuge resource conflict has been fought on the battlefield of public relations and information, and this has distinguished the success of the grassroots movement fighting oil development. Furthermore, if we interpret that broad term of globalization as including the power of the corporate-owned mass media to shape hearts and minds through incessant public relations campaigns, then it is unwise for the oil corporations, the embodiment of "resource globalization," to damage themselves publicly for possibly several billion barrels of oil. Their activities overseas, and the resource wars that they are causing on every continent, are certainly under the radar screen of the American public, which is now the victim of the corporate-controlled U.S. media.

The American public, due to the public relations campaign championed by the large coalition of U.S. environmental organizations, has pushed congressional representatives to vote against refuge drilling. The issue is a *national* poster child of environmental "success." Unfortunately, the American public is unaware, for the most part, of oil company activities overseas, and access to information of their activities is now virtually limited to the Internet, where global nongovernmental organizations publish and provide data on the "truth" about what is going on behind the incessant public relations campaigns in the mass media, where distortion and image have replaced facts.

Nevertheless, my purpose is to point out that the giant oil companies get what they want, and if they really needed the Arctic Refuge *economically*, then they would get it. In the next two chapters I will continue a discussion from chapter 1 illustrating how the Alaskan political delegation, led by Ted Stevens, has pushed the opening of the refuge for political ideological as well as sheer economic reasons. If there is a distinction between politicians and business executives, though the line is now virtually obscured by the corporate takeover of the state, then politicians such as Ted Stevens are motivated by monumental egos, driven to create legacies of power. It is common to bunch political and economic interests together, but in the Alaska case, I would argue that the worldview of the big oil executives—such as Lord Browne of BP and his president of Alaska Exploration, Steve Marshall—boils down to strictly economic reasons, not political, as with a politician such as Ted Stevens, who views the people in his Alaskan state as his children. The oil companies' "worldview" is strictly economic, cutting costs to make bigger profits; companies' strenuous efforts to lobby to lower their taxes as well as deregulate governmental (environmental) oversight over their practices fit in with this goal.

Perhaps their most successful strategy in keeping with a globalist agenda is cost shifting: cutting their costs, their taxes, while the public ends up actually paying for corporate welfare and corporate ventures through taxation. The perfect case of this is seen with the U.S. Senate's approval of tens of billions of dollars of taxpayer money "laundered" through the "public" governmental Pentagon to finance defense contract corporations (including oil companies and oil service companies such as Halliburton). Cost shifting is the very point of globalization: get the public to finance, for example, through "public" institutions, such as the World Bank's new private oil ventures in foreign lands, by companies such as ExxonMobil that construct new pipelines in places such as Chad and Cameroon, displacing hundreds of more or less traditional communities. Oil companies are committing atrocities all over the world, but they are not publicized in the United States because ExxonMobil, BP, Unocal, and ChevronTexaco board members either cross-sit on the boards of mass media companies, or they have heavy cross-investments, or simply fund the programs.[18]

The "old and the new" of globalization have been fused with the rise of the American neoconservative Bush administration: the "old" industrial economy of the oil powers has seemingly combined with the "new" high-tech virtual information economy of the great media corporations such as General Electric, Disney, and Fox (Rupert Murdoch) to deal a serious blow to the future prospects of democratic access to truthful information. The corporate Republican agenda is fueled by the energy corporations, and they have locked up the American avenues to information, the real crime against democracy. The corporate media is shaping hearts and minds, feeding the public with disinformation, and omitting valuable facts of what the public should know about corporations such as the oil giants, shapers of our entire foreign policy.

The oil industry is not part of the "old industrial economy," as fossil fuel energy drives the entire cyberworld "virtual" economy.[19] The oil company directors and board members sit on major media corporate boards, as noted. If the oil companies fail to provide oil and natural gas, then the mass media as well as computers roll to a stop. Oil runs the world, and according to global scientists, it is killing the world.[20]

ALASKA'S OIL COMPANIES, THE NORTH SLOPE, AND THE ARCTIC REFUGE

First, I should provide an important note concerning methodology and the gathering of information relating to the Arctic Refuge. I attempted in a fair manner to request in-person interviews with the main oil company actors in the debate. I requested interviews with BP Exploration Alaska and its president, Steve Marshall, as well as with ExxonMobil and Phillips Petroleum. These requests were declined. Thus this chapter relies upon secondary textual references and citations to attempt to discern the views and tactics of the oil companies concerning the refuge itself as well as broader questions concerning future uses of resources, development, global capitalism, human and indigenous rights, and the human relationship to the earth. Other actors provided opinions on the oil companies involved in Alaska, and Richard Fineberg qualifies as an expert on the industry, having worked within it and Alaskan government for many years. My primary information concerning the industry in this chapter is taken mostly from the Fineberg interview, as well as from several other environmental activists who will be cited. Please note that I was invited to an interview with Judy Brady, the director of the Alaska Oil and Gas Association in Anchorage, and when she read my consent form and topic concerning the refuge, she asked me to leave her office, rudely declining an interview. I deceived no one in garnering the interview over the phone. I made every effort in good faith to interview a key individual from the oil side of the debate, and I was rudely treated and refused.

Nevertheless, in keeping with the other requests made to interview oil representatives, I learned that the very methodological process I applied, to interview expert actors, appeared to verify one of my theses concerning the secretive tactics employed by the pro-drilling proponents, with the exception of Arctic Power, which I will discuss in chapter 4. The very actions employed by pro-oil proponents seemed to demonstrate an intolerance for dialog and openness to information, appearing to coincide with the characteristics of the neoconservative worldview and value system displayed by the current dominant thinking in the corporate-Republican federal administration.

The penchant for secrecy has been documented and analyzed by Joseph Stiglitz, the winner of the 2001 Nobel Prize in Economics. In *Globalization and Its Discontents*, Stiglitz comments:

> My research on information made me particularly attentive to the consequences of the lack of information. . . . This is why in the discussion of reform I emphasize the necessity for increased (economic) transparency, improving the information that citizens have about what these institutions do, allowing those who are affected by the policies to have a greater say in their formulation. The analysis of the role of information in political institutions evolved quite naturally from my earlier work on the role of information in economics.[21]

While Stiglitz was referring to his experience with the World Bank and International Monetary Fund, his ideas apply as well to the behavior of the elitist political-economic alliance involved in the Alaskan oil development dispute. Except for the lobbying group, Arctic Power, the powerful actors of the main three oil companies and the offices of Ted Stevens declined or refused to speak to me about the Arctic Refuge issues. The increased "privatization" of information and lack of transparency about economic practice in my interview process starkly contrasted with the "public-minded" access to information provided by numerous expert sources from the anti-drilling side of the debate. I will further discuss this in part 2. In keeping with Stiglitz' comments, the arrogant tendency toward secrecy and lack of transparency is fundamentally antidemocratic, and this process can be seen in the strategies and tactics of the oil companies in the Alaskan debate, certainly verified in the methodological attempt to gain access to interviews.

ALASKA'S OIL GIANTS: GLOBAL TO LOCAL PLAYERS

The oil corporations involved in Alaska's North Slope, and subsequently the Arctic Refuge, hold a powerful monopoly over the oil production and transportation in the state as well as the state government. Since 2000, British Petroleum, ExxonMobil, and Conoco-Phillips have controlled virtually all of the Alaskan oil production and transportation through the trans-Alaska pipeline.

In late 1999, the Federal Trade Commission (FTC) permitted the $81 billion merger of Exxon and Mobil, making it the second largest company in the world. This prompted BP-Amoco to attempt a merger with ARCO, the original discoverer of oil in the giant Prudhoe Bay field. BP merged with

ARCO, but only after a bitter grassroots fight in Alaska, whereby a citizen-led coalition named "Backbone" contested the merger as it was reviewed by the FTC. Fineberg and three former Alaska state governors led Backbone in the effort to block a merger that would have given BP virtual control over production and the trans-Alaska pipeline, ensuring its monopolistic control over the oil in the state, and subsequently its stranglehold over the state government. The FTC, influenced by Backbone, required BP to divest its newly acquired ARCO interests in the North Slope on condition of permitting the merger. BP took control of ARCO's other assets outside of Alaska but sold its North Slope holdings to Phillips Petroleum, resulting in the present tripartite split of Alaska oil shares.

BP originally became interested in Alaska in 1957, when it decided to diversify its original Middle East interests and dependency upon those politically volatile interests (Iran, for example) to expand into the Western Hemisphere. After ARCO and its silent partner, Standard Jersey (Exxon), hit oil at Prudhoe Bay in 1968, BP became the third major power on the North Slope along with those two. BP, ARCO, and Jersey organized to build the Alaska pipeline, along with companies with much smaller interests. It gradually became the dominant power in Alaskan oil political economics after it acquired Standard Oil of Ohio (SOHIO) in 1987. For perspective, SOHIO, through its Alaskan oil profits, had jumped from seventy-third on the Fortune 500 list before Prudhoe Bay to third on the list in 1980. According to Fineberg: "No other company has ever gone up that far in the Fortune 500 in four years. That's how big Prudhoe Bay was and is." BP had acquired John D. Rockefeller's original company SOHIO to assure it of "downstream" outlets of Alaskan oil, that is, refineries and gas stations.

The takeover of SOHIO in the late 1980s made BP a visibly powerful player in Alaskan economics. Then, in 1998, BP bought Amoco for $60 billion, becoming the second largest private oil company in the world. When BP announced in 1999 that it was going to buy ARCO, another major player in Alaskan oil production, for $29 billion, the state was on the verge of becoming victim to outright monopoly.

The Classic Oil State

There is no other state in the U.S. where a single industry provides, every year, approximately 80 percent of the state's general fund, and roughly two-thirds of the state budget. As Fineberg states: "There isn't any other state that comes close to being so dependent on oil; where do you have three companies that control 90% of production profits, as with BP, Phillips, and Exxon?"

The merger by BP with ARCO, as mentioned, prompted a major battle in the state of Alaska. Then Governor Tony Knowles, an ex-oil man, favored the BP merger and increased monopolistic control over the state's oil. The citizens' group, Backbone, was created by people such as Fineberg and the three former governors in response to the perceived lack of "backbone" by the state legislature in standing up to the governor's office's full support of the BP merger. According to Fineberg:

> Then Governor Knowles caved in completely to represent the BP line. The protocol of BP's proposed agreement with the state and actual agreement with the state was called a development charter, what it would do if there were a merger. This was how they governed the (American) colonies, with charters. There is a charter between BP and the State of Alaska—they have lived up to a formal agreement based on what they would do if a merger were permitted.[22]

The merger went through, as did the BP state charter, however, it was revised by a ruling of the FTC, as the FTC required BP (and the state of Alaska, its partner through the "charter for development") to divest BP's Alaskan ARCO shares, shares that were sold to Phillips. Concerning Knowles, the governor's office, and BP, Fineberg states: "What is a charter? The King's dispensation to control a colony. The state bureaucrats had no spine to fight the governor, they caved in, so the citizens formed Backbone to fight the merger. We were saved by the FTC, not the state government, which had caved in to BP on the charter. BP had a win-win situation."[23] Exxon had sued to block the merger, and coupled with the FTC's ruling, oil power in Alaska became divided three ways, rather than one way, by BP. Fineberg believes the outcome greatly benefited the state of Alaska: "This solved a thorny, outstanding problem to Alaska's benefit. Both the Phillips acquisition of ARCO Alaska and the equalization at Prudhoe Bay were tremendous outcomes for Alaska (compared to a single company's monopoly); both were opposed by the State of Alaska and neither were part of the Governor's "Charter For Alaska.""[24]

The result, since 2000, is that three companies now own roughly one-third each of the oil industry in Alaska, as the divestiture of ARCO shares to Phillips greatly enhanced the latter's power in Alaska (Phillips's share in the North Slope and the pipeline is now approximately 30 percent). Phillips is aggressively working to open the Arctic Refuge. We have seen how it is expanding in strength, gaining contracts in Iraq and the Caspian Sea, for example.

Indeed, this has become a "win-win" situation for BP in its control over Alaskan oil. In the latest (required yearly in the charter) 2003 "Charter for

Development Report" sent by BP Exploration President Steve Marshall to now Governor Frank Murkowski, Marshall explains that the report

> describes our actions in 2002 to meet our commitments to the State of Alaska as outlined in the Charter document signed Dec. 2, 1999, and amended March 15, 2000. In 2002, we remained Alaska's No. 1 private investor, with a capital budget of over $640 million. Through this investment we realized a nine percent increase in production and secured more than $750 million in capital allocation for 2003, a sum that is 20% higher than the average annual capital expenditures during the 1990's. In addition, Alaskan companies received 85 percent of $1.1 billion spent with third-party (oil) service providers, further underpinning the Alaskan oil field economy.[25]

Marshall goes on to state:

> We continue to concentrate on producing the multibillion barrels of oil in place and lowering our operating cost. We have enough known oil and gas resources in our Alaskan portfolio to sustain production at current rates for the next 50 years, and enough proven resources to maintain current rates for 20 years. BP also contributed $5.3 million to the community in 2002 to a variety of organizations that make life better for all Alaskans. Part of our commitment is manifested in the BP Energy Center, which opened its doors to the public last year and is a source of immense pride for us. Utilization by community groups is extremely high and the feedback we receive on this service is very positive."[26]

This letter verifies the tremendous economic power wielded by BP over the state of Alaska government and communities. While ExxonMobil remains overtly low-key and secretive in Alaska since its oil spill in 1989 in Prince William Sound, a national catastrophe, BP takes center stage for its control over the pipeline, profits, and contributions to the state, as evidenced in Marshall's letter to Murkowski. Money buys political and civil legitimacy, according to the corporate worldview, and profit transcends all other considerations such as social and economic justice, environmental sustainability, and political democratic practice. Of course, the rhetoric of BP champions itself as stewards of these virtues. Reality is something different than image, however.

Public Relations and the Arctic Refuge

The corporate oil giants involved in Alaska's North Slope and Arctic Refuge are currently reaping big profits from the exploration, production, and transportation of oil throughout the developing world, from Africa to Iraq to the Caspian, Southeast Asia, and South America. They are benefiting from weak or nonexistent political and legal regulation, corrupt political allies, and weaker opposition than encountered, for example, with the powerful environmental organizations in the United States. In the developing world, as in Iraq, Bolivia, Columbia, Georgia, or Aceh, resistance is outright violent.[27] Resistance to oil development in the Arctic Refuge is not "yet violent," according to Alaska State Representative Sharon Cissna.[28] It has been a war of ideas and information, thus far distinct from the resource wars of the developing world. The oil companies involved have been forced to go underground, so to speak, due to incredible public relations pressure created by U.S. environmental groups.

The oil companies cannot afford bad publicity; they thrive upon both image and secrecy. In Exxon's case, the 1989 oil spill in Prince William Sound severely damaged its national image and reputation, though this has not slowed its progress throughout the world. It is the "silent partner" in the tripartite power arrangement in Alaskan oil political economy. By its own admission, it owns the majority of gas rights on the North Slope and thus will benefit greatly from a newly proposed gas pipeline that will transport Prudhoe Bay gas to the lower 48, primarily Southern California and its insatiable energy market.[29] It would profit from drilling in the refuge, for as stated earlier, it holds the majority of subsurface rights, however, it is keeping a low profile for public relations purposes.

The oil companies in Alaska would be pleased if the U.S. Congress allowed drilling in the refuge, and they are pushing this privately, but the issue has become such a public relations nightmare for them that they are happy making their continued profits from Prudhoe Bay, pipeline tariffs, and exceptional overseas opportunities where they do not have to fight a public relations war on home ground. Much debate has centered on "who" is really pushing drilling in the Arctic Refuge, the oil companies or the state of Alaska. The case is much more subtle than to merely say the oil companies are passive players, and it is the state pushing the development because it is starved for money. Of course, the oil companies are pushing the development, said one former oil worker, an Anglo who has lived in the Gwich'in Arctic Village for many years and who worked on the North Slope for twenty-five years. Compared to extracting tens of billions of barrels of oil out of the developing world, as in Iraq, where it is relatively cheap to extract from the desert a high grade of quality oil, of course the Arctic Refuge is not as attractive profitwise. Nevertheless, the oil companies would make money exceeding their costs. We are talking about comparing billions to millions of dollars when speaking of the oil companies, and of course the refuge may not be compared to Iraq, for example, for magnitude of oil and profit.

Thus publicly the state of Alaska, its congressional delegation, its governor, and its public lobbying group, Arctic Power, are, in the words of one expert environmental activist, "carrying the water" for the oil companies. The state of Alaska politicians and their cronies in the Bush-Cheney administration are the front men and women for the powerful companies that remain silent except for their marketing efforts to appear "green" and sensitive to social justice in relentless public relations campaigns.

BP is the outstanding example of a corporate oil behemoth that has proclaimed itself as a green company, based upon its public relations campaign. In a 2000 speech, Lord Browne of BP declared that his company now stood for "Beyond Petroleum." Much of this rhetoric derives from BP's endorsement of the Kyoto climate change accord, however, BP actually has become, since endorsing the accord, one of the world's largest contributors to global warming since merging with ARCO in 2000. Together with ARCO, BP accounts for 3 percent of the world's fossil fuel emissions; it is the fourth largest carbon producer on the planet.[30]

BP also stakes its image as the "solar" oil company, having purchased U.S. Solarex and the French APEX solar companies. It also installed solar panels in 200 *gas stations* around the world—not *solar stations*. Yet the image does not match the actual investment portfolio. According to Athan Manuel of the U.S. Public Interest Research Group: "Almost 100%—99.95% to be exact—of BP's recent investments are in fossil fuels. Its solar investments have actually declined to less than .01% of the overall company portfolio. BP spent $100 million, more than double this solar investment, on legal and advisory fees for buying ARCO. And finally, for every $10,000 BP spent on oil exploration and development in 1998, only $16 was spent on solar energy."[31]

Greenpeace, the U.S. Public Interest Research Group, and Trillium Asset Management of Boston—the "ethical investment company"—co-filed a resolution against BP to force the company to abandon lobbying efforts to open the Arctic Refuge, and in 2000, at the annual BP shareholder meeting, a full 13 percent of the shareholders forced management to abandon any public support and lobbying to open the Arctic Refuge.[32] Following the 2000 vote, BP continued to remain quiet and noncommittal concerning opening the refuge. In June 2003, BP Alaska responded by phone to my request for an interview. It stated: " We don't take a position on ANWR either way. BP does not take a public position on ANWR. It is public record that BP is expanding current infrastructure in the Prudhoe Bay area, but for cost reasons is not expanding into the National Petroleum Reserve and has sold leases in NPR to another oil company (Phillips)."[33]

However, due to unrelenting pressure from the Alaska Coalition, in April 2004, BP issued a formal public statement during its annual London shareholders' meeting, publicly announcing that drilling in the Refuge is "not part of the company's current business plan."[34] BP shareholders, influenced and pressured by anti-drilling groups in the Alaska Coalition, wrote a letter to BP CEO John Browne, expressing "concern that investment values could be negatively affected" by drilling and operating in the refuge. BP investors are worried that negative public relations over the famous Arctic Refuge would harm their overall profit margins, as the company drills in the Gulf of Mexico, Columbia, and the Caspian Sea, to name but a few regions.

In the Caspian region alone, BP will begin pumping $1 million of oil *per hour* through its "BTC" pipeline running from the Caspian Sea at Baku, Azerbaijan, to Ceyhan, Turkey, by 2005. The 1,100 mile pipeline was built using 80,000 joints and 150,000 sections of pipe: the amount of steel used equaled that of 100 million cars. BP expects to export 1 million barrels of oil per day through this pipeline, garnering the company enormous profits, as it works closely with the politically corrupt regimes in Azerbaijan and Georgia.[35]

The pipeline travels through dangerously politically unstable war-torn regions, such as in the Nagorno-Karabakh of Azerbaijan (which has produced 1 million refugees), and Tbilisi, Georgia, where Chechen fighters in the Pentezi Gorge regularly threaten to kidnap oil company employees. The U.S. military, ironically, is stationed in Tbilisi and guards the interests of the British-owned BP. Essentially, American taxpayers are paying their military to protect the oil interests and profits of a foreign-owned company. The Caspian BTC pipeline will enable BP—"Beyond Petroleum"—to capture and control a large share of the global oil market, up to 25 percent. The pipeline passes through regions populated by desperately poor local populations, but BP still manages to work closely with corrupt politicians such as President Aliyev of Azerbaijan, whose brother owns all of the gas in Georgia.

John Browne is a shrewd oilman, sensitive to the need for a sophisticated public relations campaign. No other oil company (except Royal Dutch Shell) has devoted so much effort to advertising itself as a socially responsible, "green" corporation. Nevertheless, for all of its marketing and image making, it is still letting Ted Stevens, Frank Murkowski, and Arctic Power, "corporate front men" through the state of Alaska, pursue the dirty work in a high-profile public relations war. This is a war that the oil companies would rather leave alone while they pursue far better profits and far larger quantities of oil outside of the United States. If Congress votes to open the refuge, then the oil companies will proceed to drill and make a profit, but they are not about to hurt their image, presently, to do so.

In the Spring of 2003, drilling proponents were defeated in a deciding Senate vote by 52 to 48, a slim margin of two votes. In the spring of 2005, the Senate drilling proponents attached the ANWR vote to a 2006 budget resolution, framing the refuge as a potential source of revenue. The Senate

Republican majority gained four seats in the November 2004 election, enabling drilling proponents to win a 51–49 majority vote in spring of 2005. Senate Republicans avoided a Democratic filibuster by attaching the ANWR vote to a budget resolution, requiring only a majority vote. Sixty votes are needed to defeat a filibuster. Final approval for drilling depends upon a House of Representatives vote late in 2005, as the House decides upon its own 2006 budget resolution.[36]

Chapter 4

The Corporate State

We live in a thoroughly corporatized society, where unelected and unaccountable corporate executives dictate our choices regarding media, education, transportation, forms of energy, health care, pay, housing, to the very food we eat. The fundamental public policy decisions regarding how our society should be organized are being made for us. . . . We are not self-governing citizens; we are merely labor units and consumers.

—David Cobb, The Program on Corporations, Law, and Democracy

A recurring theme resonates in the discussion of the actors setting the stage in the resource conflict of the ANWR. Indeed, it is a fundamental clash of worldviews, between values of economic growth and environmental conservation and between material and spiritual interpretations of the worth and value of nature.

But the heart of the issue is one with profound implications at the national and global levels, and this speaks to prospects of an ominous future predicated upon the sheer power of the private corporate-business sector to control public institutions and publicly elected officials. We may view the example of Alaska and the oil companies there as a regional microcosm of a deeper and broader political-economic dynamic pervading the national and global stage with a dangerous virus. This disease constitutes the very nature of upcoming economic-political "wars" in the next several decades: and that is the dismantling of the public sphere and governance by the private sector, the systematic destruction of public government for private profit.[1]

In the data in the previous chapter we saw how the major oil players in Alaska quietly, behind "PR screens" at home in the United States—using smoke and mirrors— proceed to make huge profits overseas, as in Iraq. The oil companies routinely "co-opt" political allies throughout poor developing countries, contracting with those allies and their state oil companies to reap hefty profits. They are in effect doing the same thing in Alaska, at the regional level, using political figures and institutions such as the Alaska delegation, state, and lobby group Arctic Power to take the heat off of them in the public sector. The "corporate age" of the late twentieth century and twenty-first century is characterized by the privatization of public interests, officials, and policy. This is the long-term strategy of huge business and corporate powers, as they have, in effect, declared war on anything public in nature, on public governance and representative democratic practice.

To implement this ideological economic strategy, as illustrated in the previous chapter, the corporations—in this case, oil—have tactically used the mass media to appropriate the very language of democracy and social justice, and environmental responsibility and stewardship, the arguments used by their opponents. In the next chapter I will discuss how the pro-drilling advocates in the Arctic Refuge issue tactically appropriate the very language of their enemies, and how the manipulation of the "facts" and misinformation is part of the public relations war.

Presently, however, let us further examine the monopolization of the oil industry in Alaska and how the industry uses its political "front men" at the state and national levels to garner greater power and profits. Some scholars have argued that the principles of political ecology, involving how economic elites co-opt political partners in the developing world to cause great environmental and human rights damage at the local level, are not applicable to developed world cases. Try arguing this to activists and leaders of the Gwich'in tribe in Alaska, who may lose their entire form of physical and cultural survival if drilling is allowed to permeate the Arctic Refuge. With the rise of corporate monopolization and power over public policy making in the United States, it now seems outdated and irrelevant to argue that "Third World" practices of political cronyism and corruption cannot be applied to a democratic state such as the United States. They certainly may be applied and will be borne out in the coming years as corrupt political economic partners continue to dismantle representative democracy in the United States, as the latter appears more and more as a corrupt developing country separating rich elites from poor masses.[2] If the United States were a genuine democracy, then political ecological arguments could not be applied so readily to First World resource conflicts such as the Arctic Refuge. But the United States is no longer a democracy, and with corporate monopolization, the same trends are taking place in the United States as in the developing world, through the abuse of public policy, governance, and the utter disregard for the poor and the environment. National boundaries of the "nation-state" are falling away, replaced by global separations of rich and poor.

The challenge in the Arctic Refuge has been to "name the enemy," as evidence of Starr's thesis. The anti-development coalition has fought a tough public relations war, a battle of words, concepts, and scientific evidence. While it managed to force BP to pull out of the public campaign to open the refuge to drilling, it is fighting tooth and nail with the oil corporations' front men, the Alaska congressional delegation, the governor, and the previous governor (Tony Knowles, a Democrat).

As Fineberg observes, oil company influence on Alaskan politicians is so thorough as almost to be unique in the United States: "The power structure between the State of Alaska and the three oil companies (BP, Phillips, and the silent partner ExxonMobil) is unprecedented in the U.S. Oil industry dominates in many ways, they shape public perceptions and what gets on the radar screens of people, what is or isn't a problem. They mold perceptions, and that power is indirectly exercised and more directly exercised in contributions to politicians, campaign financing."[3]

The oil power is exercised over state politicians in Alaska more than in any other state. Former Governor Knowles is a Democrat who is planning to run for the Senate representing Alaska in the next election cycle, ironically challenging the current governor's daughter, Lisa Murkowski, who was appointed by her father to finish out his Senate term when he became governor in January 2003. The Alaskan political power structure is run by a few powerful individuals; individuals, according to one Anchorage environmental activist, who are "definitely in bed with" the oil executives of the three oil companies.[4]

Ted Stevens, Frank Murkowski, Don Young, Tony Knowles, and Lisa Murkowski form the Alaskan insiders' political clique and power structure that is inseparable from oil special interests. In fact, there is only a rhetorical division between these Alaskan politicians as distinct from BP, Phillips, and ExxonMobil. If the citizens group Backbone had not vigorously protested Governor Tony Knowles's partnership—the development charter—with BP, then BP would now control the entire state in an iron monopoly, solidifying its control over American domestic oil production and sales. According to the 2003 BP Report:

> Following a series of mergers and acquisitions with Amoco, ARCO, Burmah Castrol and Vastar, by 2001 BP had become the largest oil and gas producer and one of the largest gasoline retailers in the United States. At the end of 2001, we had nearly $40 billion of fixed assets in the U.S., with operations in almost every state. In May 2002, BP was, overall, the

sixth largest company by market capitalization on the New York Stock Exchange. U.S. investors own some 35 percent of the company's shares."[5]

It appears as though the foreign national BP is controlling the colonies, not only in Alaska but at the national level as well.

MONOPSONY OVER THE STATE

If BP had succeeded in taking over ARCO's Alaskan shares in 2000, then it might have gained control over the U.S. domestic market. BP, as noted in Marshall's letter to Murkowski, is reaping bigger profits in Alaska each year, almost 10 percent a year, though production has leveled off since the boom of the late 1970s. At its peak production, Prudhoe Bay produced 1.5 million bpd, though now it produces 500,000 per day. However, some curious facts have been uncovered not only by Richard Fineberg, the long-time Alaskan oil expert, but by the state of Alaska's Department of Natural Resources Oil and Gas Regulatory Commission.

BP now controls 51 percent of the trans-Alaska pipeline system (TAPS), and if the FTC had allowed it to take over ARCO's Alaskan assets, then BP would have controlled the pipeline and Alaskan oil industry. Instead of three companies now buying all of Alaska's oil from state contract leases, the 2000 merger would have left one in total control, and quite possibly in control of the entire U.S. market. If one seller controls a market, you have a monopoly; if one buyer controls the market, the result is a "monopsony."

Beth Kertulla is a state representative for the state of Alaska, representing Juneau. I had an opportunity to interview her at her parents' home outside of Anchorage, while her father was present. Her father, Jay Kertulla, was in the Alaskan State Legislature for thirty-two years, and he passed more bills than any other legislator in the history of Alaska. Both Kertullas are Democrats and dedicated to the state government of Alaska. According to Jay Kertulla, Alaska is now a "corporate state," and he blames a 1985 legal agreement contracted between the oil companies and the State Department of Law. A November 2002 ruling by the Alaska Regulatory Commission claimed that the oil companies in charge of pipeline tariffs overcharged competing oil producers on the North Slope by $9.9 billion over just and reasonable "costs" between 1977 and 1996.[6]

The state of Alaska is losing revenues each year at present, and Jay Kertulla estimates that this loss is exponential: "We lost $100 million this year, and it will be $200 million next year."[7] (Fineberg has estimated the figure to be between $100 and $120 million a year.)

One reason the state has lost revenue to the oil companies in Alaska is because pipeline tariffs, controlled primarily by BP, exceeded costs by 57 percent. In 1985, state lawyers caved in to the pipeline owners, a consortium of seven companies led by BP, to end eight years of litigation. According to Parker: "Historically, the (Regulatory) Commission and its predecessors favored the widely accepted depreciated operating cost methodology permitting pipeline operators to charge tariffs sufficient to cover repayment of investment, operating cost, taxes, and fair rate of return on investment."[8] However, the 1985 agreement between state attorneys and the oil companies agreed to an alternative methodology that allowed the pipeline operators to charge tariffs 57 percent over their costs. That 57 percent profit was ingeniously included as cost, once the state oil royalties and taxes were collected *after* all of the oil transportation "costs" or expenses were tabulated. The tariff is a shipping cost. According to Fineberg, for every dollar per barrel of oil that costs go up, the state of Alaska loses $0.21 per barrel in reduced royalty and severance tax payments. This may seem slight, but as Fineberg explains:

> One example of a giveaway in the TAPS tariff that was clearly identified in the Regulatory Commission decision on the pipeline is the per-barrel profit allowance that is built into the tariff agreement ($0.65 per barrel). The more the North Slope exceeds production forecasts, the more profit the industry takes in. Increased production of, for example, 100,000 barrels per day results in additional profits of $65,000 that day at no increased cost. Since pipeline tariffs reduce state revenues by approximately $0.21 per dollar, the State loses $13,550 on that increased production.[9]

In other words, this is creative accounting by BP, Phillips, and ExxonMobil: their actual profits are counted as shipping costs. Fineberg has conducted extensive research into what he calls the "pipeline tariff theory," or how a company controlling the transportation of oil essentially controls the market. Conoco, Fineberg contends, had been driven out of Alaska by BP and its partners, even though it was renting a prime oil field on the North Slope. It could not justify the tariff charges against its production costs, and it was losing profits. The shipping tariff is how BP drove its competition out of the state. Fineberg has visited the Caspian basin and believes that within ten years BP may end up controlling Caspian oil through control of the main pipeline. Apparently, the oil production operators are nervous.

The pipeline is not the only way that state revenue is affected negatively; oil prices critically control markets and determine profit shares. Oil revenue in Alaska is roughly divided three ways: 50 percent to industry, 25 percent to the federal government, and 25 percent to the State of Alaska. Pricing of oil per barrel also determines how the state loses money. Once oil exceeds costs of production and transportation, somewhere between $7.35 and $10 a barrel, any profit over that base is divided three ways, with the oil companies receiving 50 percent, as opposed to 25 percent each for the federal and regional governments. For example, if oil is at $30 a barrel (presently it is moving past $65 a barrel), then the net revenue is $20 to $22.65 a barrel. The state of Alaska collects only one dollar per barrel for every two that the companies make as prices rise.

Thus it is greatly to the benefit of BP to drive out competition using the pipeline than to become a "monopsony" by controlling the prices of Alaskan oil traveling interstate to the U.S. West Coast (California) and Hawaii, the two largest consumers. Again, according to worldwide oil experts, oil prices will only continue to climb in the future as production peaks and declines. The consumers will pay, and the oil companies will harvest tremendous profits through higher pricing with level or decreased production.

State politicians such as the Kertullas term this as evidence that the oil companies thoroughly dominate Alaska through manipulating the tax structure. Beth Kertulla, in her second term as representative for Juneau, possesses extensive expertise in working with and against the oil companies. After law school she worked for ten years in the Alaska State attorney general's office, having studied environmental law. She worked on oil and gas issues for the state as well as issues relating to the pipeline, and she brought with her a powerful understanding of the oil and gas industry to the state legislature. She represented the state in numerous court cases pitted against oil company attorneys. Her father, Jay, the retired thirty-two-year legislator, joined former Governor Jay Hammond and Fineberg in forming Backbone to fight the BP merger in 2000.

Beth Kertulla represents a state-level politician who is very worried about how big business dominates and runs her state government: "The hard part is when you run up against a monolithic industry, which the oil industry is in Alaska. They seem to want to stamp out all criticism; they don't want any disagreement, and won't tolerate it at all. By and large the oil industry is getting *our* oil for very little or nothing because of the tax structure, and seem to want no questioning of what they are doing—and this [is] wrong."[10]

Not only are the three major oil companies in Alaska shifting their profits from pipeline tariffs into the cost column, effectively, they also benefit from a tax structure that is part of the earlier 1985 state law concerning oil fields on the North Slope. According to Beth Kertulla, "In the tax structure there is an economic limiting factor connected to 'aging oil fields,' supposedly, but the way it was written it now applies to new fields as well." That is, the big three oil companies are benefiting from depreciating taxes connected to increasingly aging fields: not only do the taxes depreciate yearly for existing fields, but the tax breaks apply to new fields as well.

The state, according to the Kertullas, is losing money at an exponential pace, every year. "The state is at a crossroads in how to deal with the future permanent fund and taxation. We should be stepping back and looking at the oil industry as we have a regressive tax structure now. The state will see a decrease in revenue because of the tax structure, over the next ten years, though production levels will stay the same or increase." In fact, of the $110 million or more a year that the state could gain just if the pipeline fees were lowered, reflecting true shipping costs, about $33 million would go into the State Permanent Fund. As it is, many Alaskans believe that the Permanent Fund is in jeopardy, and that the state may curtail the fund's yearly payments to Alaskan residents in the very near future.

The boom days for the state government are over, then, however, the big three oil companies are enjoying massive profits. As noted, BP announced to Murkowski that it enjoyed a 9 percent profit over the previous year, in 2002, roughly equaling the plus-$100 million that the state lost that year.

Yet given this crisis to state government, neoconservative big business ally Governor Frank Murkowski is cutting back state public services rather than helping state advocates such as Kertulla rewrite the tax structure and tax the oil companies for their increasing profits.

It is important to note that just because state government advocates such as Jay and Beth Kertulla would like to see the oil companies pay their fair taxes, complaining about oil company monopolization, and are against drilling in the refuge, this does not mean that they are against oil development in general as a form of revenue. Remember, the state of Alaska has received generous monies for decades from oil, and it is rare to find anyone in the state government against fossil fuel extraction and use in general, as are the environmental and Gwich'in advocates in this case.

People have different thematic agendas in the Arctic Refuge debate, some overlapping and some diverging. Jay Kertulla noted in the interview that his wife's family had been part of the oil empire in Oklahoma, so anti-oil development was not part of the Kertulla agenda—anti-industry monopolization (monopsony) was, if it hurt state coffers. This is why research over the refuge unearths very complex variances of people, ideas, and values. For example, the Kertullas constituted one of my best interviews, and these were honest, decent people, even though I would not agree with them about continued oil development given the sophisticated arguments by global scientists concerning global warming caused by fossil fuel use. Interestingly, in Arctic Village, the Indians were arguing about global warming, placing the argument in a larger context than mere amounts of revenue to state coffers in one local area of the world. I further discuss the Gwich'in views on global warm-ing in chapter 6.

Beth Kertulla poses an interesting case, as she is one of only five state politicians, three representatives, and two senators who have stood against drilling in the Arctic Refuge. (Another is Rep. Sharon Cissna, whom I also interviewed.) Kertulla is against drilling, interestingly, not because of strictly conservation reasons—she thinks that the oil companies could drill ("if they wanted to") without harming the landscape, the main issue for the environ-mental community—but because she has visited the Gwich'in Arctic Village and firmly believes that this is an issue of human and indigenous rights. She is not completely against drilling and is pro-oil development in Alaska: "I am for development, I have helped write leases, but I want to see the indigenous people respected. I am just more skeptical than others who say outright that it (the refuge) cannot be developed safely environmentally."

THE OIL COMPANY FRONT MEN

Ironically, the powerful Alaskan political allies of the oil companies, Ted Stevens, Frank Murkowski, Lisa Murkowski, Don Young, and Tony Knowles,[11] actually use this shift from public to private funding, that they instrumentally create politically, to argue the need to drill in the Arctic Refuge, to fill state coffers, when it is they who have enabled the oil com-panies to benefit from increased profits, paying lower taxes. The Alaskan "regional" case is virtually reflective of what is happening at the national level, and it is a perfect marriage of the Alaskan neoconservative Republi-can elites, exemplified by Stevens, with big oil and big business in general, and the Bush-Cheney administration.

If ever there were a clear example of a few powerful political elites allied with big industry, it is Alaska. Stevens, Murkowski, and Young are longtime Washington insiders with close ties to the oil companies as well as the Bush-Cheney administration. The corridor of influence runs straight from the Alaskan delegation and Alaskan oil to the federal government. Ted Stevens is one of the most powerful men in Washington, D.C., and has been the primary drumbeater of the Alaskan oil industry in advocating drilling in the Arctic Refuge over the past decades. What has made the grassroots fight against drilling in the Arctic Refuge so remarkable is that the indigenous Gwich'in Indians and their environmental and religious/human rights allies are pitted against such powerful forces, such as the oil companies, Ted Stevens, Dick Cheney, and George Bush.

Ted Stevens has served in the U.S. Senate since he was "appointed " in 1968—thirty-five years, and he is currently one of the most powerful men in

Washington, D.C., a close ally of the Bush administration and innumerable big corporate sponsors and contributors. He personifies the neoconservative Republican close to big business. At eighty-two years old, currently in his seventh term in the Senate, he is Senate President Pro Tempore and chair of the powerful Senate Appropriations Committee, the committee funneling the tens of billions of taxpayer dollars into the military-corporate takeover of Iraq. No other Republican in the U.S. Congress is more instrumental than Stevens in securing corporate welfare subsidies for large defense and oil contractors and companies, at public expense.

As the senator for Alaska, he is the most powerful politician by far out of the state, and he far outdistances Frank Murkowski both in ability and influence. Stevens never was initially elected to the U.S. Senate in 1968. According to Donald Craig Mitchell, his appointment by Governor Wally Hickel was an example of "odious skullduggery" in which Stevens, a state Senate Republican in 1968, managed to manipulate state law to take over a federal Senate seat.[12]

Stevens had always been ruthlessly ambitious in his goal to become a U.S. senator, but by 1968 he had lost two elections for the Senate. Alaskan Democrats controlled the delegation in those days, until Stevens turned the tide with dirty political tactics. At the time the two Democrats, Ernest Gruening—who had beaten Stevens in 1964 for the Senate—and Bob Bartlett were aging and victims of poor health. The state had to plan for contingency of replacing one in the event of death. All fourteen Republicans in the state Senate, led by Stevens, set about to change the state law, which required a Senate successor to come from the same party. The bill was passed, by Republican majority, and Stevens's mentor, Governor Hickel, signed it without even reading it. Sure enough, Bob Bartlett died, and Hickel appointed Stevens as successor in 1968. One state Democrat (Nick Begich) noted that Stevens could not get elected, so he engineered a coup enabling an appointment. They have not pushed him out of the office since, in thirty-five years. The man is power hungry and believes himself *to be Alaska*.

The Republicans have controlled Alaska ever since. Representative Don Young is serving his sixteen term, first elected in 1973. Frank Murkowski, the new governor, was first elected to the U.S. Senate in 1980, and when he left to become the current governor, his seat was taken over by his Republican daughter, Lisa Murkowski. Alaska is staunchly Republican, and it constantly argues against big government. This is very hypocritical, say Alaskan conservationists, in that Stevens is known in Washington, D.C., as the "king of pork," bringing in more federal taxpayer dollars per capita to his state than any other. Stevens is not well known among citizens in the "lower 48," but he is a linchpin for Washington Republican power, and one of the Senate's closet allies to the Bush administration.

Stevens has spearheaded the Alaskan State's drive to open the Arctic Refuge to drilling. Because the oil companies have pulled out of public advocacy for the drilling, Stevens has publicly excoriated the industry for letting the state take the heat. Arctic Power, the "NGO" that was created ten years ago to lobby solely for the opening of the Arctic Refuge, is the mouthpiece for Stevens, Murkowski, and the Bush administration. (Their ideas and arguments as representative of the neoconservative corporate Republican ideology will be the subject of the next chapter.) Since he took office in 1968, Ted Stevens has lobbied for the oil industry to open the Arctic Refuge, and he claims that he "made a deal" with the Democrats in 1980 to allow them passage of the ANILCA only if the refuge were to remain accessible to drilling. (The ANILCA stipulated only that the refuge should be *studied* for effects of development on the wildlife and land, for seven years, not that it would be open to drilling.) Stevens is the most arrogant and relentless supporter of drilling in the Arctic Refuge. Stevens, Young, and Murkowski are blatant oil "front men," pursuing the development interests of these corporations. Just observe the data on oil contributions to these three, contributions from the same companies trying to drill in the Arctic Refuge.

From 1993 through December 1998, Don Young, as chair of the House Resources Committee, received more hard money from BP, Exxon, ARCO, and Chevron political action committees (PACs) than any other member of Congress, $54,698. Young is also on the Select Committee for Homeland Security and is the chair of the House Transportation and Infrastructure Committee. Frank Murkowski, chair of the Senate Energy and Natural Resources Committee from 1993 to 1998, received the second largest amount of PAC money from these companies, $22,500. Kay Hutchinson, the Republican from the oil state of Texas and an avid advocate of drilling in the refuge, received the most from these companies, $44,699. Of the top ten senators receiving money from these companies in this period, Ted Stevens ranked sixth, receiving $24,750.

From 1993 to 1998, the top ten recipients of PAC (hard) money from these oil companies were all Republicans, both in the Senate and the House.[13] Senators in the top ten included ardent drilling proponents and supporters (now) of the current Bush administration, Larry Craig of Idaho, and James Inhofe of Oklahoma.

In Ted Stevens's 2000 profile of political contributions, the oil and gas industry tops the list, with $160,000, followed by an array of monies from other PACs from the megacorporate community, including defense contractors. Stevens is the quintessential big business-friendly Republican. From 1995 to 2000, his contributions totaled $3,501,660, and 80.4 percent of these monies came from business. Interestingly, a full 18.4 percent of these monies were undisclosed.[14]

During Stevens last Senatorial race in 2002, he raised $3,155,116, and received 78 percent of the Alaskan vote, as compared to his Democratic opponent, who only raised $894 and received only 11 percent of the vote.[15]

This is a blatant example of a corporate-political relationship, an outright instance of "buying" the politician, where one individual receives over $3,000,000 for a campaign, and the Democrat receives $900. As Alaskan oil experts and state legislators have attested, already noted, there is no other state in the country where top-down political-economic power is so ensconced, where one industry controls the entire state, and of that industry, only three companies control the oil (it would have been one, BP, if not for the grassroots protest).

It should also be noted that Veco Corporation, originally an Alaskan oil service company, and now a transnational corporation with interests in, for example, Kazakhstan and the Caspian Sea, was the number-one contributor to Stevens in 2000. Veco is pushing hard for the opening of the Arctic Refuge and has much to gain financially. A number of oil service companies are pushing to open the refuge, some state, some national (offices in Alaska), and some from native corporations, such as the North Slope Native Corporation, Natchik (a global company). Interestingly, Veco, a main contributor to Stevens, owns the *Anchorage Times,* a vociferous local mouthpiece constantly arguing for drilling in the refuge.[16]

Observing data from the 2001–2002 period of corporate contributions to politicians, Stevens received monies from BP, Halliburton, ExxonMobil, and Anadarko Petroleum (a company trying to expand on the North Slope and seeking leases for ANWR). His portfolio of financial contributions lists a who's who of corporate America, and just this period lists over 500 corporate PACs that contributed money to his war chest. Some of these included Chevron, Shell, Ford, Phillips, Marathon Oil, Columbia Energy, Duke Energy, Sabre Energy, Sempra Energy, Tesoro Petroleum, El Paso Energy, the defense contractors Bechtel and Fluor (in Iraq), big tobacco, Goldman Sachs, Citigroup, major airlines, and Walt Disney.[17] Stevens is *the* corporate front man, as these figures illustrate.

Frank Murkowski, the ally of big oil in the Alaskan governor's office, received $1,649,128 in his 1997–2002 campaign portfolio, and 88.4 percent of this money was from business, 5 percent from labor. He disclosed only 76.0 percent of his contributions.[18]

The figures denoting disclosure are disturbing for Murkowski and Stevens, but they appear to confirm the efforts of the oil companies and other large corporations to hide their contributions from the public. They thrive upon secrecy and image in public relations. The obvious upshot of the figures presented is the clear overlap of oil and political Republican interests.

OIL-GREASING NATIONAL POLITICS

The influence of the Alaskan delegation at the national level is obvious, given the number of seats that Stevens and Young hold on powerful committees. Governor Murkowski, the former senator, like Stevens and Young, is very close to the Republican Bush administration. Alaskan regional politics then truly overlaps with the federal administration. The oil industry forms an umbrella over the elite regional and federal Republican politicians.

The oil and gas industry provided a total of $159,146,548 in contributions—individual, PAC, and soft money—to federal candidates for election cycles between 1990 and 2004.[19] For the all-important 2000 election cycle, when the Bush and Cheney ticket won the presidential election, oil contributions hit an all-time high of over $34 million, with a soft-money contribution of $16 million, and almost $11 million from individuals ($7 million from PACs). Soft money constitutes unregulated, and unlimited, contributions to political parties. If the numbers are any indicators of an increasing overlap between oil money and Republican political power, then we can see that in 2000, 78 percent of oil money went to federal Republicans; in 2002, 80 percent went to Republicans; and in 2004, 82 percent went to the Republicans.[20]

Of course, Democrats are not immune from taking contributions from oil companies, according to a report by the Center for Public Integrity: "(Documents) show the Democratic Party's propensity to solicit donations based on its legislative agenda and rarely seen connection to the oil corporations. One such call sheet dated November 13, 1995, instructs a caller to ask British Petroleum for a contribution of $85,000."[21] According to one Democratic National Committee call sheet: "The (Clinton) Administration helped them out on two major issues this year, first dealing with deep water drilling in the Gulf of Mexico, and the other Alaska North Slope trade, dealing with oil imports from foreign-owned companies."[22]

Other Democratic National Committee call sheets have shown similar connections to other companies such as Texaco (now ChevronTexaco), where solicitors were instructed to tell how "the President helped out the oil industry by supporting them on drilling issues." The fund-raisers would then ask for $35,000.

While the Democrats are certainly not immune from money pandering from the oil companies—even though the Democrats in the Senate like to make a poster child out of the Arctic Refuge, to appear as "conservationists"—they pale in comparison to Republicans for the percentages received, as cited earlier.

The same report connects large corporations that have access to federal lawmakers through fund-raising events. During the 2001 Republican National Committee Gala, "executives who gave $20,000 or more could request which Republican lawmakers and cabinet secretaries they wanted to dine with." Frank Murkowski was among the energy regulatory legislators requested by the $38 billion energy company, Reliant Energy, to sit at their table at the gala. The legislators included Republican power brokers all backing the new Cheney energy policy, and of course all of whom back the effort to drill in the Arctic Refuge: Murkowski; Billy Tauzin, chair of the House Committee on Energy and Commerce; Senator Don Nickles of Oklahoma; Senator Larry Craig of Idaho; Energy Secretary Spencer Abraham; and Interior Secretary Gale Norton. The Republican-energy cadre is a formidable one and comprises a relatively small circle at the top, with the Alaskan politicians enjoying a special place at the center.

THE ARCTIC REFUGE AND THE BUSH-CHENEY ENERGY PLAN

In 1980, the ANILCA legislation stipulated that the Arctic Refuge would neither be designated as wilderness nor be opened to oil exploration. From 1980 forward, the refuge became famous as a "gray area," neither fully protected nor open to development. In this sense it has transcended itself to become a symbol of a fundamental clash of values. These values have been manifested in the long political battle, pitting oil companies and their political "front men" against the environmental, indigenous, and religious/human rights coalition.

The ANILCA in 1980 called for a seven-year "scientific evaluation" by the Department of the Interior of the Arctic Refuge to explore the possible consequences of drilling in the coastal plain area. In 1987, the department, charged with management of the refuge, issued its long-awaited report to Congress, recommending that the entire coastal plain be leased for immediate oil development. The Natural Resources Defense Council, representing eight powerful national environmental groups, including the Wilderness Society, National Wildlife Federation, and Sierra Club, went to court to challenge the Department of the Interior's finding. The Gwich'in Steering Committee also filed a suit on behalf of the indigenous community involved, concerning possible effects on the Porcupine Caribou herd that calves in the coastal plain area.

In 1988, the Natural Resources Defense Council, the trustees for Alaska, and the National Wildlife Federation issued their own report challenging the findings of the Department of the Interior. The report was the first of a number of scientific studies by environmental groups detailing the massive environmental damage caused by North Slope development, challenging the public relations campaign of pro-drilling advocates.[23]

The Arctic Refuge debate may be viewed as a public relations "war," a war of ideas, scientific evidence, and deep-seated values, between the big business and the environmental groups, with the state and national politicians sandwiched in between. Since 1987, the war over what constitutes environmental and scientific "evidence," concerning developmental damage or lack thereof on the North Slope, and by probable extension, the Arctic Refuge, has been waged by oil and environmental lobbyists in the halls of Congress, seeking to sway the votes of the Republicans and Democrats.

In 1989, an attempt to open the refuge was squashed when the Exxon Valdez disaster in Prince William Sound dealt a blow to the image of the oil companies. (Since then, ExxonMobil has kept a very low profile in Alaska, although it managed to avoid paying millions in punitive damages in lawsuits in Alaska.)

In 1995, both the House and Senate approved drilling for the coastal plain, attaching a provision for drilling to a budget bill. President Clinton rescued the refuge at that time, vetoing the entire budget bill. Nevertheless, the Alaskan delegation continued to pursue its "white whale," and Stevens has taken on the role of a relentless Ahab, with Murkowski as his first mate. When Bush and Cheney took over the executive branch of government in 2000, Stevens, Murkowski, and Young became enamored with their renewed chances to open the refuge for drilling.

In October 2001, Murkowski and Senator Jim Inhofe from Oklahoma tried to attach a drilling provision to a massive $345 billion defense bill, immediately following the World Trade Center attack. Murkowski and other Republicans tried to convince senators that opening the refuge was now a matter of national energy security. Murkowski exploited the New York tragedy to attempt to open the ANWR, playing upon national fears concerning oil imports. Larry Craig and Trent Lott fortified the Republican line on drilling in the name of energy security, however, Democrat Tom Daschle, always the spearhead against drilling, managed to keep the ANWR provision out of the defense bill.

The Republican-crafted energy bill of 2002 (S.517), a product of Cheney's secret energy task force in the spring of 2001, included an amendment introduced by Murkowski to open the Arctic Refuge to drilling. This time, the desperate Murkowski "tried to swing deals to gain more Democratic votes, at one point offering to use some of the revenues from the oil leases to pay for benefits for laid-off steel workers."[24] Actually, Murkowski and his Republican allies had said back in the fall of 2001 that they would try to attach Arctic Refuge drilling "to virtually any bill that would come to the Senate floor."[25] The attempt was defeated in the Senate by a vote of 54–46.

In the spring of 2003, another attempt was defeated. "Last week Alaska's senators tried to keep an ANWR drilling measure in the Senate's budget bill. Their effort failed 52–48."[26] Following this defeat, Stevens was furious: "I'm mad enough to eat nails right now. I just don't like it when people don't keep their word to me. People who vote against this today are voting against me—and I will not forget it."[27]

Seven Republicans had voted with the Democrats to remove the ANWR from the budget resolution. The lobbying battle between pro-drilling advocates such as Arctic Power versus environmental and Gwich'in groups had always been furious, but before the 2003 vote, these sides were both targeting four senators perceived to be sitting on the fence: Lincoln and Pryor, both Arkansas Democrats; Smith, the Republican from Oregon; and Coleman, a Minnesota Republican. All four ended up voting against drilling, due to the influence of the environmental lobby.

Later, Stevens, the chair of the Appropriations Committee, said that three senators had reneged on commitments to him, voting against drilling. He vowed that he would remember these senators as he was writing annual spending bills: "You bet your bottom dollar, if they can't keep their word to me, why should I keep my word to them? Why should I give my word?"[28]

These incidents are important in understanding the general and persistent intolerance and arrogance that Stevens has portrayed throughout multiple efforts to gain drilling access for his allies in the oil industry, as well as to buffer state coffers. Stevens's ideas and tactics illustrate those of the quintessential neoconservative or neoliberal and are reflective of the Bush-Cheney mentality. He does not live up to the typical rhetoric of the neoconservative, however, in reducing state spending: his Appropriations Committee allowed $87 billion for the "war on terrorism" in Iraq and Afghanistan, awarding billions in contracts to oil companies, oil service companies, "security" firms, and defense contractors. Furthermore, his (along with both of the Murkowskis, Young, and Tony Knowles) rhetoric of blasting non-Alaskan Americans for their utter misunderstanding of Alaska's local environment and oil industry is thoroughly specious and hypocritical as the "king of pork" brings more federal tax dollars to his state per capita than any other.

This is not the action of a free marketeer, a so-called traditional Republican. He is instrumental in working with the Bush administration to push America further into insoluble debt. The Brookings Institution believes that a conservative estimate for federal government debt in a Bush-Cheney-style administration from 2005 to 2015 would reach $4 trillion over ten years, with the implementation of permanent tax cuts for corporations and wealthy individuals (those earning over $200,000 a year) and the partial privatization of Social Security. Just the partial privatization of Social Security would account for $2 trillion of debt over ten years.[29]

Unofficial estimates of the entire national debt, including personal, household, and government figures, are over $51 trillion. Boston University economist Laurence J. Kotlikoff argues that the government's actual fiscal gap—the difference between expenditures and receipts is $45 trillion, a figure derived from a study commissioned in 2002 by former U.S. treasury secretary Paul O'Neill. After the 2003 medicare drug benefit is added into the equation, the debt reaches $51 trillion. Furthermore if a 3.6 percent interest rate is allowed to compound on this figure over the next fifteen years, the total will reach $76 trillion, assuming the government pays nothing back during this period. Kotlikoff notes that the entire net worth of the American people in 2002 was $40 trillion, $11 trillion less than the $51 trillion debt or fiscal gap—thus making the country technically bankrupt.[30]

Politicians such as Stevens are shifting public funds into private coffers: he, along with the rest of the Alaska delegation, just managed, through the Bush Energy Bill, to award $21 billion in loans to BP and Phillips in Alaska to build a new gas pipeline that will transport gas to the lower 48 states, primarily California.

Of course, this coincides with a new Senate bill that will provide $100 billion in tax breaks to businesses over the next ten years. Tax breaks, subsidies, and loans, all at the expense of the public sector. This would be easy to fix if elected officials were not allowed to take any monies from the private sector, only from public funds as in Arizona at the state level. However, we have seen from the data that federal level politicians are bought and paid for by the corporate community, exemplified by the Alaskan delegation. Government documents show that Energy Secretary Spencer Abraham met with more than 100 representatives of energy companies and corporate associations from January to May 2001, during Cheney's secret task force meetings. BP, ExxonMobil, ChevronTexaco, and the Independent Petroleum Association of America were among the powerful corporate interests forming the energy policy.[31]

The head of Congress' General Accounting Office (GAO) was going to sue Cheney for refusal to provide full disclosure of the spring 2001 energy policy meetings. Ted Stevens met with Comptroller General David Walker, and it was speculated by high sources in the GAO that Stevens threatened to cut funding to the GAO, as head of the Appropriations Committee, unless Walker dropped the lawsuit.[32]

Sadly, we must question whether the Arctic Refuge is but a diversionary tactic calculated by the oil industry to shift environmentalist and public attention away from what the industry truly covets: tax breaks and energy subsidies paid by the taxpayers. The aid to energy firms in the Bush-Cheney energy bill includes provisions for up to $558 million in annual funding for coal, oil, and natural gas research and development; the loan guarantees for the Alaskan gas pipeline; the creation of a new Energy Department R&D program to support ultra-deepwater oil drilling technologies that could be used to find more oil in the Gulf of Mexico (is it coincidental that BP controls the drilling in the Gulf?); and, importantly, a little-known provision to allow Indian tribes to lease tribal land and rights-of-way for oil, gas, and other energy exploration.[33]

Indeed, even a Sierra Club lobbyist admitted: "Certainly we had great worries that by focusing our (lobbying) efforts on Arctic drilling, we would not devote resources to other issues such as tax incentives and subsidies for the oil and gas industry. Some of these things slipped under the radar; there wasn't a floor fight in the House on those provisions."[34]

The environmental lobby has targeted Tom Daschle, Joe Lieberman, and John Kerry as the Democratic Senatorial champions in protecting the ANWR. Even Arctic Power told me in an interview, which will be discussed in the following chapter, that these three senators, along with Richard Gephardt, are the nemeses of the pro-drilling lobby. However, the problem lies in viewing the Arctic Refuge as an isolated issue from the rest of the energy bill that just passed the Senate. Tom Daschle himself—with Trent Lott, the arch-conservative who wants to drill in the refuge—added an amendment, giving $14.5 billion in tax credits for the energy sector, including tax breaks for oil and natural gas exploration.[35] The Arctic Refuge has created an image for liberal senators seeking to appear as friends of the environment, as environmentalists poured their monies and lobbying efforts into the issue of the ANWR.

The political machinations need to be understood within a broader framework of what is really at stake: corporate power has thoroughly co-opted representatives of the public, and this includes corporate Democrats such as Lieberman, Daschle, Kerry, and Gephardt, who are all wealthy individuals. When a campaign such as ANWR focuses too tightly upon a conservation issue, ignoring deeper political-economic signals of corruption and subversion of representative democratic practice, then a cancerous system quietly gets worse as liberals worry about pandering to politicians merely looking to appear as "good environmentalists." It is like taking aspirin for cancer. Daschle and Lieberman want the spotlight for saving the Gwich'in and stopping refuge development, but both fully support the energy bill and its oil tax breaks and subsidies, and along with Kerry and Gephardt, join the Republicans in funding $87 billion for the oil war on Iraq, vastly benefiting oil companies and defense contractors, among others. The hypocrisy is real: corporate money has infested national politics, and there is little difference now between Democrats and Republicans, in the corporate state. The real difference is between the wealthy and the poor, in the age of corporate globalization, and the rhetoric of liberal politicians who themselves are quite wealthy just does not bear much substantive fruit.

Chapter 5

The Culture of Corporation Spin

Corporations now *govern* society, perhaps more than governments themselves do; yet ironically, it is their very power, much of which they have gained through economic globalization, that makes them vulnerable. As is true of any ruling institution, the corporation now attracts mistrust, fear, and demands for accountability from an increasingly anxious public. Today's corporate leaders understand, as did their predecessors, that work is needed to regain and maintain the public's trust. And they, like their predecessors, are seeking to soften the corporation's image by presenting it as human, benevolent, and socially responsible.

—Joel Bakan, *The Corporation: The Pathological Pursuit of Profit and Power*

The collusion of high-level corporate and political power has, unfortunately, resulted in a domination of the mass media. Recent political deregulation in the summer of 2003 by the U.S. Federal Communications Commission has led to greater monopolization of the media by a few mammoth corporations. This development has further eroded the democratic process and the subsequent access to truthful information and knowledge.

Corporate control over the dissemination of information and ideas is fundamental to the long-term strategy of the big business community, and the oil companies are no exception to this rule. In the previous chapter, we saw how business corrupts and dominates political representatives and policy making. If there is any such thing as "long-term" strategy to business thinking, it pertains to making profits, period. As evidenced in the previous discussion of the political-economic powers involved over the Arctic Refuge debate, it goes without saying that their "worldview" is decidedly materialistic, economic, and centered upon elitist power, drastically departing from the values of the opposition in the fight over the Arctic Refuge. In part 2 I will explore the nature of these latter values derived from interviews with participants in the debate.

To elaborate upon Fineberg's opinion, the oil companies in Alaska have taken up two priorities as their strategy to monopolize profit as power: one, to "buy" politicians through campaign contributions, in turn garnering tax breaks and subsidies, for example; and two, to capture the hearts and minds of common people through the artful dissemination of public relations campaigns, including monetary contributions to communities and incessant television advertisements. Both of these "tactics," one for the elite politicians and one for the public, are intended to ensure strategic goals of maximizing profit and cutting cost. Both tactics involve an employment of the sheer power of money to purchase political and social legitimacy.

The second tactic is the subject of this chapter, the "art" of disseminating misinformation in our new era of "corporate spin" at the dawn of the twenty-first century. Never has the process of capturing hearts and minds come so easily to political-economic elites as it does presently, given the sophistication of mass electronic media, the embodiment of "techno-capitalism."

As mentioned previously, a war of information and ideas, not bullets, has characterized the battle for the Arctic Refuge. The battle is for ideological legitimacy, with both sides—the business worldview and the environmental worldview—vying to press their ideas and values upon political decision makers and the public. In a grand view of temporal and spatial scales, the ideological and axiological (pertaining to values) debate over the Arctic Refuge concerns a clash of business and environmental values, with the public and politicians squeezed in between, so to speak, as profiteering developers war with conservationists and ecologists. As this war develops, both ideological positions seek to press their arguments upon the minds and values of politicians and the public.

Obviously the conflict entails many individual and group interests, overlapping and diverging within each of the major camps. Nevertheless, it is imperative to keep foremost in mind the major ideological platforms inherent with the positions and to not become lost in the plethora of details in this multifaceted subject. In dealing with the history and politics of the ANWR, it is easy to lose sight of the forest through the trees. My intent is not to cover all of the details in this subject but to focus upon a political ecological approach and methodology concerned with political economic power and injustice at the global scale, and how "ANWR" signifies the broader clash over capitalist versus social justice and ecological claims.

These claims are now the subject of what quite possibly will be the twenty-first century's greatest source of conflict and debate, the relationship of humans to the natural world, of which they are part. The pro-development and anti-development positions, though not by all means simplistically categorical, revolve around this seminal question or dilemma. The positions taken by the Arctic Refuge participants illustrate assumed ideas and values concerning how humans shall perceive and live with or against nature.

To complete this first section on the pro-oil development actors, I would like to discuss the ideas and concepts utilized in the viewpoint of Arctic Power, the formal lobbying group for the state of Alaska—and may we say informally—for the oil companies that have chosen to avoid the negative publicity in the campaign. In discussing the ideas constituting the position of Arctic Power, in essence the mouthpiece of Stevens, Murkowski, Young, and the oil companies, it is important to understand the role of their ideological position within a theoretical context of political-economic legitimacy.

Manfred Steger provides a helpful theoretical definition of ideology that pertains to the particular issue of battling ideologies over the Arctic Refuge:

> Most political and social theorists define ideology as a system of widely shared ideas, guiding norms and values, and regulative ideals accepted as fact or truth by some group. Ideologies offer individuals a more or less coherent picture of the world not only as it is, but also as it should be. In doing so, they organize the tremendous complexity of human experience into simple and understandable images that, in turn, provide people with a normative orientation in time and space, and in means and ends.[1]

Yet ideology always contains a political dimension, asserts Steger, and "is ultimately about the many ways in which power is exercised, justified, and altered in society." Thus the alliance of the oil companies and their neoconservative political allies forms an ideology that is an expression of top-down economic power, an articulation of assumed beliefs as to how social classes should be divided (unequally and vertically), as well as to how this upper class stands by its perceived right to infinitely exploit natural resources for its own profit.

The indigenous people, conservationists, and religious leaders fighting against oil development in the Arctic Refuge provide their own "counter" ideologies, worldviews, and even political tactics in their contestation of what they perceive to be an *ecologically unsustainable* economic growth ideology conveyed by the "carbon club."

The language, as well as the very process of delivery, seemed to markedly distinguish the experts I interviewed from the two sides of the Arctic Refuge debate. As noted, the very fact that the Stevens and Murkowski offices either flat out refused to talk (Stevens) or did not bother to respond (Murkowski) indicated a contempt for the very process of dialogue, the

backbone of democratic practice. Nevertheless, Arctic Power as the lobbying tool of Stevens, Murkowski, and Young did speak quite candidly
and at length.

The ideas expressed by Arctic Power provide a lens through which to
view the general platforms of the political-economic neoconservatives who
are pushing the oil development in the Arctic Refuge. Arctic Power was
created in the early 1990s by the state and oil companies with the express
intention to serve as a lobby group to open up the Arctic Refuge to drilling.
Arctic Power, officially funded by "state of Alaska" monies, receives an average
of $1.25 million every three months from public state monies (another ex-
ample of how the oil industry shifts its private costs to public expense). While
it focuses solely on the refuge, its ideas are fully representative of the corporate neoconservative ideology now dominating the federal political landscape.
In this sense the interview was especially helpful and illuminating to observe
firsthand the business/neoconservative value system and the political tactics
employed as demonstrative of those beliefs or values. In essence, the language
and tone used in the interview constitute the operational tactics employed by
the neoconservatives in the Arctic Refuge public relations battle.

In discussing its ideology, it is first helpful to frame Arctic Power's positions within what Manfred Steger refers to as the three hallmarks of ideological presentation: distortion, legitimation, and integration.[2]

Distortion, states Steger, is "the production of contorted images of social
reality. Most importantly, the process of distortion hides the contrast between
things as they may be envisioned in theory and things as they play themselves
out on the plane of material reality."[3] Distortion is central in the presentation
of Arctic Power's ideas, as representative of Stevens and Murkowski, for they
continually attempt to project their own negative weaknesses onto the opposition, primarily the environmentalists. The burden of "falsehood" and misinformation is attributed over and over to the environmentalists, while they,
the neoconservatives, protect truth and the scientific "facts."

Legitimation is the need for any authority to establish its right to rule
in the face of public scrutiny and possible contestation of that right to rule.
The battle of ideas for the Arctic Refuge lies precisely within this plane of
action: the local conflict may be extrapolated to represent the global battle
heating up between corporate elites (and their political front men) and
common (poorer) people fighting to preserve democratic, public, and ecologically sustainable values. According to Steger: "There will always remain
some discrepancy between the popular belief in the authority's right to rule
and the authority's claim to the right to rule. It is one of ideology's functions to supply the people with additional justification in order to narrow
this gap."[4] The Arctic Refuge debate precisely addresses this gap, and Arctic
Power was created by the Alaskan delegation and the oil companies as a

mouthpiece to launch a public relations campaign to attempt to counter the powerful *public contestation* of grassroots information and ideas assembled by the Alaska Coalition.

The integrative function of ideology, as derived from anthropologist Clifford Geertz, stabilizes and preserves social (and economic and political) identities of individuals and groups. The conservative function of identity overtly applies to the Alaska case, in that any challenge to the legitimacy of the most powerful group or class is met with fierce resistance: the oil companies and politicians refuse to have their power challenged, let alone by environmentalists and indigenous people. As Steger notes: "Such rigid forms of resistance to change contribute to turning beliefs and ideas into a dogmatic defense of dominant power structures."[5] Indeed, language reinforces power structures and is used by dominant political-economic groups or classes to gain the consent of the subordinate groups, without having to revert to physical coercion. Language becomes fundamental to reinforcing the legitimacy of one's power in the age of corporate public relations. If they do not have to resort to using force, as the oil companies have repeatedly used in developing countries, then they will use the power of ideology, propaganda, and image as in the case of the Arctic Refuge.

In much of the United States at present, the corporate attempt to capture hearts and minds by integrating the public into the dominant neoconservative worldview is working, with the media as the tool. However, the story of one area of land in the Arctic has challenged this "integrative" process and evoked tremendous emotion and passion on both sides, one attempting to challenge the dominant political-economic order, the other resisting change by tooth and nail to preserve the perceived *weltanschauung* of American Manifest Destiny.

ARCTIC POWER: THE FRONT NGO FOR THE CARBON CLUB

In *The Carbon War*, possibly the best book written to date on the politics of global warming, oil industry scientist and expert Jeremy Leggett provides an insider's view into what he refers to as the "foot soldiers" of the oil industry, the "carbon club."[6] As he recounts over a decade of international political negotiations with the intergovernmental panel on climate change, Leggett explains how the oil companies employ front organizations, such as the "Global Climate Coalition," led by people such as Don Pearlman, to do their bidding and political lobbying.[7]

Arctic Power is another oil front NGO, though a regional invention that lobbies at the national level, certainly not at the level of the Global Climate Coalition. Its ideas and tone within the interview reflected what Leggett observed while trying to discuss global warming with higher-ups in the oil industry:

I felt that I had discovered something very important here. The most basic information on the global warming debate, it seemed, was not getting through to people . . . I had a similar experience at the World Climate Conference, where I had taken part in a public debate with BP's then managing director. It seemed that a kind of subtle corporate information shield was at work. People in the carbon-fuel industries were able to exchange perceived wisdoms about global warming in a comfortable, mutually supportive milieu into which few opportunities were offered for the insertion of worrying extraneous information. When information was aired widely in the industry, it was often spurious.[8]

These insights apply directly to the carbon war in Alaska, and the attitudes generated by the Alaskan carbon club are the same of which Leggett speaks. There is little toleration of the opposition or opposing information: any knowledge provided from outside of the power structure must be false, a product of deceitful misinformation. Dissent is not allowed, as alternative ideas and values threaten the status quo of the power structure.

For example, in responding to a question regarding what the basic issues of the Arctic Refuge debate are all about, the Arctic Power representative said:

These are the same simplistic issues as 10–15 years ago, as the facts go, but they are so emotionally charged that it has created a very polarized situation. The basic issue is that Alaska is so far away from the rest of the country, and we have an understanding of oil development—we're very comfortable with it, we all know people who worked in the industry on the (North) Slope, it is not a controversial issue in the state. Polls show that 75% or higher support drilling. We know the facts about the caribou and the way these issues get portrayed nationally is so far from the facts. But people have no way of knowing that, because it's been portrayed as an environmental issue and it's not.[9]

A few signifiers jump out from this statement. The word "facts" is used not only three times in this particular quote but is referred to repeatedly throughout the interview. Also, not one of the anti-drilling interviewees attempted to portray the ANWR debate as "simplistic." If anything, it is a myriad of complex subtleties, in history, ideas, and actors. Reference is always made to the "fact" that Americans from the "lower 48" do not understand the Alaskan "resource development" culture, implying a resentment of outsiders who do not understand the regional and local situation. This coincides with the neoconservative dislike for federal government, an almost inherent Republican mentality characteristic to the state, or at least Anchorage, the dominant population center.

Nevertheless, the rhetoric does not bear out the "facts," as the "King of Pork" Ted Stevens, a primary voice and power behind Arctic Power, brings more federal money per capita into the state than anywhere else in the country. These funds are derived from the taxpayers in the "lower 48" who are ignorant about Alaska, according to Arctic Power, and who should have no say about whether Alaskans want to drill or not.

The old axiom holds true, that to cut through the rhetorical smokescreen, one needs to follow the money trail. We have seen data on how the neoconservatives in U.S. business and politics are not freemarketeers at all but live by a devised and calculated manipulation of the public sector, using public government to enhance private subsidies and profits. There is nothing "free market or laissez faire" about corporate monopolization and welfare.

Regarding polling statistics, environmental activists pointed out that the polls vary according to who is funding the study, obviously, so the "75%" cited is subject to skepticism. This polling number was produced from a firm in Anchorage funded by the pro-drilling groups. One environmental activist said that the public opinion in Alaska is actually swinging toward *not* drilling in the Arctic Refuge: he contended that 40 percent of Alaskans now support conservation of the refuge. Arctic Power likes to speak of "Alaskans" as a whole versus outsiders who do not know the issues, however, Alaskans are diverse in their opinions and realize that this is a very complex issue.

The language and tone of Arctic Power is one of condescension and exclusion: there is no point in having any discussion over the issue because there *is no* issue. It is assumed that the oil development interests hold the sole rights to discussion. It reminds us of Beth Kertulla's statement that the oil companies in Alaska will not allow any dissent; the very process of democratic dialogue is disallowed. This then results in a kind of epistemological dictatorship, where opposing views and concepts are not even given an opportunity to fight on a level playing field. This is very similar if not identical to stances taken by the Bush-Cheney-Rove administration, where any process of multilateral dialogic process is annulled.

It is interesting to analyze neoconservative corporate thinking, for it invariably projects incivility, intolerance, and hypocrisy—a lack of reasonableness—onto the opposition, constantly shifting the negative imagery to the perceived "enemy." It has been noted that Karl Rove, the neoconservative ideologist and policymaker behind George Bush, is a specialist in shifting negative imagery onto the opponents of the neoconservative agenda: "(His) most obvious talent lay in conceiving of a devastating negative attack."[10]

Perhaps the most obvious tactic employed by the oil industry in general, and certainly voiced through Arctic Power, is the attempt to greenwash, and thus neutralize, the environmental arguments. Arctic Power, unlike the anti-drilling groups, refused from the outset to even frame the debate as one pitting economic development versus conservation, economic growth versus the environment. In its opinion, the oil industry in Alaska has proven over the past thirty years on the North Slope that it is a viable environmental steward, and that it cares about protecting the environment with sound technologies. "We have proven that you can have protected environments with development." Thus the oil industry co-opts the language of the opposition by referring to "sustainable development," that amorphous catchall term that has come to the aid of unsustainable developers.

When asked about the report published in the spring of 2003 by the National Academy of Sciences, detailing thirty years of environmental pollution and severe damage to North Slope environments as well as to native cultures, Arctic Power merely acknowledged that it knew of the report: "Some of these reports are politically influenced." I retorted that indeed they are influenced, for the pro-drilling lobby paid to have the report researched and published, yet the findings thoroughly contradicted the intent of the oil lobby. Senator Joe Lieberman latched onto the report the day it was released, citing the findings as evidence to support making the ANWR a permanent wilderness.

The realities of North Slope oil development diverge sharply from the corporate spin propagated by the industry. Pamela A. Miller has extensively researched North Slope development and environmental degradation:

> Prudhoe Bay and 24 other producing fields today sprawl across 1,000 square miles, an area the size of Rhode Island. There are more than 4,700 exploratory and production wells, 225 production and exploratory drill pads, over 500 miles of roads, 1,100 miles of trunk and feeder pipelines, two refineries, 20 airports, 115 pads for living quarters and other support facilities, five docks and gravel causeways, 36 gravel mines, and a total of 27 production plants, gas processing facilities, seawater treatment plants, and power plants."[11]

The environmental record of this development sprawl has been anything but kind to the environment and native cultures. Scientific data on the North Slope show that air pollution from Prudhoe Bay has been measured 200 miles away in Barrow, Alaska. Miller states that industry

> annually emits approximately 70,413 tons of nitrogen oxides, which contribute to smog and acid rain. This is more than twice the amount emitted by Washington, D.C., according to the Environmental Protection Agency, and more than many other cities. Other regulated pollutants include 1,470 tons of sulfur dioxide, 6,199 tons of particulate matter, 11,560 tons of carbon monoxide, and 2,647 tons of volatile organic com-

pounds emitted annually, according to industry records submitted to the Alaska Department of Environmental Conservation.[12]

Concerning greenhouse gases, North Slope industry annually releases 24,000 metric tons of methane and 7.3 to 40 million metric tons of carbon dioxide.

In regard to spillage, the North Slope fields and trans-Alaska pipeline have produced 423 annual oil spills since 1996, and there "were 2,958 spills between 1996 and 2002, totaling more than 1.7 million gallons of toxic substances, most commonly diesel, crude oil, and hydraulic oil."[13]

This barrage of statistics is not meant to overwhelm the reader with excessive data; to the contrary, it is necessary to illustrate the scientific "facts" that seem to undermine claims of legitimacy by the oil lobby. The Arctic is an extremely fragile environment, and the devastation of thirty years of development has rendered areas unrecoverable. The National Academy of Sciences has projected that the significant effects of existing development on the North Slope will continue to expand and adversely influence wild areas far beyond the immediate area of development. That is, damage to the Arctic is far-reaching.

The worst "synergistic" damage is in the form of global warming. Governments, scientists, and activists throughout the Arctic are debating what to do about melting ice sheets, glaciers, sinking tundra, the massive release of methane, the loss of wildlife, and the effects on native cultures in the circumpolar region. Indigenous activists in Alaska argue this point with force:

> Science has confirmed what Alaska Natives, such as the Yupik (Eskimo) and Gwich'in, have been saying for many years: something is happening with the weather, and it is affecting the air, water, land, animals, and, in turn, affecting the people. Though the whole world is warming, climate change has a more drastic effect on the geographical north, hitting Alaska, the Northwest Territories, and Siberia the hardest. Global temperatures do not rise evenly. Over the past 35 years, these northern areas have experienced a temperature rise that is five times greater than the global average of approximately one degree F. One degree, even five degrees, may not seem like much, but consider this: the difference between the average atmospheric temperature during the last geologic ice age and today is only nine degrees F. That change took thousands of years to produce, but the massive burning of fossil fuels, ever expanding since 1900, is creating rapid change, especially over the past few decades.[14]

Arctic Power, as a voice of the oil lobby, had this response when asked about whether fossil fuels were responsible for global warming:

I'm skeptical about the whole issue; it's a chicken-little situation, fossil fuel use doesn't contribute. There are natural causes, like cows and methane gas. I can't believe that people can focus so narrowly that this warming is man-made, when climate has fluctuated so much through history. The Arctic world used to be tropical, that is why we have oil here from dinosaurs. I agree about temperatures and our climate is changing; what I don't agree with is that fossil fuels are to blame. How can a tropical environment with dinosaurs then become covered with ice? That's a huge swing in climate.

At this point I was having trouble following the logical train of thought: this oil lobby representative was invoking a very poor sense of geological history to explain the five-degree change in temperature to the Arctic over the past several decades. The group wants to invoke "science," but at every turn it has a complete contempt for science.

The oil industry in Alaska, unbeknownst to much of the public, has been hit hard with fines and penalties relating to disregard for environmental regulations. In 2002, BP was hit with separate fines of $675,000 (spill cleanup problems) and $300,000 (delaying installation of leak detection systems). It was fined $412,000 in 2001 and $22 million in 2000 (federal court, criminal, and civil). The BP (native) oil service company contractor Doyon was fined $3 million in 1998 for intentionally dumping hazardous wastes down Endicott wells. In 1993, BP was penalized another $51,000.

These data seem to contradict Arctic Power's rhetoric: so much for "environmental stewardship" and the notion of corporate self-policed governance. When asked about how to respond to criticisms concerning North Slope damage, Arctic Power responded: "They measure spills on the Slope by teaspoons. There are different ways to use statistics to prove a point. People that have this inherent fear of development and oil companies are going to criticize Prudhoe Bay, but those *knowledgeable and comfortable* about oil, especially from other countries like Russia, come here to take tours. We give so many tours. These oil tourists can't believe we are so clean on the North Slope."

In fact, BP has stopped giving tours to members of Congress who are trying to decide on the Arctic Refuge. They may be giving tours to Russian oil officials, of course, since Tony Knowles and the oil industry are trying to bolster cross-border investments with Russia, as Siberia contains an estimated 40 percent of the world's reserves. Many Americans are working in the Siberian fields, and oil is why Bush and President Putin remain cooperative. It is also difficult to say that "other countries" are comfortable with oil development, when much of the developing world is protesting oil development, from South America to Asia to the Middle East and Africa.

The Spin of Misinformation

The Alaska oil lobby has continually painted the issue as one of national energy security, trying to parlay the World Trade Tower incident into an argument for the need for domestic oil development. According to the Arctic Power representative: "We import 60% of oil from countries that don't have the governments and regulations to protect their environments like we do. Let's get the oil from where it is the most environmentally safe, the North Slope."

We have already seen the data on how environmentally safe the North Slope is, and in response to the argument concerning domestic energy security, resource economist Pete Morton writes:

> The U.S. is a high cost oil producer with just 1–3 percent of global oil reserves. . . . The expected value of economically recoverable oil in the Arctic Refuge represents between 0 and three-tenths of one percent (0.3%) of global supply. . . . Assuming oil is found, production of Arctic oil can be expected to range from approximately 200,000 to one million barrels a day for a decade or so. This represents between 1 and 5 percent of what the nation consumes daily.[15]

Fineberg estimates that the refuge would likely peak at 400,000 barrels a day, far from the figures cited by Stevens, Murkowski, and Arctic Power (1 million a day, for decades).

Still, the real point in all of this is not the precise number of barrels that the ANWR would produce. As Fineberg notes, the only real "energy security" lies not in further oil development, whether overseas or at home, but in conservation, both in civil practice and governmental support and regulation. Furthermore, as we will see in part 2, strictly economic arguments miss the big picture, especially with regard to global warming and massive changes to the environment.

The oil lobby has also consistently portrayed the issue as one of job growth: Arctic Power's Anchorage office is in the Teamsters' building, and it likes to argue that the unions are fully behind oil development in the refuge. A 1990 study funded by the American Petroleum Institute projected that up to 735,000 jobs would be created by opening up the ANWR.[16] Gale Norton of the Department of the Interior, Stevens, and Murkowski all cite the inflated job number. Nevertheless, Morton states that drilling would result in "0 to 60,000 jobs nationwide."[17]

While Arctic Power receives support from the Teamsters, who have pushed drilling in the refuge, the argument does not hold that organized labor only supports the drilling lobby because of job growth. Drilling opponents receive strong support from the Service Employees International Union (SEIU), the largest union in the AFL-CIO, with 1.4 million members. "We need a long-term, sustained effort for working families to solve our nation's energy policy, not quick, fly-by-night solutions," said the president of SEIU.[18] "Although the Teamsters have been very visible supporters of tapping the refuge, orga-nized labor is clearly of two minds on the issue. The operating engineers, the laborers, and the building trades unions are with the Teamsters. Leaders of the United Auto Workers, Communications Workers of America, the Na-tional Writers Union, and the United Electrical, Radio, and Machine Work-ers of America have spoken out against drilling, citing environmental reasons."

Thus the divisions in labor are quite real over the issue, and it is not one-sided by any means, as Arctic Power and the Alaskan delegation would argue.

While Arctic Power asserts "that development has meant a more sus-tainable, self-reliant posture for Alaskans," Alaska State Representative Sharon Cissna has a different view. She claims that the state of Alaska does not support sustainable self-reliance at all. She is a strong advocate of sustainable community development, and her district in Anchorage, which includes the University of Alaska, is a rare model of a self-supporting community. Accord-ing to Cissna:

> This state does not support sustainable development. They try to lure big businesses into the state, bringing in money that won't stay in the state. They are just betting, making huge risks in development, such as with ANWR. They are giving huge incentives for companies to come into the state, like BP, and in order to finance that will cut monies to many local communities, as with health care. They are sacrificing sustainable busi-ness. ANWR is an example of inviting large outside corporations to come in, develop, and take the money back out with them. (Fighting opening) ANWR maybe is the most profound example of trying to build a state where people want to live, sustain one's heritage versus letting outside corporations come in to develop and leave.[19]

Cissna zeroes in on the problem of globalization: outside corporations coming in to make profits, only to leave once the monies dry up. She has an alternative vision, that of local sustainable communities, and she is working hard to implement this in policy, though her ideas are not popular in a state led by political elites allied with big money. "Oil companies only think about next year, not 50 years from now." Here Cissna targets the real issue over the ANWR, short-term profit versus long-term visions of sustainable environ-ments and communities.

Regarding jobs, Cissna's opinion is a stark contrast from the argument made by Stevens, Murkowski, and Arctic Power:

In the late 60's when oil was found we weren't looking at the social costs. Oil came into Alaska, and we were thinking about short-term jobs. Now we are thinking about jobs in the same way, little has changed. The people attracted to oil jobs are young, mobile people with not a great work history. Many who were attracted to Alaska were people who couldn't get jobs in the lower 48. We had a liquid labor pool floating to Alaska. Anybody who had any talent left Alaska. Those who didn't invest their money wisely blew it, and many of those are left here now.

Cissna noted "how the best people leave Alaska, where there is a big turnover" and little long-term social investment. She wants to create an environment where people stay. "They are not looking at long-term costs; it is about short-term greed and small thinking. Elected officials are going to think first of getting reelected."

Arctic Power had an interesting view on the perceived "most powerful actors" in the debate: "It is a small group of Senators. The focal point of the debate is so polarized; they have their own agendas that this is an environmental vote, and they are pandering to environmental NGOs [nongovernmental organizations] who are warm and fuzzy on these issues without researching them." Here is the ever-present hate for the environmentalists, again blaming *them* for lack of research and use of the scientific facts. "They [the senators] know that people will not be able to go to Alaska and research it for themselves. It's an easy vote to support the environment, when they really don't know the issue in Alaska. People like John Kerry, Lieberman, Tom Daschle: they have all refused to come to the state." This is untrue, for Lieberman has visited the Gwich'in in Arctic Village.

On the native element of the debate, Arctic Power and the oil lobby fully support the Inupiat Eskimo village of Kaktovik, as the village sits on the proposed development site. "Kaktovik Natives own this land, want to develop it, and they have no other way of supporting themselves." The oil lobby argues that these Eskimos still rely upon the caribou for subsistence, just like the Gwich'in. However, the Kaktovik Eskimos argue against oil development offshore, as it will affect their bowhead whale hunting.

The issue over Kaktovik is complicated. The mayor is a white man and friendly to the oil industry. Two different activists in Alaska, one involved with indigenous issues since the 1970s, confirmed that some type of "land swap" took place to enable the Kaktovik leaders—in this case a white man as mayor—to own the land. The subtle issue here again is one of behind-the-scenes co-optation of indigenous leaders by corporate and political elites bent on development. One long-term religious activist and scholar in Alaska told me that in the early 1980s the Prudhoe Bay oil people were flying over to the ANWR 1002 area to camp with the U.S. Fish and Game people and were bragging about how they were co-opting the Kaktovik Inupiat Eskimos by giving them helicopter rides, and so on.[17] Today, Kaktovik has schools, sewer systems, and indoor playgrounds. It has been given these from the oil industry. (In the Gwich'in chapter, I will contrast this with the poverty of Arctic Village.)

Thus co-optation of allies in local government—the same process that has happened all over the developing world—seems to explain the Kaktovik phenomenon. One Gwich'in representative told me that letters and even e-mails are received all the time from individual Kaktovik villagers who privately are against oil development on the ANWR and who support the Gwich'in stance. The upshot is that this is not as simple as Arctic Power would have one believe, but there is a long history to this, dating to the early 1980s, when the oil companies first began to "bribe" the local villagers on the prospective development site. In all of these cases of resource conflict, everywhere, it is imperative to distinguish *who* wants the money, and *who* has the most to gain. Political-economic inequality must always be accounted for first and foremost: the elites, including village leaders, have the most to gain but always claim that they have the best interests of the people at heart.

There is another extremely important point to make. Many indigenous leaders now are corporate people, and this is getting worse as Congress, receiving pressure from the Bush administration and the Interior Department, relaxes regulations allowing energy corporations to make deals with numerous tribal leaders on U.S. western lands to develop oil, gas, and minerals on tribal land.[21] The point is that one's values and beliefs determine whether one values immediate gain from money and profit or sees the value of something beyond money and greed. "All" indigenous peoples are no longer living in harmony with nature, and many have been absorbed into the capitalist paradigm. Ethnicity does not determine how one feels about ecological sustainability or capitalist growth, or socioeconomic justice, for that matter. It is a question of values, beliefs, attitudes, and ideas.

Of course, Arctic Power appears to have little respect for the Gwich'in: "That's hyped, that the Gwich'in are on a subsistence economy. Everyone is on a cash economy in this state. Gwich'in are very bitter about not becoming a corporation. The Gwich'in have been adopted by the environmental community, and the Eskimos here don't have the same weight to their voice. It's PC [politically correct] to be native now, and I just don't understand this, it's cool to be native." Actually, conversely, I learned that the Gwich'in are very proud to have not become a corporation.

Also, the Kaktovik Eskimos do receive weight to their voice, and publicity, and are supported with political power. In 2003, Richard Pombo (Republican-CA), the House Chair for the Committee on Natural Resources, convened a meeting at Kaktovik to promote the village and its "need" for oil development. Pombo is a neoconservative pushing oil development in the Arctic Refuge, and he used the Kaktovik meeting as a public relations tool to make it appear that indigenous peoples were pushing development. Thus neoconservative politicians such as Pombo, Stevens, Young, and Murkowski, along with the lobby group Arctic Power, provide a voice to the certain Kaktovik Eskimos who prefer the money associated with drilling.

Neoconservative Corporate Theology

Arctic Power typically represents what Jeremy Leggett refers to as a carbon club front NGO. Big corporations, and certainly big oil companies, now put massive efforts into public relations campaigns, attempting to convince the public that they care about ecological sustainability and social justice. Shell Oil is now spending tremendous amounts of money to appear as an environmental steward, as it has come under increasing criticism from international environmental, human rights, and indigenous activists for its activities in Nigeria's oil wars. Even National Geographic is now advertising the virtues of Shell Oil and BP ("Beyond Petroleum") as beneficent environmental stewards. Bribery takes all forms.

After comparing interviews with Arctic Power and anti-drilling representatives from various environmental, indigenous, and religious groups, it became apparent that fundamentally different worldviews were taking the stage in the Arctic Refuge clash, and that these deep-seated perspectives and values were reinforced by the very process of the communicative tactics used, in the ways actors spoke of the opposition. The Gwich'in typically, as part of their culture, ask to hear as many opinions as possible, in a remarkable *process* of what might be called democratic, indicative of fairness. The actors from the environmental and religious communities also displayed a keen sense of fairness and compassion for nature and people. I was fortunate to interview some remarkable people in this "resource war."

The striking aspect of the Arctic Power interview was the nature of the seeming intolerance for the opposition, a sense of arrogance. The ideas and the process were indicative of neoconservative economic thought in general. Behind the cursory presentation and effort to appear as an environmental steward, it was interesting that the real ideas and values poured through later in the interview. A main theme of neoconservative corporate theology is a disgust for anything public, as opposed to private control, as evidenced from this statement by Arctic Power: "12% of land in Alaska is owned by Native corporations, and less than 1% is in private hands. Compare that to Texas; they don't have any problems with what we have to go through up here. Texas is almost entirely privately held, people do what the heck they want." This expresses a disgust for federal governmental oversight and regulation, displaying a clear libertarian mentality.

It is interesting how Ted Stevens brings in so much federal money to Alaska, the most in the country per capita, yet his mouthpiece NGO Arctic Power complains about federal public lands and oversight: "Senator to Senator some of our biggest allies have been those who recognize states' rights. Two Hawaii Democrats are Stevens' strongest allies, because Natives don't have access to federal lands." To use the example of Hawaii to invoke states' rights and indigenous rights to complain about federal lands in Alaska is another specious comparison. Arctic Power typically uses the language of "indigenous rights" as a way to divert attention from the sheer drive for profit.

Neoconservative ideology and language wages war on anything public: process, lands, and dialogue. George Lakoff analyzes neoconservative thought as a top-down process, which is thoroughly social Darwinistic: "This means favoring those who control corporate wealth and power (those seen as the best people) over those who are victims (those seen as morally weak). It means removing government regulations, which get in the way of those who are disciplined. Nature is seen as a resource to be exploited. One way communication translates into government secrecy."[22]

Social Darwinism views self-interest and competition as values to be placed above all others: injustice and inequality are justified as the strong (the richest, in corporate theology) rise to the top, and the weak do not deserve compassion, they deserve what they get. Social Darwinistic values and thought, spearheaded by corporate America, are deeply ingrained at this point in history in the United States, and the spread of this vicious belief system is what is benignly referred to as "globalization."

International legal scholar Joel Bakan has expanded the discussion of corporate institutional power to specifically address the "psychopathic" characteristics of the drive for corporate profit.[23] These institutional qualities are very similar to those characterizing individual psychopaths, indicating tendencies toward irresponsibility, lack of empathy and antisocial behavior, manipulation, grandiosity, a refusal to accept responsibility for their own actions, and an inability to feel remorse. They are basically publicly and socially irresponsible in their need to realize the corporate goal, shareholder profit, and the externalization of social and environmental costs, thus putting others at risk of great harm.

Perhaps the most dangerous personality characteristic of this institutional psychopath is the overwhelming motivation to represent itself as caring, compassionate, and socially responsible. Bakan draws a parallel between the human psychopath's penchant to use charm to mask his or her own narcissistic self-absorbed behavior and that of the corporate institution. Public relations thus becomes the primary directive of the corporate sociopath, to carefully present itself to the public as a caring and compassionate "person," at once concerned with social and environmental responsibility. This presentation to the public, however, is designed to hide its own selfish motivations, the externalization of social and environmental costs onto an unsuspecting public. This public relations machine, relentless in its drive to charm the public, essentially displays sociopathic qualities, for the sociopath functions quite well in society and superficially appears quite caring and compassionate. Nevertheless, the charm masks an inherent disdain for ethical and moral concerns, norms, and rules.

In lieu of a worldview predicated upon values of predatorial self-interest and competition, tactics promoted to "destroy one's enemy," Lakoff describes the alternative to the neoconservative corporate emphasis of the bunker mentality:

> Social responsibility requires cooperation and community building over competition . . . there is a general "ethics of care" that says, "help, don't harm." To be of good character is to be empathetic and responsible. . . . Empathy and responsibility are the central values, implying other values: freedom, protection, fairness, cooperation, open communication, competence, happiness, mutual respect, and restitution as opposed to retribution.[24]

Importantly, Lakoff's progressive view of government contrasts sharply with the corporate theological distaste for regulation:

> In this view, the job of government is to care for, serve, and protect the population (especially those who are helpless), to guarantee democracy (the equal sharing of power), to promote the well-being of all, and to ensure fairness for all. The economy should be a means to these moral ends. There should be openness in government. Nature is seen as a source of nurture to be respected and preserved. Empathy and responsibility are to be promoted in every area of life, public and private.[25]

The fight over the Arctic Refuge is truly a confrontation of these respective values and worldviews, as well as their manifested political tactics. This battle is now taking place on the world stage, amid ecological, demographic, and economic crises. Part 2 turns to the progressive thinkers and actors in this global debate, as depicted in the "War for the Refuge."

Part 2

Sustainability and Justice

Chapter 6

The Environmentalists: Visions under Siege

Most of the glimpses of immortality, design, and benevolence that I see come from the natural world—from the seasons, from the beauty, from the intermeshed fabric of decay and life, and so on. Other signs exist as well, such as great and selfless love between people, but these, perhaps, are less reliable. They hint at epiphany, not at the eternity that nature proclaimed.

—Bill McKibben, *The End of Nature*

The success of the Alaska Coalition in battling oil development in the Arctic Refuge depended precisely upon bringing a diversity of interests together: environmentalists, indigenous peoples and activists, and religious community activists. Activists contend that the ANWR campaign succeeded because of broad-based support, uniting traditionally individual interest groups and developing a convergence of values. Chanda Meek, an experienced environmental and indigenous activist, commented:

The reason the Arctic National Wildlife Refuge coalition was so successful was because you have the cultural values, indigenous rights, environmental values, the global warming argument—all are there in ANWR. You can pull in a lot of different groups with different perspectives. There is a diversity of interests. You can pick and choose which groups you want to work on which aspect. The cultural aspect of ANWR is important, and that of indigenous rights: the belief that the Gwich'in should be a principal actor in what happens there.[1]

The perceived unity of diverse interests characterizing the Arctic Refuge campaign has distinguished it from many traditional U.S. environmental campaigns,

91

and the convergence of values is central to its success, as well as a resourceful
and pragmatic utilization of political organization and tactical savvy.

From the anti-drilling perspective, the key is to understand the subtleties
within and behind the purported "unity" of the coalition. The interesting
aspect of the ANWR campaign has been framed by its confluence of both
social justice and environmental values.[2] As discussed in chapter 1, the history
of the Arctic Refuge campaign from a U.S. environmentalist perspective hinged
upon the passage of the ANILCA, the effort to *preserve* wild lands and set
them aside from human development. In the traditional American environmental preservationist view, the only alternative to human incursion and
development is the setting aside of wilderness, an enclosure away from the
human footprint. What makes the Arctic Refuge debate more complicated
from within the anti-drilling perspective is that the social justice aspect—
indigenous rights and questions of aboriginal political authority—does over-
lay traditional conservationist concerns of environmentalists and challenges
traditional preservationist interpretations of how humans should interact with
"nature." Thus the case of the Arctic Refuge expands and deepens how educated "middle-class" U.S. environmentalists define their own values as a pre-
requisite to their environmental policy positions.

The Arctic Refuge issue does point to the themes of ("First World")
environmental justice and ("Third World") political ecology, precisely because
of the cultural dimension, that of indigenous rights, in this case the Gwich'in
Athabascan. Overall, the anti-drilling groups do work together and definitely
posit clear and unmistakably different value systems from those of the pro-
drilling forces and lobby.

It is only obvious that the twin values portrayed by the groups in part 1 focus
upon bald-faced greed and power; this is not a revelation. It is interesting, however, to see *how* the pro-oil development actors strategically and tactically implement their fundamental values of economic profit and political power. It is also
imperative to note that the pro-drilling "carbon club" is fixated upon short-term
profit and financial gain. There is little if any concern for future ecological and
social/cultural consequences of short-term economic development. This is important to note in any discussion of temporal scale, or "future history." In contrast,
the anti-drilling groups primarily center their arguments upon an ecologically
sustainable and socially just future, and the interviews with expert environmental,
indigenous, and religious representatives bear out these concerns.

ALTERNATIVE VISIONS: A QUESTION OF VALUES

The environmentalists traditionally argued to save the Arctic Refuge on
the grounds of wilderness preservation, the need to save intrinsic wilderness

values. They still do argue this, however, the platform has fundamentally expanded to include economic arguments and the need for sustainable development of local communities. Human rights organizations, according to one activist, have pushed traditional environmentalists to expand and transform their preservationist positions to include human rights issues, and more specifically indigenous rights.

The Sierra Club has now implemented a joint conservation-human rights "Partnership Program" with Amnesty International. According to the Sierra Club staff, their NGO is "by far" in the lead of environmental organizations when it comes to splicing social justice concerns into conservationist political platforms. The one theme where I found common ground among the environmentalists and the indigenous people in the Arctic Refuge interviews was that of ecologically sustainable development, ecological sustainability. Of course, advocates of unsustainable development—such as the fossil fuel industry—constantly use the language of sustainability as a PR tool. Nevertheless, the term has a very real meaning to the environmentalists[3] and indigenous peoples. According to environmental activists, they "are not against economic development" but are for sustainable economic development.[4] The Sierra Club representative importantly noted that this platform extends to suburban and urban environments as well, thus connecting the issue over the coastal plain with questions of local sustainability, such as those raised by Representative Cissna concerning her urban Anchorage district.

Thus individuals with very different cultural and ideological backgrounds converged on the values of ecological and economic sustainability: white politicians and environmentalists, and indigenous people. People are increasingly becoming aware that the current economic growth paradigm just is not realistic for the future, if only seen from an economic point of view. Kelly Hill Scanlon researches the Arctic Refuge for the Northern Alaska Environmental Center, a local Alaskan NGO that serves as a member of the Alaska Coalition. According to Scanlon, "Energy efficiency and waste have become the battle point for the environmental community. Wilderness as an intrinsic value was the traditional argument for environmentalists, but since many people don't appreciate that "value," energy waste and efficiency is now a central position. If energy efficiency is the argument, then ANWR is not even an issue."[5]

Indeed, Scanlon points out that the argument for wilderness as intrinsic value is still there, but the environmental community has transformed its message to appeal to economic sensibilities. This includes not only the philosophic value of wilderness but practical economic values, for example, in illustrating the value of energy efficiency. Scanlon made the astute point that the argument varies according to the location and constituency: in Fairbanks, for example, the economic argument is employed, and in Berkeley, intrinsic wilderness value may be used.

Scanlon views development as "meeting needs. Sustainable development is where the argument has to go. Traditional environmentalism has been elitist, but from the 1980s on, people have recognized this and tried to make changes. The key for the environmental community is to create long-term goals on a wide array of fronts. We are hampered by a Band-Aid approach; short-term protections require taking money away from long-term projects like sustainability and alternative energy sources."

The problem is, Scanlon notes, the neoconservative barrage and juggernaut since 1980 is forcing the Band-Aid approach. She sees the Arctic Refuge as a defensive campaign rather than as an example of making "Carteresque" structural changes in long-term environmental policy, as in pursuing alternative energy, research, and development. She worked with the National Research Energy Labs in Colorado.

The environmentalists' economic argument for energy conservation and efficiency has appealed to many grassroots supporters. Still, the intrinsic value for wilderness has been the prime driver to harness support to fight development in the Arctic Refuge. Sean McGuire, a longtime Arctic Refuge activist, contends:

> One of the most profound things about this success story is the "spiritual passion" that people have, in their need to believe that there are still some places left just as God intended, that are wild and unspoiled. Most of the people that have written and called in with grassroots support will never even see ANWR. In an age where we have over six billion people on the planet, and another billion or more every 12 years, these last wild places are a connection to a spiritual sense of well-being. The Arctic Refuge is a symbol of pristine wilderness: people will never go there, but it still means something to them.[6]

This "spiritual" awareness of the intrinsic value of nature is further underscored by the ever-increasing cross-fertilization of ties and bonds between the environmental and progressive religious communities. For example, one Sierra Club activist in Anchorage (who is also head of the Anchorage Audubon Society) also serves as a Presbyterian church elder.[7] She notes that the Sierra Club is "bonding with the religious community," and that the Sierra Club Partnerships Program, headed by Melanie Griffith in Washington, D.C., actively promotes greater interaction with ecologically minded religious organizations and groups. The National Council of Churches has partnered with the Sierra Club.

Traditional environmentalists in the United States have typically viewed the Christian religious community with great skepticism, and this basically is traced to a perceived Christian belief in dominion, or the human right to control and dominate nature. This points to a deeper philosophical rift between anthropocentric and ecocentric views toward nature, essentially questioning the assumed human right to use and exploit nature in any profitable manner. The worldview of "Manifest Destiny" was supported and legitimized by the concept of dominion, and I have already discussed the importance of Manifest Destiny in the shaping of the unconscious values of most Alaskans.

While various environmentalists are still wary of the religious community, the walls are falling as healthy linkages have been rapidly developing over the past decade, and now an environmentalist is seen as backward if he or she does not see the incredible potential of forging ties with allies in the religious and human rights communities in an effort to overcome deleterious divisions that are being exploited every day by corporate and neoconservative strategists such as Karl Rove.

If anything, the Arctic Refuge campaign by anti-drilling forces has demonstrated a remarkable ability to bring in a cross-section of interest groups and values falling across the spectrum, from "deep greens" to "light greens," from people utilizing both spiritual ecological as well as economic arguments. The secret of the success of this campaign rests upon the very coalescence of diverse interests. Karl Rove's Machiavellian (characterized by cunning and duplicity) "genius" rests upon his ability to bring heretofore divided conservative interests together, to forge alliances, and in turn to divide and conquer the progressive communities. If the "Fight for the Refuge" has represented anything for progressives, it is how to create positive, cooperative linkages between the plethora of diverse interest groups.[8]

GRASSROOTS ORGANIZING: TACTICS

As described in chapter 1, the "Alaska Coalition" was originally founded in 1970 as primarily a wilderness preservationist advocacy group, fighting to save federal public lands from development interests both within the oil industry and the state of Alaska. The coalition was instrumental in creating the ANILCA. In this sense, the Alaska Coalition since the 1970s has been spearheaded by powerful and influential professional environmental NGOs such as the Sierra Club, the Wilderness Society, the Natural Resources Defense Council, the U.S. Public Interest Research Group (PIRG), and the National Audubon Society.

These groups have wielded great influence in Washington, D.C., not only in networking together in a tightly knit group within the environmental community but in their long-term nurturing of relationships to diverse congressional members in D.C. According to one veteran activist with the Sierra Club, the coalition focuses upon consistency in lobbying efforts: the same activist will develop a relationship with a particular senator or representative, for example.

While the coalition has, for the past three decades, centered its administrative power in D.C., and continues to do so, environmental members claim that the real success in saving the coastal plain to date has evolved from the coalition's ability to harness tremendous grassroots support from across the country, in every state.

The various activists that have been associated with the Arctic Refuge campaign over the years all agree on one point: the campaign has been an "amazing" and a "remarkable" testament to the mobilization of grassroots organization, linking national-level environmentalists to regional and local grassroots advocacy. The success has relied upon strong top-to-bottom linkages as well as "unifying" disparate interests. Andrew Keller, a veteran Alaska Coalition activist and scholar, states:

> The coalition has been successful because of unification, bringing in religious groups at the human rights angle, attempts to work with farming groups, hunting groups, an energy coalition group, a wide array of groups. But the real strength lies in people in congressional districts all over the country who see slide shows, presentations, and put pressure on their politicians. The coalition has the flexibility to have members travel around the country to give presentations and educate the public. We have a combination of D.C. people, people who have a long history with the issue, and new blood is continuously brought in. We are on top of what is going on in the capital, and people across the country do the organizing (at the local level). In Alaska, we have people who have expertise on the Refuge, from Fairbanks or Anchorage, who know it intimately, from research or guiding. We coalesce experience from Alaska to D.C., to work across the country.[9]

Indeed, the Alaska Coalition is a testament to the "power of NGOs in the U.S.," according to Keller. Environmentalists such as Keller constantly team up with Gwich'in representatives to give slide show presentations on the Arctic Refuge all over the country. Keller has given many presentations on the refuge over the years, and the coalition relies upon experts acquainted with the refuge—environmentalists and indigenous representatives in concert—to educate the public and persuade people to write, call, and e-mail their congressional delegates.

One Sierra Club activist who specializes in researching the oil companies involved in the refuge and Alaska also works closely with the Gwich'in in the political realm for the ANWR campaign. Sara Chapell actually became interested in the campaign through a slide show that came to her hometown in Pennsylvania. The Gwich'in speaker in that local presentation affected her powerfully, motivating her to organize slide shows for the Sierra Club at the local level. She is a perfect example of the power of grassroots organization and how it personally influences people to become involved. She now is one of the more knowledgeable environmental and indigenous activists residing in Alaska.

The Alaska Coalition lists over 700 members on its Website,[10] an array of organizations varying from mainstream environmental organizations such as the Sierra Club to indigenous, religious, academic, labor, and sporting (hunting) groups. Of these 700 organizations, 55 are national members, the rest divided among state and local areas. The coalition Web site provides listings of members for every state in the United States. Membership varies according to locations: California lists 70 member organizations, Florida 43, Oregon 30, Texas 3, and Oklahoma 1. The latter states obviously reflect their oil interests. Local member organizations in different states illustrate the remarkable diversity of the coalition: in Minnesota, you find the United Steel Workers of America and the Institute for Agriculture and Trade Policy; in Arizona, the Apache Survival Coalition, Women for Sustainable Technology, and Friends of Buenos Aires NWR; in Louisiana, a local Baptist church; and in Florida, the Farmworker Association of Florida. National membership includes the "Republicans for Environmental Protection." While most of the members are environmental groups, the coalition has managed to bring in a rich diversity of membership.

Coalition membership includes as well diverse Canadian organizations, including the Canadian Embassy, environmental section; the Porcupine Caribou Management Board; the Vuntut Gwich'in; the Assembly of First Nations; the Canadian Arctic Resources Committee; the Canadian Nature Federation; the Council for Yukon Indians Cultural Survival; the Dawson Indian Band; the Sierra Club of Canada; the Western Canada Wilderness Committee; the Caribou Commons; and the Yukon Conservation Society. This mix represents Canada's strong recognition of, and commitment to, a perceived inextricable link of indigenous and environmental/conservationist affairs.

While the large mainstream environmental groups such as the Sierra Club and Wilderness Society were prime drivers of the original Alaska Coalition, the Alaska Wilderness League in D.C. is now the only member of the coalition that works on the Arctic Refuge full time. The Alaska Conservation Foundation in Anchorage primarily funnels funding from outside sources into members of the coalition, while the Trustees for Alaska in Anchorage is staffed with environmental attorneys who handle lawsuits on behalf of environmental organizations in Alaska. All of these organizations work closely together in the Alaska Coalition.

INSIDER ENVIRONMENTAL POLITICS

The environmentalists working within the campaign state that as a whole, the coalition is powerful because of its unity. Outsiders cannot "wedge" the coalition, and issues are taken care of "internally, like a family."[11] They note that the coalition is guarded against outsiders for its own protection, and that the power within is distributed from the national to local levels.

This all sounds very idealistic, almost bordering on perfection. Part of the problem in attaining information in interviews from coalition environmentalists is the nature of the ANWR campaign itself. It has become such a divisive and heated battle of ideologies that even some anti-drilling advocates are not willing to give interviews. The environmentalists and Gwich'in have become very distrustful of outsiders not only because so many people, from outside of the United States as well, have asked for interviews, but because pro-drilling people have actually attempted to infiltrate the environmental and Gwich'in communities to gain information to use against them. In one case security personnel from the Alyeska Pipeline Company (part of BP) posed as environmentalists in Fairbanks to try to gain inside information to use against the environmental coalition. The oil people were exposed publicly, and the story hit the papers throughout Alaska.[12]

Environmentalists inside the ANWR campaign paint a fairly homogenous picture of the "unity of the Coalition." However, one long-term American international activist, Meek, with experience in both indigenous and environmental perspectives, who has not worked directly within the American ANWR campaign, has a more subtle view toward the environmental coalition:

> In the campaigning, groups like the Alaska Wilderness Coalition mostly were helping smaller environmental groups and helping groups around the country put together a common cookie-cutter approach: writing letters to the editor, letters to congressional people. E-mail is fundamental to environmental organizing capacity, formalizing standardized arguments, using cookie-cutter framing how people should think about the issue.

The coalition working on the refuge has depended upon members watching slide shows, sending money into the Washington, D.C.-based groups, and sending out e-mails to members. They claim that grassroots support has mobilized the campaign. Still, as Brian Tokar explains, insider mainstream environmentalism remains firmly ensconced within D.C. political circles.

> Mainstream environmentalists increasingly coveted their seats in Washington's policy circles and came to identify further with those business and government interests that could bestow such access. . . . The history of mainstream environmentalism in the 1990s has been one of legislative compromise and capitulation, missed opportunities, and the ever-persistent pursuit of "influence" in a fundamentally corrupt and anti-ecological political system. Despite consistent public support for environ-

mental initiatives, and the rapid proliferation of environmental rhetoric and images, the actual condition of our air and water, the integrity of our ecosystems, and the health of our people show few signs of significant improvement. Defenders of an "insider" approach to activism argue that access to the corridors of power enables them to work more effectively for the environment. Yet as the representatives of official environmentalism become more isolated from grassroots activists, the mainstream groups became rather comfortable in their safe and non-confrontational stance.[13]

It is fair to view the environmental ANWR campaign from a more critical overview. Lakoff provides insight concerning the differences between coalitions and social movements.

> An unfortunate aspect of recent progressive politics is the focus on coalitions rather than on movements. Coalitions are based on common self-interest. They are often necessary but are usually short-term, come apart readily and are hard to maintain. Labor-environment coalitions, for example, have been less than successful. And electoral coalitions with different interest-based messages for different voting blocks have left the Democrats without a general moral vision. Movements, on the other hand, are based on shared values, values that define who we are. They have a better chance of being broad-based and lasting. In short, progressives need to be thinking in terms of a broad-based progressive-values movement, not in terms of issue coalitions.[14]

The term here is self-interest. A more cynical view of the ANWR "Coalition" may perceive that environmental activists at "the top," especially at the Washington, D.C., level, are pursuing their own political and financial gain, albeit quite pale compared to the power of the opposition, in this case, the oil companies.

In all fairness, it is questionable whether the campaign has truly linked "broad-based values" versus merely using what Meek calls a top-down cookie-cutter approach. While nonenvironmental groups from the indigenous, religious, and labor sectors have been brought in, it appears to be out of self-interest, certainly to bolster the power of Washington, D.C.-based environmental groups.

I found that actual grassroots, lower-level, local environmentalists were more willing to share their ideas and cooperate for interviews, while administrators in groups such as the D.C. Alaska Coalition, the Alaska Conservation Foundation, and the Trustees for Alaska often would not respond to letter, phone, or e-mail solicitations. Some environmentalists were extremely open and helpful, while others were indifferent or exclusionist and did not even bother to respond, such as the directors of the D.C. Alaska Coalition or the U.S. PIRG office. People would screen their calls with recorders, and then never call back. At least the BP vice president in Alaska had the courtesy to phone in response to my letter.

Despite the rhetoric, as noted by Tokar, of a commitment to grassroots action and mobilization, as well as to "national outreach," my own experience with some of the environmentalists in the interview process seemed to validate Tokar's awareness of insider environmental politics and a top-down sense of arrogance toward an earnest outside researcher. The Sierra Club was very helpful and open, as were two researchers in the local Fairbanks ENGO, the Northern Alaska Environmental Center. Unfortunately, the process seemed to validate my own skepticism toward the higher levels of the environmentalist community, that it is not as open to grassroots action and the general public as the rhetoric would have you think.

Meek, a true indigenous grassroots activist and environmental policy analyst, noted that certain Washington, D.C., groups such as the Alaska Wilderness League designed the cookie-cutter campaign strategy for the Arctic Refuge, finding a common "value" demoninator among average Americans who understood the goals of mainstream American environmentalism—but not the complexities of indigenous politics and different indigenous groups. Meek also commented on the insider mentality of the environmentalist community: "Environmentalists are very worried in talking to an interviewer about divisiveness within their ranks, as corporations will read the thesis and use strategies to use against them."

Thus in reality, the Arctic Refuge campaign is more complicated and subtle than would first appear to an "outsider." One experience in the fieldwork/ interview process revealed a definite division and tension within the environmental community involved, and this stemmed from competition over jobs and a clash of egos, a common malady in American society whether from the neoconservative right or the liberal left.

My overall experience with the environmentalists left me doubting the rhetoric of a grassroots outreach to the general public, or that these environmental organizations are really committed to a transformation of base values, which should be the hallmark of true social movements. My own view is that the American liberal (progressive) community in large part is very divided and self-interested and cannot transcend competition within its own ranks. As Lakoff notes: "A progressive vision must cut across the usual program and interest-group categories. What we need are strategic initiatives that change many things at once." For example, 2004 presidential contenders such as John Kerry and Richard Gephardt, so-called champions of defending the ANWR, joined forces to attack Howard Dean, the popular grassroots Democratic contender, the only Democrat who stood up against the oil war in Iraq.

If groups such as the Sierra Club are truly making efforts to find common value ground with human rights groups, indigenous groups, and religious groups, then this is hopeful for the future and a departure from past (American) environmental elitist politics as usual. Nevertheless, I remain skeptical, just as the ANWR case tends to reveal an issue-based approach. Some environmentalists are reaching out, indeed, but this "community" is by no means unified—it is diverse and individualistic.

One problem with the Arctic Refuge case, especially concerning environmentalists, is that I believe it dangerously borders upon being seen as only another preservationist "issue," microscopically insulated from larger (and international) fundamental questions of political economic power, and what I see to be the corporate takeover of democratic society in the United States. The bottom line, as I see it, is when corporate Democratic senators such as John Kerry, Tom Daschle, and Joe Lieberman—who love the publicity in appearing to be environmentalists while stopping drilling in the ANWR— quietly vote for every $87 billion appropriation for U.S.-led oil wars in poor undeveloped countries, voting alongside Ted Stevens and the Bush-Cheney military-oil junta. In this age of corporate globalization, any insulated "issue" becomes dangerously irrelevant unless one constantly views the global implications of the power at the top. The point of chapter 3 was to illustrate how the oil companies in Alaska operate all over the world: they are local to global players. My fear with some American environmentalists is that they are too provincially "national" and too issue based, and not focused enough on the real structural theme of our era, the corporate takeover of the state. If this were the focus, then some environmentalists would be more concerned with how corporate "Democrats" vote on corporate oil-military subsidies totaling tens of billions of dollars than with how they vote on the ANWR.

There also is a question of how well the environmental community intersects with other public interest NGOs. The energy director at Public Citizen, Ralph Nader's consumer advocacy group, noted that the "ANWR was a smokescreen and brilliant strategy" by the energy industry and GOP to keep attention away from the real nuts and bolts of the new and far-reaching energy legislation: The "ANWR is being used as a diversion. Go to all the leading environmental websites; the ANWR issue is front and center, but there is no significant mention of other provisions in the energy bills."[15] The legislation, according to Public Citizen, was designed to use the "ANWR as leverage to get more domestic oil and gas tax breaks."

A leading D.C. lobbyist for the Sierra Club admitted: "Certainly we had had great worries that by focusing our (lobbying) resources on Arctic drilling, we would not devote resources to other issues such as tax incentives and subsidies for the oil and gas industry. Some of these things slipped under the radar."[16] Slipped under the radar? The new energy legislation is a major neoconservative overhaul of how government deregulates oversight and control over corporations. Oil and gas subsidies are much more than "issues." They comprise a fundamental restructuring of democratic governance, of creation of the corporate state. This seems naïve at best. We have to wonder whether the environmental groups in the ANWR campaign truly interlink with other NGOs, such as those focusing on corporations. But PIRG does, and along with Greenpeace, it filed the shareholder resolutions against BP that ultimately led the company to withdraw its funding of Arctic Power. However, important anti-corporate NGOs such as Corporate Watch and Project Underground are not listed as members of the Alaska Coalition. Interestingly, Corporate Watch and Project Underground are both main supporters of the Gwich'in in the fight over the refuge, however. This leads us to consider the relationship of the environmentalists and the indigenous peoples involved in the Arctic Refuge.

The ANWR: Environmentalists and the Gwich'in

The crucial relationship in the Alaska Coalition is that of the environmentalists and the Gwich'in Athabascan. The Arctic Refuge campaign brought the environmentalist and indigenous communities together, according to Meek, because of a convergence of values. Both sides capitalized on the need to save the wildlife, specifically the Porcupine caribou herd. The environmental preservationist community sought the protection of wilderness values, wildlife, and federal public lands. The Gwich'in found an overlap of values with the environmentalists because of wilderness and wildlife, of course, but because of very different reasons, and much more personal, real. The Gwich'in are fighting for nothing less than cultural survival, which includes subsistence rights to continue to hunt caribou, the animal with which they spiritually identify. In the following chapter I will discuss their relationship to the land. Their "convergence of values" with the environmental community is complicated and should not be easily taken for granted. Much of the alliance developed out of self-interest and political need for both sides, as a political necessity in battling an incredibly powerful political-economic machine.

The Sierra Club's Chapell knows the Gwich'in well and has worked closely with them in the Refuge campaign:

The Gwich'in Steering Committee is a powerful and effective voice for the people, magnifying the voices of their people. They don't really need help from outside consultants, they are smart and politically saavy Gwich'in women who have basically taken the charge from their elders, doing their work. The environmental community has taken the stance to support them in ways that are workable, somewhat financial, but more so in making sure that the Gwich'in voice has a seat at the table.[17]

Indeed, the environmentalists in D.C. have tried to give the Gwich'in greater access to political participation, grassroots participation. As Chapell observed: "If there is a hearing on native rights, sacred places, an environmental issue related to the Arctic, we make sure that the Gwich'in have an opportunity to testify in front of Congress. Or they speak firsthand to the media at a press conference. There is a big political morass out there, so political access is much more important than giving financial resources."

Chapell recognizes the deep cultural differences between the Gwich'in and the environmentalists that underscore their various values and goals of seeking subsistence versus environmental preservationism: "We don't have the experiences of the Gwich'in, I did not grow up butchering caribou. There is no reason for me to go on talking about that, it's not genuine. When we do have people traveling around the lower 48 doing slide shows, we try to have a Gwich'in delegate present, to try to match an environmental speaker with a Gwich'in spokesperson, equally. They speak from Gwich'in experience."

Chapell first became motivated to join the ANWR campaign after hearing one such Gwich'in speaker in her Pennsylvania hometown: " Until that slide show I had no idea there was a group of people so marginalized by a decision that would be made in Washington, D.C. It speaks to the power of grassroots environmental evangelism. The personal connection was the difference, meeting people that would be affected by the political decisions."

Still, the environmentalists have been running the campaign, and they have the power. Environmental activist Scanlon referred to the Gwich'in as bringing "the human wilderness component" into the campaign. "The Gwich'in have symbolic power. They are the symbol of ANWR. They have power, but it is not really theirs. It is a matter of mutual use: the Gwich'in are a willing participant, they are willing to be used for their own political gain, but it is mutual gain."

If the Gwich'in and environmental communities are willing to use each other for political gain, with the latter gaining the most political capital, then there is a more fundamental separation between the two within the American context. Indigenous activist Meek is very familiar with the Canadian political system and its willingness to incorporate indigenous politics into all phases of governmental decision making, including environmental policy. According to her, there is a big difference between Canadian and American environmentalists:

It seems to me that there is a gulf between indigenous activists and environmentalist activists in Alaska. I knew a former environmental activist from Alaska who viewed native corporations as representative of native communities. While there are native corporations in Canada, they are not as powerful as those in Alaska. He said that ANWR was no big deal, that it was not the most important issue in Alaska. He didn't care about indigenous rights. The history of American protected areas is a history of removing the original inhabitants and land managers.

In contrast, in Canada indigenous rights are inseparable from discussions of environmental sustainability. The notion of Canadian environmental-indigenous justice is very different from that of American environmental preservationism. Meek explains: "[American] environmentalists want to lock up land, set it aside, imposing a regime hurting local communities. There are multiple uses for any landscape. Deep ecology is unrealistic for communication with various parties. In Canada you don't have the David Ortons of the world. American preservationists are unrealistic, imposing cultural imperialism."

Thus maybe the overlap of values in the ANWR campaign is more a matter of political advantage for the environmentalists, to build an issue-based coalition. Meek has a different view concerning the treatment of the Gwich'in in the ANWR campaign:

> It's not as if the Gwich'in Steering Committee got a million dollars to work on ANWR, but I'll bet some environmental groups did. Those groups have a lot of pull in Congress and D.C. and can pull in big financial resources like the Natural Resources Defense Council, the Wilderness Society, the Sierra Club. The Alaska Coalition, however, is not a wealthy group. The Indians never get the money. The success in blocking drilling is not because of the Gwich'in, it is because most senators can feel good about voting against ANWR due to the fact that there was so much public pressure created from the campaigning. The senators wouldn't lose any political capital by voting against it. If they didn't have direct political consequences, they voted against it; it was a poster child.

A closer inspection of the Arctic Refuge environmentalist campaign reveals more subtlety and complexity than first perceived at a superficial level. The campaign's success was contingent upon a public relations barrage orchestrated by the main environmental groups in D.C., capitalizing on the symbol of the Gwich'in, the "human wilderness component." Indeed, grassroots action was mobilized throughout local areas of the entire country, which was a remarkable feat of organization, even if was a "cookie-cutter" approach. Overall, however, the "coalition" does not seem to have reached the status of a social movement, if a true convergence of values is required, with a common future vision. One possible interpretation is that political expediency and opportunism motivated the D.C. environmentalists to bring in disparate interest groups.

This chapter is only meant to provide a more realistic, critical approach to an overview of the ANWR narrative. It is dangerous to ignore critical subtleties and complex diversities in participant values: indigenous activists themselves will point out that there is an uneasy marriage between American environmental preservationists and indigenous goals and values. Through my firsthand observation with the actors in the refuge conflict, the indigenous and the religious community representatives seemed to challenge my ideas the most, expanding my views and portraying uneasy subtleties within the issue.

The Gwich'in, to whom I will now turn, placed the ANWR debate truly within a larger global context, fundamentally drawing upon the crisis of global warming. The Gwich'in argue for the twin themes of human-ecological sustainability *and* their need for political self-determination, expanding upon the environmental preservationist model. In essence, the refuge war has left them squeezed in between three major actors, the oil company-Alaska State complex, the federal government, and the environmental preservationists. They are the real "heroes" in this story.

Chapter 7

The Gwich'in: A Fight to the End

Conquest through colonization by industrial nations destroyed millions of indigenous peoples and countless cultural groups. Most surviving indigenous groups lost their political independence and now only have a precarious control over resources. As of 1997, an estimated 220 million indigenous peoples were scattered over the world, usually in remote areas that are prime targets for resource development by outside interests.

—John Bodley, *Victims of Progress*

The story of the Gwich'in battle against oil development in Alaska is currently taking place all over the world, in remote areas. The theme is the same, as indigenous cultures fight for their lives, their lands, and the very worlds they have known.[1] In the Gwich'in case with the ANWR, the difference is that they are trying to use the political vote to stave off resource extraction: as Representative Cissna commented, it has not become violent "yet."

Bodley's *Victims of Progress* probably serves as the best historical and theoretical overview through which to view the Gwich'in battle. The idea of temporal and spatial scales brings the Gwich'in and the Arctic Refuge into focus. This battle is being fought against a larger canvas of what Bodley refers to as the clash of large-scale, modern industrial *commercial* societies with small-scale traditionally subsistence-based cultures. The fight over the ANWR may be viewed as a classic historical clash of scale and values: the large (global) dominant commercial culture and its inherent capitalist value system threatening the very life of a local-level and extremely small group of people representing and advocating local sustainability. The ANWR is a perfect example of the global-level capitalist resource extraction machine attempting

107

to run over and destroy any traditional small culture in its path. These traditional peoples are "in the way" of "progress and manifest destiny."

The current story of the Gwich'in may be perceived as a physical and symbolic last stand against the entire American capitalist value system that has committed genocide and ecocide against American tribal peoples for the past 400 years. It is as though the inexorable machine of manifest destiny has reached the limit of its acquisitive value system on a stretch of U.S. territory lying above the Arctic Circle, where a battle of values is being waged of historical and global proportions. A unified Gwich'in nation is fighting much more than just black oil, but the very beliefs that have propelled genocide and ecocide in this country. They represent hope for an alternative future, advocating values for local, small-scale, ecologically sustainable communities that are simultaneously culturally, economically, and politically self-determinant.

THE GWICH'IN CULTURE AND NATION

The central, most exciting feature of my interview process in Alaska was my bush plane flight into Arctic Village, which lies 200 miles north of Fairbanks, 110 miles north of the Arctic Circle. Arctic Village is historically known in the Gwich'in language as Vashraii K'oo, which translates to "Steep Bank by the Creek." The Gwich'in were nomadic before they settled into Arctic Village, which is the farthest north of any Indian village in the United States. The contested calving ground of the porcupine caribou herd in the coastal plain of the Arctic Refuge is 200 miles north of Arctic Village. Arctic Village rests between hills on three sides, lying just on the south side of the Brooks Range. Flying north from Fairbanks, the Alaskan landscape is riddled with tundra ponds and lakes, with rivers coursing through seemingly infinite Arctic plains. The terrain is immense.

In the language of the Gwich'in Steering Committee, Arctic Village is part of the "Native Village of Venetie Tribal Government" land, a sovereign area established in 1943. The Native Village of Venetie Tribal Government is the governing body over 1.8 million acres of private tribal land, which includes the villages of Venetie and Arctic Village. There are nine tribal council members, chiefs, who oversee the tribal government. Each village has a traditional council as well, managing community affairs. Each community has a "traditional chief" who is the authority over traditional tribal laws, advising the village councils about traditional laws and values, for guidance in governing the community.[2]

From the outset, it is important to understand the fundamental rift between how the Gwich'in view themselves, as a sovereign tribal entity, and how the U.S. government views them. In 1998, the U.S. Supreme Court ruled 9–0 that the Gwich'in of Venetie and Arctic Village do not qualify for

"Indian country" status, giving them reservation status as commonly found in the lower 48. This was a rebuke by the federal government concerning legal and political autonomy, not whether the Gwich'in owned the 1.8 million acres. The Gwich'in land is private—one needs permission to enter their area. The U.S. government and the U.S. Supreme Court refused to recognize their tribal government sovereignty. The U.S. government sees the Gwich'in not as a sovereign "nation" but as private landholders. This is absurd, since these people have lived in their ancestral areas for possibly 30,000 years, compared to over 200 years of existence of the U.S. government.

Arctic Village is a small Gwich'in Athabascan community of 130–180 people, with three dirt roads and one small plane strip. In the summer, people drive small multiwheel motorcycles with heavy tires, and I saw only one old pickup truck in the village. In the winter, they drive snow machines to get around. The Gwich'in of Arctic Village and Venetie (the bush plane stops in Venetie on trips to and from Arctic Village) are materially poor people: one may walk the length of the village in ten minutes, and it is composed of mostly one-room log cabins. They have repeatedly turned down monetary offers from oil companies and offers to build new facilities—all modern conveniences enjoyed by the Inupiat Eskimos at Kaktovik.[3]

The Gwich'in community is a very small kin-based community. Arctic Village, for example, is composed of several extended families. Bob Childers, an indigenous and environmental activist, worked with the Gwich'in for over twenty-five years and helped bring them into the ANWR debate. Childers notes one cross-cultural difference concerning the Gwich'in: "Working with the Gwich'in is about working with clans and extended families, not institutions."[4] Venetie and Arctic Village have a joint tribal council of nine ranked chiefs. The day I arrived in Arctic Village, the tribal council of chiefs was meeting for its annual event. My plane stopped in Venetie along the way to pick up chiefs attending the meeting in Arctic Village.

I was invited into Arctic Village by one Gwich'in tribal representative, for two days.[5] This was an extremely short period, granted, however, it appeared that the invitation *meant* for the trip to be brief. For those unfamiliar with the extended history of the ANWR campaign, outlined in chapter 2, it is difficult to fathom how many people both nationally and internationally have visited Arctic Village. One Gwich'in told me that it is like having people knock on the door of your home every day, year after year. There is no end to it for them. They are caught in between: they need the allies, and they need people friendly to their cause to tell their story, however, at the same, they just want to be *left alone*. One Gwich'in gave forty interviews in one week alone to outside visitors to Arctic Village.

To the Gwich'in, as well as other actors in the long ANWR campaign, so many types of people have come through the evolving door for so many years, only to make quick exits, pursuing their own political, research, and commercial interests, for example. In a sense the process has become so overwhelming as to be a cause for cynicism. The Gwich'in have been used and exploited by so many "anti-drilling" individuals and groups, using the "poster children" to further personal and interest group gain. In the big picture, the example of the Gwich'in is a sad testament to exploitation, even from their own anti-drilling "side."

The Gwich'in are not political or legal by nature. They traditionally do not even think in those terms. They were, for thousands of years, nomadic hunters and gatherers, taking life from hunting caribou. Thus they have had to become assimilated into the dominant white legal-political culture just to attempt to develop allies and work within the system to fight oil development and their loss of aboriginal land rights. This assimilation process has caused great debate and division within the Gwich'in villages, and I witnessed this firsthand. Foremost, it appears in the attitude of the elders, who are frustrated with the perceived loss of their traditional ways, coupled with a frustration with the younger generation that—more and more—is living in white urban society, attending white colleges, and learning white "worldviews." One elder lamented the fact that all of his children live on the outside, and that maybe he sees them once a year for Christmas. A trip into Arctic Village—albeit a brief one—reveals a prideful people, fiercely proud of their culture, history, and relationship to the land. Still, it would be naïve, like many environmentalists who have never been to Arctic Village, to paint the Gwich'in as a homogenously traditional people still thoroughly living a life of pure subsistence. Meek, who has researched and worked with many indigenous communities, commented that she "can't think of one that is strictly a subsistence economy." The Gwich'in still hunt caribou, of course, but they do not wear caribou skins, unless it is for a special ritual event.

They appear to be materially very poor people but simultaneously rich in other ways, such as kinship ties. However, one can see the tragic subtleties in their community, especially in the gulf between the older generation and the younger. One elder commented that the culture would be gone in three to four years. This frustration and sense of tragic loss is borne of a consciousness of one's cultural and family history, the unbroken chain of clan lineage and continued connection to the same land over generations. These deep feelings, connecting a memory of the past to the present and future, are not really understood and appreciated by people like myself growing up in an urban, commercialized culture. Gwich'in respect for history, history of family, and the land is practically diametrically opposite to white American disregard for history and what one owes to the past. The two cultures could not be more different.

I can try to speak of the way the Gwich'in perceive their connection to the land, and to their ancestors, but this is only a superficial approximation. The best I can do is portray the tremendous gulf between our cultures. Childers, who probably spent more time with the Gwich'in over the past twenty-five years than any other white man, explains: "Getting along with native folks can be tough, but the Gwich'in are the toughest. They don't take it from anybody, they are very prideful." After I arrived in the late morning in the village, I was instructed to wait in my small cabin until my Gwich'in representative—the one who invited me—came to see me. I grew frustrated as the day passed, into the evening, waiting for the interview. At 10 P.M. this person knocked on my door, with child in tow. According to Childers, this was typical, and I was ignored intentionally: "It took seven years before anyone talked to me on the street in Arctic Village. One Gwich'in told me, 'Well, all you white guys look alike.' " In my case, that particular interview was postponed until late the next day.

There is a great cultural divide, even among the Gwich'in and their environmentalist allies. According to Childers: "The Gwich'in did not want to support the environmentalist 'wilderness' position, because that is a foreign concept to them, not being able to do things as they always have. They have wanted things as they have always been, and for us to get the hell out of their face." This involves a deeper, subtler fundamental divide over how the whites from Bodley's consumer culture—including environmentalists who want to set nature aside—see nature, in contrast to the Gwich'in. Childers continues: "It is a question of the wilderness concept versus subsistence. In the American worldview there are only two or three boxes, and in one box is 'wilderness,' to protect and preserve. To the indigenous worldview, the white view of 'wilderness' is that where humans don't belong, they don't have a place. They see the land exactly as you see your backyard. The concept of wilderness doesn't fit, it's not 'wild' to them if you have lived there your whole life. There is an assumption of separation in white American thought, between the idea of the primitive versus that of the civilized. The primitive represents that which you can't control. There is a fear of the primitive, that which you can't control."

The Gwich'in are now speaking of ecological sustainability, using the term to expand upon that of subsistence. Both, in essence, refer to need, meeting basic needs in a balance with nature and resources, in contrast to the insatiable commercial want exemplified in the global American society and culture.[6] Gwich'in culture actually represents a true sense of sustainability, if the term broadly includes a commitment to seeking a human balance with the natural world, an equilibrium, as well as a sense of communal social democratic structure. The Gwich'in live in fifteen small villages, totaling 7,000 people, spreading from eastern Alaska to western Canada. They live simply and take only what they need to survive.

> We live a very simple and humble life in our communities, and although it may seem that we are not very advanced in modern adequacy we love

our homeland and way of life. We are healthy and content in our community and homeland. We believe that we are a very fortunate people to
have a healthy ecosystem, which sustains us and a living culture to pass
on to our future generations, as well as the conveniences of modern
times. . . . In our day-to-day life we balance our traditional lifestyle with
the current. This is our approach, to live in the best of both worlds. We
try to ensure that our culture thrives in the face of modern times. Balance
is the key. In the community there are modern facilities and conveniences
as well. We have two stores, a post office, a clinic, school, washeteria
(showers and laundry facilities), and a council office. Our school and
offices are equipped with computers and the Internet. Some homes enjoy
satellite television as well. We have telephones, VCRs, and microwaves,
etc. Although we do have these modern conveniences, we do not have
running water or indoor plumbing in our homes, nor do we have indoor
heating, as woodstoves provide warmth in our homes. We do have to
haul our wood and water for these purposes.[7]

The Gwich'in are proud of their lifestyle and the fact that they never accepted
the terms of the ANCSA. They kept their land and turned down the money.
They are the rebels in the state of Alaska and have refused to become co-
opted indigenous people, or corporate indigenous people—taking the money
and sacrificing one's history, culture, language, spirituality, and connection to
the land. Where most indigenous peoples in the United States are increasingly succumbing to capitalist influence, in gambling and cooperating with oil
and mining companies to extract resources from their tribal lands, the Gwich'in
are a most remarkable exception.

THE CONNECTION TO THE LAND

Faith Gemmill, a member of the Gwich'in Steering Committee, explains
the deep spiritual connection between the Gwich'in and the land.

Indigenous Peoples have a spiritual obligation to uphold the sacredness
of life, as well as uphold the integrity of the Earth. We are given life
from the Earth. We relate to the Earth as our Mother—we understand
that the role of our mother is a life-giving force that nurtures, protects,
and promotes life. The integral role and values Mother Earth has
nurtured within us is that we are responsible for the assurance of life.
These teachings entail the essence of our life and spirit of our peoples,
which are not negotiable nor compromised. Exploitation of our lands is
to sever the umbilical cord between our Mother and our Peoples. If this

cord is severed, it would threaten the survival and well-being of our future generations.[8]

Every Gwich'in speaks of the sacred connection to the Earth, to the land. While the ANWR is a federally managed area of land contested by oil companies, state and federal government, and environmentalists, to the Gwich'in it is a sacred place, where their caribou give birth and nurse the young in the summer. The Gwich'in call themselves the "caribou people," and they have a spiritual connection to the caribou, the animal upon which they have depended for subsistence for hundreds of generations.

> We have a spiritual connection to caribou. They are everything to us— the food on our table, they were shelter to us before. It's our story, it's in our songs. We do a caribou hunt dance. We used to be nomadic people, we'd follow the food, wherever we could gather the food. We used to live a very basic life, simple life based on needs, not greed. Without caribou our people wouldn't have survived after Western culture came to us with disease that wiped out a lot of our people. There used to be 100,000 of us, now there are less than 7,000. Our people used to die only of old age, but today after the change that has come to our country, our people are dying of cancer, heart disease, drug and alcohol-related death. That's what development put upon us. If there is more development it will get worse.[9]

The land, nature is everything to traditional Gwich'in learning. One Gwich'in told me proudly how he grew up in Arctic Village, climbing and exploring every hill and mountain within sight of the village. He was part of that land as a child, and as an elder, he continued to see it as his life. He said that they are losing the land, of which the caribou are part; that is, they lose their land, they lose their humanity. The land was and is their heritage, their race.

> The caribou are God's way of giving us life. They are too sacred for self-interest. Politics is not in our (traditional) system. When the caribou migrate they use the energy of this planet. Now the energy is all screwed up. It is a matter of spirituality and the global environment. You can't rely on money out here; these are the cycles of nature. Without the cycle of life, without ANWR, the cycle of life is over, all for money. Oil is unnatural; fossil fuels lead to global warming.[10]

Another Gwich'in spoke in similar terms, emphasizing how this battle over the refuge was really a question of how humans relate to nature, the natural cycle, and other humans. To the Gwich'in, the process of how humans interact is everything. Childers, the Gwich'in activist, noted: "To the Gwich'in the visiting is the meat of it, between people. The process of visiting round the campfire, speaking only in Gwich'in, meeting with people all night."

The Gwich'in culture, then, is characterized by an integral relationship to the surrounding land and the other clans, people in the village upon whom they depend for survival. It is said that each Gwich'in knows the land intimately, every aspect of it in detail, for 200 miles in circumference of each village. This is an amazing thing to comprehend for a Western, "urbanized" mind.

One Gwich'in said that the ANWR has become the pinnacle of a struggle of big companies and powerful government pitted against the poor (he emphasized to me that he meant "poor" in the material aspect, not in that of pride). He said that in the indigenous worldview, the question is about our role as human beings and our relationship to life and other beings. This, he said, contrasts with the Western corporate worldview, one based on hierarchy and power. Indigenous organization of leadership and social structure, he said, may be seen as a reverse triangle, as the leaders seek to uphold the will of the people.

In a very real sense, Gwich'in communitarian ethics is an excellent example of social democracy on a small scale, a village scale. According to Childers, Gwich'in truly practice democracy in the way and process that they make decisions and consult with each other. If there is a natural democracy, it is enshrined in Gwich'in culture: "You cannot get five Gwich'in to agree on anything. They are very comfortable in airing their differences in public. They tell you to speak to different people to get different views." This sounds like an inherent democracy, encouraging difference of opinion, and extended discussion. The Gwich'in are unique in that they practice a true form of communitarian social structure, depending upon each other, yet they think for themselves, as emphasized by Childers.

I found this to be true in my brief experience in the village, as the Gwich'in are very outspoken, and some are actually belligerent in their candid appraisals of what they perceive to be the destruction of their natural lands and way of life.

The Gwich'in are angry about profound environmental change to their traditional land and ecosystem. Every tribal member to whom I spoke expressed a combination of anger and deep sadness over environmental change to the land. It actually snowed while I was in Arctic Village, in the middle of July. According to elders, it was the first time in their entire lives that they had ever witnessed snow at this time of year, and they were blaming global warming and severe disruption to the global climate.

Importantly, the Gwich'in to whom I spoke with did not want to speak of the ANWR issue as just a separate or freestanding issue. When they speak of the caribou, they will tell you that the caribou migration patterns have been disrupted; one village member told me that they have not seen caribou in the area for two years. One villager complained that the massive stream of outside "hunters and hikers" flying into the Arctic Refuge has disrupted the migratory pattern of the animals. It is not just oil development, then, that threatens the animals and Gwich'in subsistence. Masses of people, from both sides of the political spectrum—including backpackers, environmentalists, wildlife and resource biologists, and academic researchers—are streaming into the ANWR, changing the land with the human footprint. I saw groups of hunters, backpackers, and researchers getting ready to take off in bush planes for the refuge area and the Brooks Range. The Gwich'in are being swamped with outside hunters and eco-tourists. The problem, the Gwich'in will tell you, is not just oil but too many non-native people invading their landscape. Basically, they just want to be left alone.

The caribou, for generations, followed the same migration route, and this route always flowed through Arctic Village. Thus in the springs and summers the Gwich'in would take the caribou they needed for subsistence, as the animals respectively traveled north to the coastal plain birthing grounds, and again south before the fall, back to Canada for the winter. These patterns are now changing dramatically. The oil people and hunters are not the only ones disrupting the caribou: the Alaska Coalition of environmentalists is now tracking the caribou with radio collars on the animals. Many wildlife biologists and scientists, urban environmentalists, and anthropologists are imposing their own brand of cultural and ecological imperialism upon the traditional indigenous peoples—this was asserted by three expert "white" long-term indigenous activists. The Gwich'in are caught in between dualing forces from the dominant global commercial culture, the resource extractors, and the resource "managers," the environmental scientists.

These people see their very way of life beginning to vanish, and it is not theoretical to them, it is real. *To them, global warming is not a theoretical debate, it is a daily and yearly reality,* as it now snows in the middle of summer, and much of the previously year-round ice and snow of the Arctic is now melting. The permafrost under the tundra is melting. The Arctic region in Alaska is warming at a rate "10 times faster than regions in the rest of the world. Scientists say the average winter temperature in Alaska has risen by 4 Celsius in the past 40 years. Many Alaskans say the state itself is partly to blame, because they believe its own oil resources are helping to drive climate change. They say the ice is melting and the weather warming, with disastrous results."[11] Another study by the National Aeronautics and Space Administration (NASA) reports: "The historic loss of sea ice seen in the Arctic in recent years is tied to widespread warming in the polar region that is increasing at a rate of more than 2 degrees per decade."[12]

I was impressed with how the Gwich'in feel their natural surroundings, how they are connected to every rhythm and change in nature. When it snowed, one villager mentioned that snow at that time of year was harmful to the natural cycle, that the cold would kill the new plants and the baby birds, the chicks. The natural cycles and the climate have been terribly disrupted, according to the villagers.

The Gwich'in as a whole perceived that their local disruption was at once a global phenomenon, an absolute local to global linkage. Others from the anti-drilling side of the Arctic Refuge debate did not speak overtly of global warming, but more typically about saving and preserving the land, and wilderness values. *The Gwich'in all spoke of massive environmental disruption, at a global level.* They live with temperature change and warming on a daily basis, and it is affecting whether they can eat. *Global climate change is not an ideological issue for them, it is one of the stomach and survival.*

It is clear to the Gwich'in at the (extreme) local level—an isolated village of 150 people north of the Arctic Circle—that a massive change to nature is taking place, and that industrial society is to blame. Their local experiences and observations confirm what global scientists such as Jeremy Leggett have been saying for twenty years. After it snowed, one Gwich'in rode by on his four-wheeler, introduced himself in a friendly manner, and then commented on the climate change, the change to nature. I asked what he thought of the refuge and of the snow in the summer. He replied angrily: "Why ask me? You guys are the ones who are supposed to have the answers. Why don't you figure it out!" He also meant that "we"—consumer culture—caused this mess, and that they are paying for it, with the loss of their culture, their livelihoods, their lives. Other experts interviewed, non-Gwich'in, lamented that the average Alaskan could care less about what happens to the Gwich'in in these isolated villages, that the retort "let them move to Anchorage" is a common refrain.

In the Gwich'in worldview, every aspect in nature is linked, part of a wider web of life, of which humans are but one part. The Gwich'in do not speak of the Arctic Refuge separately, because they do not think of it as a section of land to be divided up with political and legal jurisdictions. It is a sacred place, where the caribou give birth, give life—in turn giving life to the native people. Their way of seeing the world could not be more different than those people who are attempting to take oil out of the ground only for profit. Granted, many natives have now become swallowed up by the money worldview, driven by greed. These are the corporate natives—usually tribal elites targeted and co-opted by wealthy white corporate and political leaders—but they are to be distinguished from people such as the Gwich'in, who believe in and advocate sustainability rather than profit.

Gwich'in Activism

The Gwich'in have a long history of political activism, and the Gwich'in Steering Committee has become well known the world over because of the fight over the Arctic Refuge. Sarah James is now an international figure and won the prestigious Goldman Prize, awarded yearly to worldwide indigenous activists.

Nevertheless, few are aware of the history of Gwich'in political involvement over the ANWR, dating to the late 1970s. The seed of the fight against oil development in the Arctic Refuge was planted and nurtured by the vision of one man, Gwich'in Chief Jonathan Solomon, from Fort Yukon. Bob Childers, who worked with Solomon for over twenty-five years, states that the Gwich'in were unworried about development in the Arctic Refuge until the passage of the 1978 provision in the ANILCA that allowed government seismic exploration for oil. Until that time, they assumed that the wildlife area was unthreatened.

According to Childers, Solomon was the spark from this period forward: "Jonathan was born with a wide-angle lens on the world. It was his first instinct to make this an international issue, and he insisted that this go to Old Crow (the Gwich'in on the Canadian side of the border). There was not a single Gwich'in indigenous person that understood the importance of that until 1988, unlike Solomon. Most people have a very provincial view. Solomon was a visionary."

Childers explains that in the late 1970s and early 1980s, it was very difficult for the Gwich'in to make any progress in the halls of Washington, D.C., in attempting to lobby congressmen on the ANILCA and the fate of the coastal plain. At one point in the late 1970s "the Gwich'in, led by Solomon, started beating drums in the congressional office hallways, and the Senators were so startled that they came running out of their offices. They started to listen to Solomon, because he was the Mayor of Fort Yukon, as well as the Chief. Politicians could care less if you are a Chief, but if you are a Mayor, you are something."

By 1987, Solomon was the first to frame the ANWR issue as one of human rights, indigenous rights. Environmental groups such as the World Wildlife Fund and Robert Redford's Institute for Resource Management were attempting to work with the Gwich'in, but to place the issue within a context of conservation. By 1988, Solomon met with Gwich'in leaders, brought the entire Gwich'in nation together, including the villages in Canada, and characterized this as a battle for human rights.

Childers, who has worked on both sides of indigenous and environmental activism, says that "it is now fashionable to have coalitions of environmental, human rights, indigenous, and religious activists." However, in 1988, it was not, and Solomon importantly pushed the Gwich'in to not only frame the issue within an international context by bringing in the Canadian Gwich'in but to create a platform for a human rights battle.

In 1988, the Gwich'in Steering Committee was created to collectively represent the Alaskan and Canadian Gwich'in. The committee was designed to have four representatives, with four alternates, evenly divided between Alaskan and Canadian communities in four regions, two on each side of the border. Interestingly, Childers noted that "the Canadian Gwich'in always had a greater affiliation to their government." Childers helped place Sarah James on the Steering Committee: "Sarah stuck out early on, as a health care aide and coordinator in Arctic Village. I wanted her on the committee, and she has been on there ever since. Originally, however, she was way too provincial to see the bigger picture, and Solomon was the engine in all of this. Solomon may be a sonofabitch and hard to deal with, but he has been one of the best street-smart politicians I have ever seen."

Jonathan Solomon understood in 1988 that the Gwich'in needed to build alliances with other tribal groups. They sent one delegate from Arctic Village to the annual meeting of the National Council of American Indians (NCAI). Childers states that "the power of the NCAI since 1988 has kept the oil development from proceeding in the coastal plain. One week after that NCAI meeting we had (anti-drilling) resolutions from the NCAI, Indigenous Survival International, and the entire Gwich'in Nation. We had momentum from then on. North Slope oil has never been able to break that seal of support, that unity behind the Gwich'in."

It is valuable to tell Childers' story, for it reveals the important background to the current success enjoyed by the younger, rising Gwich'in activists and leaders. Much of the ANWR limelight has been focused upon the large environmental groups, for their "grassroots success." In contrast, few people even know of Solomon's vision and persistence, his tenacity in bringing the entire Gwich'in nation together as well as forging powerful alliances with other national indigenous organizations such as the NCAI. According to Childers, Solomon's entire story has never been told, never documented.

This history of the indigenous alliance in the ANWR campaign also points to the difference between the positions of the environmental and indigenous campaigns. They have superficially overlapped, for political purposes, over wilderness values, but have diverged in important ways. Normally an interviewer would never hear Childers' story, only the popular environmental side. What gives Childers' views so much weight is that he started out as an environmental researcher and activist out of the University of California at Santa Cruz, but he then transformed into an indigenous activist, by his own assessment: "I wanted to do both, but after two to three years I understood that you can't do both.

You're either an indigenous rights activist or a greenie. These are not brown-skinned environmentalists, they are Native people. Many environmental activists out there are hallucinating, the two don't overlap. The Natives are not urban environmentalists, they meet only on mutual ground." Indeed, most people never hear of the Gwich'in alliances with other indigenous organizations, which since 1988, in Childers perspective, have deterred refuge development.

Solomon's groundbreaking activism cleared the way for current young Gwich'in leaders who are challenging unsustainable development in Alaska—specifically oil—as well as the ANCSA. The issues of native land claims and native sovereignty are inseparable, of course, from the overall problem of oil development in Alaska, since the ANCSA was created by politicians such as Ted Stevens and Wally Hickel, in conjunction with oil interests, to nullify any later native land claims that may have stood in the way of the oil pipeline. The ANCSA was passed in 1971 without a vote from the Alaskan native population, or the American people. "The discovery of oil on the North Slope pushed Congress to enact the Alaska Claims Settlement Act in 1971, which took nearly all of the land from indigenous control and allowed the industry and state to gain access to the resources. It set up a tool to divide and exploit the Indigenous Peoples, their traditional lands, and resources."[13]

The Gwich'in leaders have recently allied with other Alaskan native tribes and leaders to form the Alaska Native Oil and Gas Working Group. The new coalition is an exciting attempt to challenge the major political-economic forces driving unsustainable development in Alaska, and the world. Hundreds of Alaskan native leaders from all over Alaska are forging an alliance to challenge the legitimacy of the ANCSA and oil development.

> Concerns over unsustainable oil and gas development with environmental and cultural consequences for Alaska Natives created the need for grassroots community groups to come together. This process was supported by international organizations like Project Underground and the Indigenous Environmental Network through the Indigenous Mining Campaign. The communities and the activists are challenging the oil industry in Alaska, sort of the "sacred cow" of Alaskan politics, the source of state revenue, and individual check to Alaskans (which many refer to as "bribe or shush money"), and indeed the lunch money for most politicians—whether state or federal.[14]

The policy statement of the new Oil and Gas Working Group speaks to both ecological sustainability and self-determination.

> The Alaska Native Oil and Gas Working Group rejects the Alaska Native Claims Settlement Act as an illegitimate infringement on our right to

sovereignty and self-determination. ANCSA has allowed the "takings" of our aboriginal lands to be exploited by natural resource extraction corporations with no commitment to building and maintaining sustainable and healthy communities. We are honored to share, reach out, and network with Alaska Natives, other Indigenous tribes and organizations, and support groups who want to defend our inherent rights to our lands, waters, and cultural way of life from unsustainable energy policies advanced by corporations whose goal is to disenfranchise, separate, and eradicate Alaska's Native peoples.[15]

The creation of this alliance "from below" is indicative of the fundamental challenges taking place against the oil industry, in Alaska and around the globe. One Gwich'in representative told me that he is networking with approximately 100 formal and informal organizations, both nationally and internationally. He spoke of the urgency in the needs for his people. Power is now more subtle than it was historically, he said, but the history of the ANWR and ANCSA is unquestionably a fight against massive greed, wealth, and power. He emphasized that the ANWR narrative history requires an understanding of the "whole" history, including the extinguishment of aboriginal land rights.

The alliance of natives in the Oil and Gas Working Group represents a rising tide of indigenous activism, led by young native leaders eager to confront the corporate worldview.

ANCSA has successfully removed tribal people from control over their ancestral lands and destiny. Because our lands are run by corporate Indians and not our traditional leaders, we have lost our way and our wisdom. As long as a "profit at all cost" is the motto of these corporate entities, Alaska Natives are left to defend themselves—including their distinct culture—from corporate raiders, government, and greed. ANCSA has splintered Native people over money, at a time when we need to come together to save what remains of our wild lands and subsistence ways of life.[16]

There is a clash of values and worldviews taking place between the Alaska natives, as evidenced in these words. Arctic Power and the oil interests would have the public believe that "most" Alaska natives are for oil development and the monetary benefits accompanying that development, and that the Gwich'in are the intransigent rebels, but in reality we see in the example of the Alaska Oil and Gas Working Group a cross-section of natives—of which the Gwich'in are only part—seeking an end to unsustainable development and profiteering that is ruining their environments and cultures.

This coalition, what I would term a native "movement," posits a coalescence of values, a common vision for the future.

As global warming, resource wars, increased demand on diminishing supplies, and the people's demand for a cleaner future bring to an end the age of oil, Alaskan Natives will be left with devastated lands, fractured cultures, and a broken economy. At that point, shares in Native Corporations that have built their profits on oil exploitation will be worthless. There is a powerful movement of Alaska Natives who are challenging the oil industry. We demand our rights to a safe and healthy environment, from which we can feed ourselves and build sustainable economies.[17]

A broad spectrum of Alaska natives has been complaining about global warming for years now. In a 1998 Greenpeace report, Art Ivanoff, chair of the nonprofit organization, Arctic Network, and a native resident from Unalakleet, Alaska, stated: "Traditional activities, such as hunting, fishing, and gathering of plants, are crucial to Alaskan Native peoples' way of life. Even subtle changes in temperature over the long term can affect our ability to live as our parents and grandparents have—we need a healthy environment to fully preserve our traditional values, culture, and spirituality."[18]

Native testimonies over a two-year period contributed to the release of the 1998 joint Greenpeace and Arctic Network report "Answers from the Ice Edge," which included native testimonies from seven Bering and Chukchi Sea villages—Eskimos—detailing their firsthand experiences with global warming. The cosponsors attempted to give the Western science of global warming a human face, in an unprecedented documentation of climate change at the native community, local level in the Alaskan Arctic.

Gwich'in natives are not the only ones objecting to development of the Arctic Refuge. In a April 1, 2003, article in the *Anchorage Daily News*, the Eskimo mayor of Nuiqsut, a village west of the ANWR and Prudhoe Bay, near the Beaufort Sea Coast, explained that oil development on the North Slope has caused heavy environmental damage to the entire region, along with cultural breakdown among the villages:

Air pollution isn't the only problem. We have water quality changes, land use conflicts, oil spills, noise pollution, increased traffic, and disturbance to fish and wildlife species. And the social fabric of the community is under stress. Truancy, vandalism, domestic violence, alcohol, and drug abuse and suicide are all increasing. . . . And how does all of this affect global warming? Remember that all of these sprawling pipelines will eventually go under water, and the plates of ice will rise. Then what will happen to the oil facilities? When the pristine white wonderland that we live in becomes a black wasteland, it will be too late.[19]

There is a concerted Alaskan native movement now aimed at the oil industry and its political partners. It is critical to understand that this involves a cross section of Alaska natives, supported by other national and international groups of native and non-native organizations. Gwich'in leaders and activists are now attending international conferences and meeting with other indigenous peoples such as the native Hawaiians and the Maoris in New Zealand. They are networking from the local to the global level.

OPEN-ENDED RESISTANCE OR STATE PROTECTION?

The "statement of principles" of the Alaska Native Oil and Gas Working Group explicitly calls for an inherent right to self-determination for all indigenous peoples, and it rejects the ANCSA as an illegitimate infringement upon that right to self-determination. The statement interestingly incorporates principles of sustainability similar to those long advocated by political green parties: "We are committed to a moratorium on all new exploration for oil, gas, and coal as a first step towards the full phase-out of fossil fuels with a just transition to sustainable jobs, energy, and environment. We take this position based on our concern over the disproportionate social, cultural, spiritual, environmental, and climate impacts on indigenous peoples, particularly in Alaska."[20]

The key to the stated principles of this organization lies in the vision, not merely in the resistance to big oil and its allies in state and federal government. The indigenous people are calling for a "just" and sustainable future, as well as "sustainable economic solutions for our communities." The principles include commitments to "upholding and promoting the integrity of our traditional cultures and values," as well as an "intergenerational approach, which honors the wisdom and guidance of our elders and that values the role of our youth." These indigenous people are networking with other groups and individuals from the local to global level, attempting to share a common vision based on mutual values of social justice and ecological sustainability.

They state that the decisions made by the group originate from indigenous members of the communities affected, and that nonindigenous "supporters" will be included at the "prerogative of the decision-making members." They also welcome all individuals and representatives from communities and organizations that adhere to the principles.

These "principles" state a common purpose for indigenous peoples sharing a worldview that is polar opposite to the "corporate natives" and others embracing the economic growth paradigm. However, it is unclear how this vision for locally just economic and ecological sustainability is to be concretely enacted, politically and legally. Meek notes that mere resistance is bound to fail in the face of corporate power unless local indigenous communities are protected by constitutional codes. The federal government should have an obligation and a duty to consult on activities on Indian land. Tribes need to be politically and legally recognized as their own nations, so a confederal relationship might exist between the autonomous community at the local level and the federal government, codified in the constitution. The economic decisions need to be made primarily at the local community level, in consultation with the federal government, thus a decentralized "bottom-up" arrangement would give greater autonomy and decision-making power to community members.

While indigenous communities are networking with environmental groups all the time, there is still a vast gulf between the two, if the large environmental organization is perceived as centralized and "top down," battling the corporation at the expense of the local community. One religious community representative stated that many indigenous communities in Alaska, Eskimo and Indian alike, are very distrustful of large environmental organizations seeking to impose preservationist sanctions against corporate development, ignoring the need for indigenous subsistence. To these indigenous communities, it is a question of political authority, as well as subsistence and sustainability.

Open-ended resistance does not bode well for indigenous communities fighting corporate development. If the state does not protect the community from the corporation, then the corporation will keep coming back over and over until it wins. In the United States, the Gwich'in have private land but were denied tribal government recognition by the federal government. The new energy bill passed by the U.S. Republican administration and Congress (drafted behind closed doors) gives corporations *more* power than before to negotiate with tribal leaders to develop oil, gas, and coal on native and government lands. In essence, the U.S. government, at the behest of corporate lobbying, is abdicating its power to the business community. Meek notes that states must protect native communities from corporations, and that environmental NGOs will not stem the tide: "NGOs are not going to save the world."

We cannot abandon the nation-state system in favor of some amorphous and ill-defined vision of global civil society, which will just lead to chaos and anarchy, a world where the massive corporations will win every time. The problem is privatization of the public sphere, public-spirited institutions. However, privatization will merely lead to further fragmentation and chaos, lawlessness, and ecological breakdown. The only viable alternative is the "new" kind of state, where local communities are given autonomous economic control to develop sustainably, while a strong and healthy federal government protects local rights in the national constitution. The goal would be to protect healthy "bioregions," where local communities control their own sustainable economies, using renewable resources, self-determinant in their own political decision making, while in consultation and cooperation with the federal government.

The Gwich'in did articulate to me their proscribed goal concerning political autonomy: "Our current goal, which is informally agreed to, is to work towards the greatest level of self-determination and self-governance that we are able to attain within the U.S. system. There is talk of other approaches, but none that have been formalized through a decision of a major gathering of our nation."[21] Given the directions of the current U.S. corporate state, however, their prospects do not look good. Without permanent federal recognition and protection—as in making the ANWR a protected bioregion—the oil industry and its allies in the state of Alaska will keep pushing for renewed yearly votes to open the refuge, without end.

Chapter 8

The Religious Community: Philosophers of the Arctic National Wildlife Refuge

Governments, corporations, and, sadly, even religious institutions have undermined or stolen the capacity of aboriginal peoples to survive. Often this has been undertaken with strongly held ideals of progress. In this, it represents an ongoing and ancient struggle of civilizations. In our present global context, this has reached an urgent and critical point of crisis.

—Mark MacDonald, bishop of Alaska,
2004 London address to BP shareholders

There is a rising awareness among leaders in the progressive religious community that a vital cross section of shared interests and values concerning social justice and ecological sustainability must lead to further political cooperation between groups fighting unsustainable corporate development.

The Alaska Coalition is supported by numerous religious organizations, including the National Episcopal Church, the Religious Action Center of Reform Judaism, the Central Conference of American Rabbis, the Coalition on the Environment and Jewish Life, the United Methodist Church, the Earth Ministry, the National Council of the Churches of Christ, the Justice and Witness Ministries, the Presbyterian Church, the Evangelical Lutheran Church in America, and the St. Thomas Orthodox Church. This formal list does not count the growing number of progressive individuals and organizations in the religious community currently supporting and working with other political advocates in the indigenous and environmental communities.

Some of the most exciting and intellectually challenging insights and ideas regarding the current and future state of corporate globalization are emanating from the progressive community. It is imperative to distinguish religious progressives in the United States from the present Christian Right, which, thanks to Karl Rove's strategy making, has dangerously allied with the U.S. big business and Republican communities. We have seen how a polarization of values has characterized the Arctic Refuge debate between prodrilling and anti-oil forces, and this division can be seen in no better venue than within the religious community. The battle over deeply held beliefs, ideas, and values in the ANWR fight serves as a fascinating example, a metaphor, for a much larger conflict over values now taking place at the global and historic levels, both spatially and temporally.

While religious progressives have always held fast about what they perceive to be the primary issue of social justice, they are now regularly advocating ecological sustainability, cross-fertilizing their concerns with environmental advocates. I found the religious leaders in the ANWR case particularly sensitive and intellectually aware of the complex history and subtle dynamics taking place within the refuge conflict, as well as the predicament of the Gwich'in. The progressive religious community is extremely concerned with the growing problems of social, economic, and political injustice, particularly human rights of the poor.

Again, it is important to distinguish that ever-present ideological division between progressives and neoconservatives, for it fully carries over into the religious community. Many environmentalists do not really appreciate the potential contribution that religious progressives have to offer in building important alliances for future resource battles or wars against corporate greed, unsustainable development, and human rights abuse. The environmental community has too often mistakenly and superficially bunched all religious representatives together, without recognizing the vast division over values taking place *within* the religious community.

These politically progressive and well-educated religious leaders bring tremendous perspective to the table, along with an impassioned yet reasoned commitment to long-term values of social, economic, and environmental justice. Their presence and voice are probably essential in "social movement building," in strengthening the value base of those attempting to counter and provide an alternative to the capitalist-driven unsustainable growth paradigm.

Perhaps no setting has better illustrated this real and potential contribution than in the Arctic Refuge conflict. The U.S. Episcopal Church has been a principal driver and major player in the struggle to protect the indigenous and human rights of the Gwich'in, who have been Episcopalian for 100 years.

The Gwich'in themselves, at the turn of the twentieth century, sought out the Episcopal Church. It was not thrust upon them. According to one source in the religious community, the Gwich'in turn to the church was " a completely different game, it was not pushed upon them."[1] Faith Gemmill of the Gwich'in Steering Committee comments on the Gwich'in and the Episcopal Church: "My great-grandfather was one of the first Episcopal ministers; he helped translate the Bible to our language. We say the Lord's Prayer in our language, sing traditional hymns in our language."[2]

The Gwich'in see a close connection between their own traditional spirituality and Christianity. The Episcopal bishop of Alaska, Mark MacDonald, explains: "Gwich'in Christianity has become a way to affirm and embrace the old ways and the new ways, without losing cultural cohesiveness and solidarity. The Gwich'in are brilliant theologians. Gwich'in traditional culture is much closer to Christianity and Jesus than the dominating culture—Christian or not."[3]

MacDonald provided the most philosophical of all of the interviews, and he placed the example of the conflict within a far broader level of scale, both globally and historically. Bob Childers, the Gwich'in advisor and advocate, began working with Bishop MacDonald in the early 1990s:

> He is the church's leading national and international expert on indigenous issues. He grew up in Indian country, his father was an accountant for several Indian tribes on a reservation in Minnesota. He had a ministry there and also spent five years in Navajo country. MacDonald is the most successful person from the religious community dealing with indigenous missions *in the world*. He is one of my big heroes in all of this.[4]

The web of political action in the history of the ANWR actually brought seemingly disparate actors together. Federal Fish and Wildlife biologists, stewards of the ANWR, actually spoke privately with representatives of the Episcopal Church back in the 1980s, urging the church to take action to help the Gwich'in. The biologists had firsthand knowledge of oil company employees bragging about how the companies had co-opted the Kaktovik Inupiat into taking a pro-drill stance by offering them material rewards. The oil people figured that opening the ANWR would be easy.

The Episcopal Church then worked with Gwich'in leaders and Bob Childers to develop a political stance and platform. According to Childers, MacDonald's assistant, Reverend Scott Fisher, was a key figure at the local level in mobilizing support for the Gwich'in, and then MacDonald took the issue to a national level: "Bishop MacDonald made the big change, he moved this from one of the items on the Episcopal agenda to a top issue on the national Episcopal agenda." Fisher had consulted with Jonathan Solomon, the longtime Gwich'in activist, then Fisher consulted with Childers. The linkage grew in strength, spreading outward from the local to the national level. In the early 1990s the Alaska church took a position against developing the ANWR in support of the Gwich'in and human rights. Then the Episcopal Church in Washington, D.C., spread the word to other churches throughout the country.

THE NATIVE-HUMAN RIGHTS ISSUE:
TWENTY-FIRST CENTURY RESOURCE WARS

Bishop MacDonald, an international expert and voice on native rights in the Episcopal Church, first heard about the Arctic Refuge issue from his mentor, Dr. Helen Peterson, who had been a major player in American Indian rights issues since the 1950s. Peterson had served as the head of the National Congress of American Indians.

The ANWR first reached MacDonald's consciousness in the late 1980s, and Peterson helped MacDonald see the ANWR within the context of other native issues, and as a human rights and tribal issue, not only an environmental one. In this sense the Episcopal Church, thanks to the work of MacDonald, may be viewed as a model for how religious progressives may become more involved in supporting victims in future political ecological and environmental justice conflicts. The national bishops of the Episcopal Church have continued to vote unanimously in favor of supporting the Gwich'in in fighting the development of the ANWR.

Bishop MacDonald commented upon his background in the Arctic Refuge campaign: "In 1990 a group of us took an extended trip throughout Alaskan villages, and at this time I met Jonathan Solomon. I was not yet a major player, but was aware of the people pursuing the ANWR campaign at the level of national advocacy. To me it was so compelling because it was a combination of Native, human rights, and environmental issues."[5]

MacDonald has evolved since 1990 to become one of the most critical players in the debate, demonstrating a unique, remarkable philosophical perspective of the conflict, as well as a sharp sense of political and psychological acumen. He believes that one way to describe the ANWR is "as a model, as one of the first battles of the next 100 years, of how people live, how they see the environment and indigenous issues—a place where our fundamental values are being formed, shaped, and decided. This is a precursor of the next century."

MacDonald's ideas and experience with the debate confirm my thesis that the ANWR is fundamentally a clash of worldviews, a conflict of global and historical significance reaching far beyond the physical bounds of the Arctic coast:

> It's a clash of the past, of traditions and ideas that have served people well for thousands and thousands of years, with a view of development that is beginning to clash within the dominant society as well. Voices are saying that we have to approach this from a different point of view; we can't drill our way out of energy dependency, we can't drill our way out of bad policy, and we can't spend our way out of greed. There are so many aspects of this [ANWR], that it really is a defining issue.

MacDonald's insights and overall perspective of the conflict confirms that this is a grand narrative of multiple actors and values, ideologies, all overlapping and converging in complex ways. Fundamentally, however, he sees this case as one of many future conflicts where indigenous rights and environmental concerns converge:

> Environmental issues are not isolated from native issues. Aboriginal rights and the development mentality of first world nation-states are very much linked together. I am very sensitized to these issues and how they will affect poor people, indigenous people. There is a heightened sensitivity not only by the victims of development, but to the fact that the ideas, values, and approaches that threaten the environment also threaten indigenous people.

Critically, MacDonald echoes the worries coming from within indigenous communities, concerning the split between "corporate Natives" and those such as the Gwich'in seeking to retain sustainable communities: "They are also developing a heightened awareness that their own values and approaches as indigenous people are seen as dangerous from a developmental point of view. I find it sad that there are Native people on both sides of the issue. I try, as the Gwich'in do, to show a tremendous amount of respect for different opinions, and also be aware of the political complexities."

The Episcopal Church's stand on human rights is fundamental to the anti-drilling platform. The environmental and human rights elements, as already discussed, have not always coincided and worked in tandem. MacDonald notes that he is an environmentalist, but emphatically states that his vocal stand and political activism on the ANWR issue first and foremost originates from a commitment to indigenous and human rights:

> I consider myself an environmentalist but I worry when I listen to environmentalists who don't seem to understand the human rights issues involved, and that makes me very nervous. It is a potential problem. I think there is a potential conflict [between human rights and environmental issues], as you are dealing with people, ideologies, and cultures that don't always mix well, or don't speak to each other well. For example, some of us spoke with the National Wildlife Federation before they took their historic stand against developing ANWR. One Gwich'in got a big lecture from the environmentalists when he said that development isn't so bad.

Thus MacDonald and the church view the ANWR predominantly through a lens of indigenous and human rights, though they have allied with the environmental community:

As a diocese we are very aware that we are part of a coalition predominantly made up of indigenous organizations related to the Anglican community around the world. We understand that a big part of our central identity is being indigenous. We also have other responsibilities, and there are political nuances. I am not a big fan of gaming in the lower 48, but because tribes are sovereign, and they have been forced into this situation because of treaty funding cuts, I think it is no one's business to preach to them, even though in-house I can see the raising of big issues of whether it is good, bad, or indifferent. I personally would have a big problem if the Gwich'in wanted drilling, and I would express that opinion. Nevertheless, I would also defend the natives' rights to make their own decisions.

Thus the complexities of a situation such as the ANWR reveal convergences and divergences of values, even within the "anti-drilling camp," and the indigenous-human rights aspect of the matrix truly creates the defining nuance in the conflict, challenging deeply held belief systems.

A STUDY OF DEEP-SEATED VALUES

I have discussed the vicious polarization of emotions and stances that have evolved through the evolution of the Arctic Refuge debate. This issue has transcended itself, and it signifies a dynamic taking place of something far more crucial and elemental than a mere physical battle for oil over a piece of land on the Arctic Coast. Bishop MacDonald possesses a penetrating insight into the deeper forces at work in this polarized debate, for the Arctic Refuge is really representative of an uneasy challenge to the fundamental, day-to-day values of the average spoiled American. No player in the refuge matrix has more experience with this conflict of values than MacDonald. He has taken a very unpopular position in defending the Gwich'in, even within his own church, and he has stood his ground, while often under vicious fire:

> The pain that is going on is a testimony that something is going on of major importance, at a deeper level of values. These opponents get the fact that for me the Gwich'in and their survival is the big thing here. I would still be against drilling if the Gwich'in were not in this, but not going public and not willing to take so much criticism. In Alaska and elsewhere in the United States, in the mainline press they tend to avoid the human rights issues. When we are getting into that realm we are getting to the deeper parts of the issues that people want to avoid.

Indeed, the Gwich'in piece of the ANWR puzzle strikes at the core of this topic, creating tremendous hostilities, hatreds, and confrontations.

A powerful, underlying sense of racism and cultural imperialism inherited from the mentality of Manifest Destiny seems to be rearing its head in the Arctic Refuge conflict. MacDonald states:

It's complex because it is somewhat hidden. It's almost as if the native people are invisible, are relics of the past. I think America has a difficult time dealing with its own lack of logic in its relationship to native peoples: on the one hand, some feel guilty in the way they have treated indigenous peoples, but fundamentally the attitudes have changed very little from beginning to end. The unsaid feeling is that "we discovered this land and now we will use it any way we want; we are very sorry we messed up your life but if you know what is good for you you'll go to Anchorage." You hear this all the time, it is often articulated.

The modern theme of colonization is ever present in the ANWR, the implicit inherited belief in the power of the dominant commercial culture to bring "progress" to uncivilized peoples and undeveloped landscapes. This mind-set and belief system are currently destroying the remaining traditional cultures and natural environments left in the world, not only in the Arctic. Bishop MacDonald and the national Episcopal stance appear to be very sensitive to this global dynamic taking place in Alaska, to this fight over deep values: "You have these deep feelings of guilt, acquisitiveness, and greed, mixed with shame, all of these things. The implications are tragic in what we have shown in our capacity to hurt people. There are also fears that there 'won't be enough for my family and me.' All of these things come together into a kind of awful web. It is very difficult to deal with, break open, and display."

What is really taking place here is the beginning of a painful paradigm shift within the grand narrative, as alternative, positive visions for the future confront dominant yet outworn values in the American commercial, capitalist culture. American values of materialism, greed, egoism, and competition (social Darwinism, survival of the richest) are being contested on an axiological battleground that will extend into the upcoming decades.

MacDonald perceives that this paradigm shift is taking place in the way the ANWR is contested, in the approaches used by the opponents:

What the natives are saying is like a mirror toward what the American public has been trying to avoid—doing with less, changing one's lifestyle. Even environmentalists try to avoid it, as if the Gwich'in and their views in this raise fundamental questions: about how we live our day-to-day lives, what is important, our families, our homes. It is a mirror that is held up to the dominant culture, in a way that the dominant culture finds difficult to sustain any gaze upon. They see it for an instant, then walk away.

MacDonald almost seems to view the other actors in this drama as though he is looking down upon the entire tragedy, understanding of its past and its future, and the motivations of the separate actors. MacDonald has resided in Alaska as the bishop for six years, transplanted from the lower 48, and this may be why he has a better overview of the situation. The value conflict over the Arctic Refuge has produced ugly confrontations inside Alaska, where the real battle is taking place. The vote may be taken inside the Senate in Washington, D.C., but the real battle, the pitched confrontation over beliefs and values, is being fought on Alaskan soil. "A lot of Alaskan hopes, fears, insecurities, and difficulties seem to be coagulating over ANWR. It is a fundamentally defining issue for the state, but sadly there is a tremendous amount of bitterness and resentment in this. It has become very personal for people like Ted Stevens."

The ANWR matrix is a fascinating web of actors all connected to each other. Ted Stevens, the great voice for the pro-oil coalition, is an Episcopalian, ironically a member of MacDonald's Alaskan diocese, an organization standing by the Gwich'in. Only the ANWR could bring these two supposedly disparate individuals together. A group of Episcopal bishops made a national statement in backing anti-oil forces, writing a letter to President Clinton and asking him to protect the refuge by making it a national monument. Stevens happened to be in Anchorage at the time and ran into MacDonald in the airport, the same day the statement was sent to Clinton. Stevens verbally exploded at Bishop MacDonald in the airport, rebuking him for his position and making a scene, in what is now a legendary incident within Alaska. Stevens' various explosions over the ANWR have become well known by now, as the members of the Senate may attest.

This incident symbolizes the divisiveness over the ANWR and shows how the Episcopal Church itself is divided over the issue. It also raises questions over one progressive individual's right to speak up against a neoconservative majority opinion. MacDonald has been vilified by many in Alaska, and within his own church, for his principled stand:

> The papers at the time misrepresented what I said. TV crews crafted interviews with me to make it look as if I were speaking for the whole . church. I am very careful in everything I say to point out that Episcopalians in Alaska differ on this. The reality is that in the Episcopal Church outside of Alaska, there is no dissension that is significant to speak of over ANWR. The bishops have unanimously voted time and again at some cost to them in their own dioceses, to support the Gwich'in.

This is the only thing they have voted on unanimously since I've been a bishop. They have shown great courage in this.

There are many heroes in the ANWR story, and Bishop MacDonald is just one, however, his particular role in the matrix is even more intriguing because of the fire he has voluntarily taken from within his own "interest group," so to speak, the Episcopal Church. The pressures have also been immense within Alaska on those wishing to speak up like MacDonald, but who are afraid to do so against the dominant values: "People have written to me to say thank-you for being a voice on this issue. People are afraid to speak up, are afraid of losing their jobs, for example. A lot of people in the state of Alaska [government] who are against development have been intimidated into silence. There are strong and violent reactions to those who speak up against drilling."

This intimidation sounds frighteningly similar to the same reactionary, militantly zealous mentality that has arisen in the United States ever since the attacks on the World Trade Center. The affluent in the United States, accustomed to a certain material lifestyle, are reacting violently to those poor people everywhere who are lashing out in anger and frustration, calling for a fair distribution of economic resources. This is all about pursuing fairness, economic equality, and a distribution of political authority: Who is doing the decision making, and is that ecologically sustainable? The ANWR is really nothing less than a challenge to the political-economic power structure, a struggle of the "weak" on the outside of that power circle who are attempting to change that structure. This struggle is backed by visionaries such as MacDonald, who understand the far-reaching, profound dynamics at stake:

> People write letters to me, some in support, and others threaten to leave the church over the ANWR issue. It is gratifying because people write with support and encouragement, and it is horrifying because so many Alaskans feel intimidated into silence. The worst thing in Alaska is to be characterized as an environmentalist. An Alaskan environmentalist is not supposed to exist but is seen as an outsider, a do-gooder with good intentions but not much awareness of what is going on.

It is fascinating how militant anger has come to dominate the ANWR issue. MacDonald explains: "The opposition tends to stereotype and carica-ture. Much of the logic of their arguments includes things like: 'You're a jerk, therefore we should drill, or you're stupid, therefore we should drill.' The passion overtakes them, and they repeat formulas, the same outworn formulas like it 'can be done safely.' "

MacDonald's support of the Gwich'in seems to be triggering the heated reaction: "People will feel bad about what earlier generations have done to native people, but they still justify wiping out the Gwich'in lifestyle for a few gallons of gas. They believe that the Gwich'in should fit the American lifestyle."

The fundamental ways of how humans relate to nature are being examined in this ANWR process, pitting an economic worldview of "progress" against deeper meanings of subsistence:

> Subsistence is at issue here: in English it means "barely getting by," but in Gwich'in and Inupiaq it means "our way of life." In Gwich'in, subsistence has a connotation of someone who is well prepared, someone who is taken care of. This lifestyle has to do with a recognition of the abundance of nature, the abundance of God's generous response to the creatures of this Earth, and also the sacrifice that other creatures make to serve the people.

Here the debate moves into the realm of spiritual ecology, examining and calling into question the very material values of what Bodley calls the "dominant commercial culture." The Gwich'in and the religious community are expanding the debate to include far deeper questions than the traditional argument provided by preservationist environmentalists, as the very meaning of subsistence is getting to the root of the issue over unsustainable capitalist growth and acquisition. The fundamental way humans relate to each other and to the nonhuman natural world is under examination in the microscope of the ANWR. To the Gwich'in, and certainly to MacDonald's mind, an alternative to the economic worldview includes a confluence of life-affirming, healing values: the quality of life, spirituality, human community, belongingness, and connectedness to others (human and nonhuman beings alike). Thus it is more than "just getting by" in the strict economic sense: it is a healthy "way of life," physically, psychologically, and spiritually.

POLITICAL AND SPIRITUAL ECOLOGY

The matrix of actors in Alaska debating critical themes of ecological sustainability and social-economic justice extends beyond the issue of the Arctic Refuge. The progressive religious community is not only working with indigenous peoples to advocate concerns for social justice and human rights, as in the case of Bishop MacDonald, but is reaching out to voice its support of environmental platforms. As cited previously, the Sierra Club is attempting to develop stronger ties with human rights organizations such as Amnesty International as well as religious organizations through their "Partnerships

Program," organized by Melanie Griffith in Washington D.C. To reiterate, the National Council of Churches has partnered with the Sierra Club.

In many intriguing instances, environmental activists are simultaneously working in their religious communities to further raise consciousness of the coalescence of social justice and ecological issues. Mary Ellen Oman, whom I interviewed in the Anchorage Sierra Club office concerning the ANWR, is also a Presbyterian Church elder. The fascinating web of actors in the Arctic Refuge conflict spins outward, creating unexpected and gratifying possibilities in research. Mary Ellen Oman arranged an interview with her Presbyterian minister, Karen Lipinczyk, an advocate of spiritual and political ecology.[6]

While Lipinczyk is not directly related to the ANWR issue, her ideas and political positions are illustrative of the progressive thinking and visions now taking shape within the religious community, combining commitments to the education of spiritual and political ecological issues.

Lipinczyk is quick to distinguish progressive Christianity from the neoconservative brand that has infiltrated current political and economic circles in the United States. She has worked with students at the University of Buffalo in an attempt to dispel the conjunction of Christian and political neoconservative agendas:

> Jesus was a political revolutionary, and social justice was his main concern. He was unequivocally for marginalized people, social ethics. We are now living in a nation that has gone crazy with materialism. Corporate capitalism is not compatible with Christianity—there is no meeting ground. Progressive Christianity is connected to all of those causes seeking to increase human understanding, peace and justice, saving the planet, and funding education. Christianity addresses how to be a faithful human being in honoring the Divine in all of life—all life.

Lipinczyk's ideas are intriguing, for they seek common ground for discourse in political and spiritual ecology, often separate fields of inquiry. Her views parallel my own argument, that the progressive religious community has a tremendous contribution to make in discussing issues relating to the environment and socioeconomic and political justice, and that political and spiritual ecology might be viewed as two sides of the same coin. For example, the presence of the Gwich'in and their views on the relationship of humans to "nature" in the ANWR discourse lends an entirely different dimension to an otherwise typical development-environmental conflict. As Bishop MacDonald emphasized, the presence of the Gwich'in worldview—their values—challenges the very assumptions and foundations of a society devoted to money, material gain, and self-centered individualism. The "spiritual ecologists," whether in this case the Gwich'in, the Episcopal bishops,

or the Presbyterian Lipinczyk, are arguing that more than political changes
or fixes will be needed to find our way out of this political ecological morass.
The crisis is deep, and one of social and environmental ethics: a fundamental
transformation of values and worldviews is needed to examine how we relate
to nature and each other.

What are the prospects for social change, for addressing political-economic
inequalities? Lipinczyk offers a view from a spiritual and political perspective:

> There is not enough will [in the United States] to change the harm that
> we are doing, nonviolently. I still believe in nonviolence, but I don't see
> the will from a critical mass. I think that means that things will get worse
> and worse. This is empire building that we are engaged in. What I hope
> will happen, if there is hope in the midst of great pain, is that when
> things fall apart, the pain will lead to will. You can only take so much
> pain and then folks start to organize, and that is when the church of the
> modern century will have to step up to the plate. Will we make the
> sacrifices to try and hold up a whole lot of pain? We will go so far down
> as to force a paradigm shift.

Thus Lipinczyk foresees a descent into chaos, which in turn will create
a new collective power, where new leaders will emerge: "Why political and
spiritual ecology now? Partly because we've evolved to the point where we can
start thinking about those things. The planet is in such crisis, maybe this is
an evolutionary aspect of epoch change and revolution. There has to be more
to accomplish, this can't be the end. In terms of classical evolution, biologically, we have reached the wall. The change has to be spiritual for epoch
change." Lipinczyk agrees that "political ecology is about studying corporate
power, and the politicians are the front guys. Complicity is the problem in
consumptive America. There is no moral compass, no critical thought. We are
the children of the corporate mass media." Thus political ecology may be
interpreted as the naming of the problem (or naming of the "enemy," in
Amory Starr's terms), while spiritual ecology may be viewed as integral to any
fundamental paradigm shift, epoch change: forward-looking normative changes
in values, in social and environmental ethics.

Concerning the role of Christianity in politics, Lipinczyk argues:

> The temporary Christian "right" does not have the strength to hold the
> crisis that is coming. The denominational structure will fall apart, and
> that is good. Religion is not about converting people or proselytizing, it
> is in building homes, communities, fighting aids—helping people. It is
> about being concerned with climate change, alternative energies, tech-

nologies, being responsible for each other. Even unsophisticated thinkers out there can make the leap from the local to the global.

We see ideological barriers being torn down with thinkers such as Lipinczyk, intellectual representatives from the progressive religious community. She has participated in interreligious dialogue, and sees progressive Christianity as being entirely compatible with other religions: "The hallmark of progressive Christianity is that we don't have the lock on truth."

Politically, her church holds international meetings, where such issues as free trade agreements, human rights, and the environment are discussed with international delegates: "These agreements are killing them. These [American] policies are so far from the founding father visions; even if they were aristocrats, the documents were good."

Thus politically active members from the religious community are supporting human rights and environmental positions, becoming vocal participants in political and spiritual ecological issues. Those at the fore are helping to reframe the debates, exposing the differences between Christian progressives and neoconservative "Christians" with underlying political-economic agendas. Much of the process now lies in the necessity to challenge and refute the incessant corporate spin of the Christian political "right."

The progressive religious actors in the matrix offer a broad perspective, infusing temporal and spatial scale, providing a grand narrative of our current social and ecological crises within the context of past and future histories. Their future contributions in political and spiritual ecology will be many, and much needed.

Chapter 9

Prophets vs. Profits: Future Scenarios and Outcomes

After all, it should now be abundantly obvious to all but the most privileged sectors of the population that the corporations, consumed with protecting their wealth and power, have an unprecedented stranglehold over government and most of what passes for political activity. Political institutions and practices have been shrouded in corruption, deceit, hypocrisy, and manipulation to such a degree that a mockery has been made of such time-honored ideals as citizen participation."

—Carl Boggs, *The End Of Politics:*
Corporate Power and the Decline of the Public Sphere

The ANWR debate is but one case or instance illustrative of the coming twenty-first-century resource wars. In one sense the Arctic Refuge may be understood as a model precursor to the coming conflicts, pitting a complex array of actors against each other, where fundamental ideas and values—worldviews—collide and polarize.

The "local" Arctic Refuge conflict is important more for its significance on the global stage, as a blueprint for naming the constellation of actors in resource wars. Methodologically, the story of the ANWR is a basic, fundamental explication of the primary participants involved: global corporations, in this case, oil; politicians and the state; environmental nongovernmental organizations; indigenous peoples and organizations; and human rights and religious organizations.

As complex as the ANWR may be, given the constellation of actors, it nevertheless provides a fairly clear model of the conflicting ideas and values involved, enabling the reader to assess the general problems presented, which carry over to resource conflicts throughout the world. The ANWR is an outstanding model, if only judging by the corporate oil actors: ExxonMobil, British Petroleum, ChevronTexaco, and Phillips are all global players, but Phillips to a lesser degree. In chapter 3, my main purpose was to demonstrate how the Alaskan oil actors are eminently powerful at the national and global levels, to provide a spatial perspective for corporate power and its influence over government.

The confluence of oil and government power is very clear in the case of Alaska and the Alaskan political delegation. I focused upon the example of Ted Stevens as an almost perfect case of neoconservative thought and values and because he is powerfully linked to the current matrix of corporate oil, military, and neoconservative theology dominating and pervading the national and international policies of the Bush-Cheney administration.

As discussed in part 1, the neoconservative theology or agenda is essentially a social Darwinistic belief system, advocating the survival of the richest, cutthroat competition and domination of the opposition, and a sociopathic thorough disinterest and disregard for social and economic justice and equality. The values engineering American corporate globalization are fundamentally socially Darwinistic, designed to create a monied aristocracy, a plutocracy. The story of the ANWR pits this plutocratic alliance of the super-rich against a phalanx of environmental, indigenous, and human rights actors.

I attempted to portray the subtle differences and potential problems within the anti-drilling coalition, noting the top-down power of the large Washington, D.C.-based environmental organizations. Nevertheless, in contrast to the pro-drilling plutocracy, anti-development forces as a whole are very much grass roots in nature, operating on mere fractions of oil lobby budgets. There is simply no comparison in the scope of power: *My primary argument is designed to portray a corporate state out of control*, where massive amounts of money determine political decision making and affect the poorest people at the local level, destroying natural environments as well.

Politicians such as Ted Stevens, Frank Murkowski, and Tony Knowles are *corporate front men*, a thesis supported by interviews with experts such as Beth and Jay Kertulla. The national government—distinct from state and local politicians—is pervaded with monetary corruption and corporate influence, and the Alaskan delegation is but a glaring example. The theme of our era, that of the corporate state, as exemplified with the powerful political influence of oil companies such as ExxonMobil and British Petroleum, seems to consist in how these secretive corporations repeatedly manage to shift their costs onto either an unsuspecting or a just apathetic public.

The neoconservative political agenda is devoted to not only helping the richest cut their taxes, a primary concern of the Bush-Cheney administration, but also to harnessing public funds from the average taxpayer to subsidize corporate costs and projects. As mentioned previously, the Alaskan oil consortium, including the state of Alaska and Ted Stevens, has managed to shift the costs of building a new gas pipeline from Alaska to the lower 48, from private industry to the public sector. This "subsidy" was included in the new energy bill of 2002. It is but one example of the new *corporate theology*, to not dismantle government but to secretively manipulate politicians to shift the costs onto the public, a public already in massive debt.

THE DUAL-STRUCTURE PROCESS

Political ecological theory constitutes a study of top-down political economic power and how it affects environmental change and social injustice at the local, regional, and global levels. In preparation for the interview process in Alaska, I reviewed a wide range of literature covering themes in political ecology, corporate globalization and political economy, oil and energy, anthropology, and ecological democracy. My goal was to push the interdisciplinary borders to attempt to illustrate the theoretical interconnections of these areas by utilizing a challenging and relevant case study of a resource war or conflict. The critical paradigm provided the appropriate methodology through which to apply political ecological theory and a top-down study of multilevel political economic power.[1] The critical paradigm or method aligns well with political ecological theory precisely because it *assumes* structural political economic inequalities from the outset, setting the framework for a normative approach, one of advocacy.

My approach toward the case study of the Arctic Refuge involves a dual-structure method, which coincides nicely with political ecological theory. Dual structure entails (1) an employment of a matrix of actors converging upon the same event or theme and (2) an overarching critical narrative placing the actors and their respective values, ideologies, and worldviews within a holistic framework. The design is to apply a literary method or narrative to political ecological themes.

My role was to learn from these key informants, some of whom had worked with this issue for decades, and to then tie their arguments into a comprehensive narrative, utilizing a literary approach. The key for me in this research design was to approach the interview process with the broadest theoretical background possible, bringing in a number of themes, including critical globalization thought and political economy, but allowing for the highest level of reflexivity generated by the interview process. That is, the critical paradigm allowed me to approach the various actors with my own assumptions concerning local to global top-down political economic power, however, the interview process itself allowed me to "reflexively" adjust my theoretical assumptions accordingly.

The interview process with Arctic Refuge actors was challenging and stimulating, especially given the highly charged nature of the debate, which has raged for decades. Interestingly, my assumptions concerning the corporate state were verified from sources where I least expected to find them: retired Alaska State Congressman Jay Kertulla and Richard Fineberg, the oil and gas expert. These men provided unexpected interviews: I had not contacted them prior to leaving for Alaska. This is an important point for future researchers gathering interviews for the coming resource conflicts or wars. While one must be well read in a variety of thematic areas in political ecological theory before approaching the interview process, it is absolutely necessary to maintain a reflexive attitude or awareness while *experiencing* the subtleties of a highly stimulating interview process. I learned something quite important while weaving my way through the matrix of the ANWR actors: one's best interviews may indeed be the ones one does not expect. I did not expect to interview the bishop of Alaska, or Bob Childers, for that matter. Both were experts on the subjects of the Gwich'in and indigenous politics (for non-natives).

The interview process for the Arctic Refuge conflict constituted the most gratifying aspect of the research project, as I was fortunate to meet some extraordinary people. The real value in studying a resource conflict such as the Arctic Refuge is to allow the key actors to inform and educate one's own worldview and to be flexible in considering how their knowledge might re-shape one's own theoretical assumptions. This is the advantage of the dual-structure methodology, applying a literary style in the "critical narrative" overview to a political ethnographic matrix of actors.

For example, the interview process reshaped my initial theoretical assumption concerning social movements. I had assumed on an academic level that the anti-drilling group alliance in the Arctic Refuge represented a hopeful example of how progressive social movements might *unify* in the future to fight corporate globalization, environmental destruction, and social injustice. One early goal of the research process was to explore the ANWR campaign to see how environmental groups were "helping" indigenous peoples (a patronizing assumption itself—more cultural imperialism?) fight unsustainable development and oil companies specifically. This sounded quite noble on a theoretical level, however, in part 2 I discussed how the interview process generated complexities and subtleties concerning the "unity" of coalition members, and that closer inspection revealed not a true social movement, as defined by Lakoff, but a collection of interest groups. This collection was in turn characterized by a top-down organizational structure led by the Washington, D.C.-based environmental groups.

The Meek, Childers, and Bishop MacDonald interviews were most interesting precisely because they had worked within both environmental and indigenous advocacy groups over a long period of time. Each of these informants pointed out the actual deep disparity between environmental and indigenous interest groups, and how the D.C.-based ENGOs bring in other interests groups (such as the Gwich'in) to bolster their own administrative power and financial resource base. As Meek noted insightfully, "The NGOs are not going to save the world." One of my initial academic assumptions was that maybe they could save the world. This was naïve at best: the reality is that the large environmental organizations are corporations themselves, though obviously on a much smaller scale than the oil companies. One cannot compare millions to billions of dollars.

Overall, the groups in part 2 of this work are fighting for positive visions for the future, in stark contrast to the corporate-political elites (exemplified in the oil mafia). However, the question of "new social movements" is a cause for serious concern and skepticism, for the actual divided nature of these interest groups merely mirrors what I perceive to be the fundamental deteriorating qualities of individualism and competition—self-interest—within American culture and values. That is, the large NGOs, such as the environmental groups, are part of the corporate state as well, and contrary to grassroots rhetoric have evolved into top-down hierarchical organizations characteristic of insider politics, pursuing their own political and financial agendas at the expense of grassroots democratic practice. My findings from various interviews lead me to conclude that fragmentation and self-interest, rather than some form of theoretical unity, characterize the so-called new social movements, or political interest groups.

On the positive side, the indigenous political advocacy groups are now networking from local to global levels, linked by Internet communications. Their alliances are expanding by the day, as witnessed by the example of Gwich'in leaders, who are global players. It is important to emphasize, however, that these are indigenous networks, primarily, and that any perceived unified alliance with the big environmental groups is a superficial observation. As Childers noted, many environmentalists are deluded into thinking that there is such an alliance. It is far more problematic and fractious. Still, the indigenous groups themselves are networking at a furious pace, and this a hopeful sign for the future.

The issue of global warming and climate change became a focal point of the Arctic Refuge debate after having visited the Gwich'in village and talking with tribal members. The fact that it snowed during my visit in mid-July, to the distress of the Gwich'in, only supported their arguments concerning disastrous climatic change. After this incident, to my mind global warming became the common denominator for all of the groups vying for political position in the ANWR conflict. Drastic climatic change enveloped all of the arguments, at that point, especially because of its dire and immediate effect on the communities in the Arctic. The issue of global warming truly linked the local to the global, in this empirical instance.

While discrepancies arose within the anti-drilling groups, their tactics as a whole were found to be relatively benign in contrast to the powerful oil mafia. The interview with Fineberg was educational and illuminating, for here was a Ph.D. in government who had served as the oil and gas advisor to the governor of Alaska in the late 1980s, an international-level oil expert who had become the principal advisor for the Alaska Coalition trying to save the Arctic Refuge.

Fineberg's published accounts on the ANWR over the years centered upon what he emphasized was the crucial point of the battle: the need to expose and challenge the disinformation campaign continually disseminated by the pro-drilling lobby. Thus the important element of media power and *how information is used* became another critical issue that emerged primarily out of the interview process, after meeting Fineberg. His testimony proved that the war over scientific information was pivotal in the ANWR dispute, the war of ideas. Fineberg contributed fundamental insights into how oil mafia tactics have shaped the debate, continuing to influence public opinion through the power of media. The Arctic Refuge is a battleground over scientific information. The various environmental groups and the United States Geo- logical Survey, for example, have produced extensive and detailed environ- mental scientific documentation on the North Slope, as cited in this work. Indigenous advocacy groups, we have seen, are using this knowledge to forge their own alliances and arguments concerning fossil fuel use and global warm- ing. These efforts are furiously countered by the tactics of the oil mafia, which must rely upon mass media advertising in an effort to "disinform" the public.

THE COMMODIFICATION OF MIND

In chapter 5, the intent was to expose and openly discuss the sophisti- cated Machiavellian corporate propaganda methods by which these business elites constantly shape and create false perceptions and beliefs among the public citizenry. We live in the age of the new corporate state, predicated upon the incessant marketing of "false truths," a constant public relations effort to legitimize capitalist greed and power wealth by employing belief images of "patriotism," "security against terrorism," and "freedom and democ- racy." These terms are becoming cliché with the corporate state and the mass media marketing machine, in an all-out effort to discredit any opponent of the corporate-business worldview. Alaska is a perfect example. Interviewed experts noted how the major oil companies, on a daily basis, inundate local and regional television programming with eco-friendly and social justice-friendly commercials attempting to legitimize the goals of the oil companies.

The subtle, real issue in globalization is the use of mass technology by corporate monopolies to brainwash hearts and minds with commercial propaganda. The insidious intent is to convince the poor and the middle class, through the relentless use of misinformation, that it is actually in their best interest to bring about greater levels of public debt while further elevating the profits of the corporate aristocracy. The mass-marketing effect in this process is likened to a "commodification of mind," creating a type of dictatorship of ideas. By reducing humans to unthinking consumers, lowering the common denominator, passivity engenders profit.

This corporate dictatorship of the media and the dispersal of information that we are seeing in the United States are coincidentally paralleled by a meteoric rise in the power of the military-oil power complex. As I discussed in the chapter on the oil companies, given the incredible rise in corporate consolidation and monopolization over the past three years, energy executives are now interfused more than ever before with mass-media corporations. General Electric is one of the largest media owners in the United States. The energy corporations are obviously inseparable from the military as well, evidenced in the invasion of Iraq, as the protesting poor must be constantly portrayed as terrorists, threats to the creation of markets and consumer passivity.

We see an unprecedented unity of media, energy, and military corporate power at the beginning of the twenty-first century, embodied in the new radical American right, in the visions of right-wing intellectuals such as Karl Rove. As seen in the example of the polarized ANWR debate, the new American corporate Republican agenda desires nothing less than the utter destruction of the opposition, the perceived enemies to markets and profits. The oil and defense industries are basically running the U.S. federal government at this point, running up massive profits at the expense of public debt. The energy-military-media triad is bombarding the public with misinformation campaigns, as exemplified in the "war on terror," as journalism has degenerated into little more than corporate marketing and public relations.

This monopolized marketing of falsehoods invoking the use of "the facts," as discussed in the example of Arctic Power, poses dire potential problems for the future dissemination of knowledge and truth. Corporate spin is continually presenting itself as a harbor for scientific truth. This creates what Jeremy Leggett describes in *The Carbon Wars* as "cognitive dissonance," as oil company spin or misinformation, for example, constantly bombards the public with falsehoods portrayed as environmental or scientific knowledge. As Leggett observed the "carbon club" lobby at work over many years during the Intergovernmental Panel on Climate Change talks and conferences, he became an expert on the use of oil company spin: "Cognitive dissonance is an uncomfortable awareness of the distance between your own view of something, and the views of the people in whose company you find yourself. It's the kind of feeling that makes you ask yourself whether you can possibly be right, or even sane, when so many others seem so sure you are wrong."[2]

THE ASCENDANCE OF PRIVATE GOVERNMENTS

One great challenge in the upcoming years will be the absolute necessity for public and democratic-spirited individuals and groups to challenge this mass marketing of corporate theology, a worldview predicated upon the ascendant values of money profit, social Darwinism, and privatization.[3] It goes without saying that political solutions such as removing big private money (whether they are formal or informal, they are still bribes) out of political campaigns and reinstituting state control over the business community— "separating business and state"— would solve many of our problems.

But is it too late to purge the U.S. federal state of pervasive money corruption when most federal politicians are joined at the hip with corporate boards and lobbyists? Unfortunately, as seen in the case of the ANWR and Alaska, there is no distinction between the business community and what we used to call "statesmen or statists," professional public policy makers. Is it possible to politically "reform" a cancerous situation? A lifelong politician and statist such as Alaska's Jay Kertulla appears disheartened and resigned in speaking of the "corporate state." Or as theologian Karen Lipinczyk suggests, will this process just get worse and worse, bottoming out with economic and spiritual chaos and anarchy, in turn forcing a critical mass change in consciousness and values?

In *The Corporation*, legal scholar Joel Bakan researches the history of the relationship between the state and corporate entities in the United States (and previously in Britain). Bakan provides an important work, reminding lay and professional readers alike that corporations are ultimately accountable to the state and its citizens:

Without the state, the corporation is weak. Literally nothing. It is therefore a mistake to believe that because corporations are now strong, the state has become weak. Economic globalization and deregulation have diminished the state's capacity to protect the public interest (through, for example, labor laws, environmental laws, and consumer protection laws) and have strengthened its power to promote corporations' interests and facilitate their profit-seeking missions (through, for example, corporate laws, property and contract laws, copyright laws, and international trade laws). Overall, however, the state's power has not been reduced. It has been redistributed, more tightly connected to the needs of corporations and less so to the public interest.[4]

At the heart of the matter, "laissez-faire" or deregulatory ideology has not resulted in a weakened state but merely a "diminishing role of the state in protecting citizens from corporations, and the expanding role of the state in protecting corporations from citizens." Bakan argues that state deregulation and industry "capture" of state regulatory agencies reflect a *redistribution* of state power: "The question is never *whether* the state regulates corporations—it always does—but *how*, and in whose interests it does so."

The problem originates in the "natural entity" conception of corporations, that they are independent persons, dating to the 1886 Supreme Court decision. Bakan reminds us that these entities are "entirely *dependent* upon the state for their creation and empowerment." He argues that the natural entity theory and related laissez-faire doctrines destabilized the legitimacy of regulations created to promote the public interest:

> Corporations cannot exist without the state, nor can markets. Deregulation does not scale back the state's involvement with corporations; it simply changes its nature. As a creation of government, the corporation must be measured against the standard applicable to all government policies: Does it serve the public interest? The nineteenth-century judges and legislators who refashioned the corporation into a self-interested institution never really abandoned that idea. Rather, with laissez-faire ideas dominant at the time, they embraced a new conception of what the public interest required. It would be served, they thought, if individuals, including corporations, were enabled to pursue their self-interest unimpeded by government.[5]

It is a grave mistake, argues Bakan, for NGOs and others to believe the state weakened and dying in the age of corporate globalism. Conversely, only the state and its regulatory agencies can rein in the business community to serve the public good: "The fact that corporate law and policy rest upon a *conception* of the public good, albeit a narrow one, only confirms that the *concept* of the public good remains the ultimate measure of the corporation's institutional worth and legitimacy."

This line of reasoning supports Steger's emphasis upon the ideological rather than "natural" character of laissez-faire doctrine. From the law perspective, Bakan provides a timely and relevant legal history of the ideological

evolution of the state-corporate relationship in the United States, as a precursor to twenty-first-century globalism. In his view, NGOs will never replace government regulatory power, as NGOs are designed primarily to educate and inform the public, similar to the journalistic function. Only the state is imbued with legal power, possessing the potential to prevent—not merely react to—corporate harm to the public good. The NGOs do not possess legal regulatory power. They file lawsuits against corporations, but this is a reactive, not a preventative, legal function. Only the state can legally revoke corporate charters, thus dissolving corporate entities that have demonstrably harmed the society and the natural environment.

GLOBAL WARMING AND RESOURCE WARS

Obviously it is impossible to foresee events upon the horizon, but energy will play a central role in political economy and the relationship between the corporations and the state during the coming decades, according to experts across the liberal to conservative spectrum. Energy, and specifically the oil companies, will influence every aspect of society in the years to come. Energy wars and conflicts will dominate global landscapes until policies embrace the values of ecologically sustainable community building. These wars will propagate in poor countries, while consumers in the United States demand ever more nonrenewable energy as they refuse to change their material, consumptive lifestyles, fueling public debt and corporate profit.

The problems are much more structural and far reaching than merely focusing upon human rights abuses in resource wars, as victimized plaintiffs try to sue big corporations such as ExxonMobil, ChevronTexaco, or Unocal, for example.[6] These are reactive attempts only, and they do not solve the main issue, the necessity of switching to sustainable energies before global warming spins synergistically out of control. When that happens—it is starting—continued PR debates on whether humans are to blame for these violent fluctuations in climatic change will be seen as ridiculously rhetorical and irrelevant.

We would not have oil and gas resource wars in the first place, in places such as the ANWR, Iraq, Columbia, Equador, Bolivia, Aceh, Burma, and Nigeria, to name but a few, if conservation measures were implemented in simple policy procedures. It does not help to keep having yearly votes on the ANWR, to keep the wolves at bay, or to keep filing reactive lawsuits against oil companies in the name of human rights abuse. Can Band-Aids cure cancer? The oil era must be perceived, by consumers and policy makers alike, as being overly destructive to nature and human societies, outdated, finished. The growth paradigm is also dangerously outdated and harmful, generating ecocide, an utter destruction of the natural world.

In the study of the Arctic Refuge, we have seen a number of diverse arguments made against the oil industry. In my view, commensurate with that of the Gwich'in, diverse scientists such as Jeremy Leggett, and other members of the global climate coalition, the base issue is that of global warming and the dire prospect of catastrophic climatic change. Leggett perhaps offers the broadest perspective derived from extensive experience with this issue:

> The problem was in the carbon arithmetic. . . . Stabilizing atmospheric greenhouse-gas concentrations required deep cuts in emissions from all fossil fuels. We had to get to a solar future running on renewable energy sources and energy efficiency as soon as possible, and right now the expanding gas industry was busy setting itself up to make things worse, not better. It was taking money away from renewables and efficiency. Given that we couldn't turn to solar power overnight, gas might have to have a role as a bridging fuel to a future running on renewables, but we had to be very aware that there was a vast amount of gas available. There was around 1,000 billion tonnes of carbon in gas below the ground, according to the best estimates then (1993), compared with some 200 billion tonnes in oil. You couldn't allow the oil industry to reinvent itself as a gas industry, especially not in the face of arithmetic like that: 300 (maybe 200) billion tonnes of carbon from fossil fuels of all kinds was probably more than enough to risk catastrophic destabilization of the climate. And on top of that came the problem of leakage. Natural gas was, after all, primarily methane. Just a 3 percent leakage of gas from the production, transportation, distribution, and use of gas and you would lose the advantages of its lower carbon intensity with respect to oil. At twice that, you were not even beating coal.[7]

This statement from a knowledgeable, expert geologist is especially pertinent to the Alaskan case and ties the local example into a global perspective. The Alaskans, even most of those fighting against oil development in the ANWR, are strongly and almost uniformly in support of a new (subsidized by the national taxpayers) gas pipeline to be built from the North Slope to the lower 48, which will generate vast amounts of money for the entire state. They do not seem to recognize the global picture of Leggett's "carbon arithmetic," which focuses upon carbon emissions as a whole, including gas. Using Leggett's arithmetic, the argument for using "cleaner" gas is a specious one, merely utilized to bring in more profit. Environmentalists themselves in Alaska will back down and support the gas pipeline for the economic benefits. So there seems to be an inconsistency if we are really viewing the global ecological picture and the need to immediately terminate the fossil fuel culture for the health of the atmosphere.

Massachusetts Institute of Technology physicist David Goodstein offers a terse yet an excellent overview and explanation of the global warming phenomenon, the carbon cycle, and a technical discussion of fossil fuels and the various alternatives to these CO_2-producing fuels.[8] The greenhouse effect is but one of several major factors that affect the delicate balance of the Earth's climate. Others include the tilted axis, the El Niño cycle, the jet stream, and various currents in the oceans.

The El Niño cycle is driven by the Pacific trade winds, a steady flow of air that crosses the equatorial Pacific from South America to Asia. These winds push sun-warmed surface water toward Asia, where it builds up and evaporates, causing the monsoon rains that characterize the South Asian climate. For reasons unknown to scientists, once every three or four years the trade winds weaken, and the warm surface water retracts across the Pacific, leading to storms in the Americas, droughts in Australia and Asia, and, overall, a great irregular disturbance in the Earth's climate.

Goodstein notes that there are a number of "more or less stable flows" in the oceans and atmosphere. One particular oceanic flow that is becoming the subject of great scientific controversy is that of the thermohaline (thermo = temperature, haline = salt) flow in the North Atlantic ocean. The flow is usually called a great "conveyor belt," for warm equatorial water pushes northward into the colder Atlantic region, where the warmer surface water is gravitationally driven downward to the bottom of the ocean as it becomes colder and saltier. The denser, sinking water creates a gravitational energy that further drives the entire flow, like a massive conveyor belt. The cold bottom water then flows southward, emerging on the surface a thousand years later. The thermohaline flow will become a subject of even greater discussion in upcoming years, for scientists worry that the rapid melting of the Arctic ice cap is disrupting the flow, as melted fresh water ice desalinates the northern Atlantic, depriving the equatorial waters from the needed salinity to gain density and subsequently to plunge to deeper depths in its southward circulation. There is evidence that 18,000 years ago, at the height of the Ice Age, when ice covered much of North America and Europe, the thermohaline flow actually moved in the opposite direction, and the surface water became saltier and denser as it flowed south.

The greenhouse effect is still the primary factor that affects our climate. The Earth's climate exists in what scientists term a *metastable state*, a balance between the three variables of Earth, the atmosphere, and space (more precisely the amount of solar radiation coming into the Earth and the atmosphere from the sun). Goodstein illustrates how this balance follows from the two physical laws of thermodynamics, which state that (1) all radiant heat energy is converted into other forms; it can never originate from nothing, nor disappear (the energy of the universe is constant), and (2) all radiant heat energy seeks equilibrium, as heat from a warmer body inevitably flows toward a cooler body (entropy).

As radiant heat energy from the sun hits our atmosphere, 30 percent is immediately reflected back into space, and clouds contribute to the reflection of radiation. As the other 70 percent arrives at the surface of the earth, this heat energy must be, in accordance with the two laws of the conversion of heat energy, reradiated outward from the surface in the form of infrared radiation. As Goodstein explains, the Earth's atmosphere possesses an inherent balance of greenhouse gases that help block 88 percent of this reradiated infrared energy leaving the surface of the Earth, so this 88 percent is then continually bounced back and forth between the surface and the greenhouse gases of water vapor, methane (most of natural gas is composed of methane), carbon dioxide, ozone, nitrous oxides, and chlorofluorocarbons. Most of the atmosphere is composed of oxygen and nitrogen, but these are transparent gases, so they neither block incoming sunlight from warming the Earth nor block the outgoing infrared radiation heading back into space. The non-transparent greenhouse gases create a balance as to how much heat energy is released back into space (12 percent) and how much warms the Earth to allow the evolution and presence of life-forms. Without this inherent balance of greenhouse gases, the Earth would freeze at a temperature of 0 degrees Fahrenheit. These "natural" greenhouse gases raise the Earth's average surface temperature to 57 degrees Fahrenheit.

Modern industrial societies, through their extraction and burning of fossil fuels over the past 150 years, have dangerously disrupted this delicate meta-stable state, which is dependent upon a balanced complex carbon cycle. This cycle is dependent upon a balance of carbon dioxide exchange between the atmosphere and the Earth. Carbon dioxide may be taken out of the atmosphere by Earth "carbon sinks," the most important of which is the ocean. The ocean may dissolve carbon dioxide, where it may be taken out of circulation for long periods, "if" that water sinks to the bottom, as in the thermohaline flow. The dissolved carbon may also be absorbed into mineral matter that sinks to the bottom of the oceans. Generally, however, as surface water tends to absorb a maximum of carbon dioxide, it only slowly exchanges with deeper waters capable of absorbing more of this greenhouse gas. This is the reason scientists are so worried about how Arctic melting is affecting the North Atlantic and the thermohaline flow. The buildup of carbon dioxide in surface waters may synergistically spin out of control due to the rapid addition of fresh, desalinated water to the ocean.

Plants and forests, of course, absorb carbon dioxide. Carbon is incorporated into all organic matter through plant photosynthesis. As some plants are eaten, notes Goodstein, "the potential energy stored in food molecules is released by turning the carbon atoms back into carbon dioxide" through the process of digestion and respiration. Just as forests absorb carbon dioxide as "sinks," they reciprocally release the CO_2 back into the atmosphere as they burn or rot.

Couple the rapid global deforestation of tropical forests due to development with the heightened pace of melting ice in the northern and southern poles, and you see how the natural carbon sinks are becoming incapable of cycling the carbon dioxide. In effect, industrial modernity, coupled with a meteoric rise in human population, is overwhelming the natural ability of the Earth to achieve its metastable state, as illustrated in the carbon cycle that sustains all life on Earth. Before the advent of the industrial age some 150 years ago, the concentration of carbon dioxide in the atmosphere averaged 275 parts per million (ppm). At the beginning of the twenty-first century, the concentration has increased over 30 percent, to nearly 400 ppm, and it is rising.

The increase in carbon dioxide in the atmosphere over the past 150 years corresponds to a rise in surface temperature over the same time span.[9] The Earth's natural greenhouse effect kept the surface at a comfortable 57-degree average for thousands of years, and then it began to rise after 1800. During the last decades of the twentieth century, the rise in temperature and carbon dioxide is almost vertical on a chart. As Goodstein notes, if we were to abruptly curtail the burning of fossil fuels in the first decade of the twenty-first century, it would take the Earth's natural carbon cycle approximately 1,000 years to restore itself to the previous concentration of carbon dioxide in the atmosphere.

Scientists cannot predict the outcome of this potentially disastrous disruption of Earth's natural carbon cycle. While scientists the world over are now developing computer models on potential future scenarios of warming and climate change, they debate and disagree over what the change will look like and how it will affect humans and nonhuman species. One recent scientific report states that increased carbon dioxide and global warming may send 1 million animal and plant species into extinction by 2050.[10]

The carbon cycle is so delicate that scientists cannot predict how dramatic increases in carbon dioxide levels will affect the total climate process. As the Earth warms, surface water evaporates. Water vapor is also a powerful greenhouse gas, therefore, the effect of the carbon dioxide is magnified. As the warming causes the polar ice caps to melt, less radiation is reflected back into space by the disappearing ice, thus exponentially increasing ground-level warming. However, inversely, greater evaporation from warming creates more clouds in the atmosphere, which block incoming sunlight, conversely reducing warming. Clouds cool the Earth's surface: without them the surface would be approximately 7 degrees Fahrenheit warmer. According to Goodstein: "The effect of adding CO_2 to the atmosphere is complex, with both negative and positive reinforcement acting in ways that will have consequences that are not well understood. Some scientists think that by cutting off the thermohaline flow alone, an increase in the greenhouse effect could result in a net cooling rather than warming of the planet."[11]

The radical disruption of the carbon cycle, in other words, could go either way. In the extreme scenarios, Earth could freeze, as massive evaporation from the surface creates clouds blocking sunlight, dropping the temperature, leading to snowfall and another ice age. Or the 88 percent of infrared radiation blocked by the natural greenhouse effect could increase, sending the Earth into a Venus-like state, where surface temperatures are hot enough to melt lead. Goodstein believes that though Venus is closer to the sun than Earth, the difference between the "expected" temperatures would not be that great. In either extreme scenario, life would cease to exist on the surface.

Until recently, climatologists and international policy makers focused primarily upon the future prospects of gradual climatic change, not sudden and drastic change. Computer scenarios utilizing mathematical modeling projected future possible outcomes caused by global warming, factoring in diverse sectors to be affected: environmental, economic, social, political, and military. The reluctance to study drastic and sudden climatic change is now itself beginning to change. Scientists and analysts have discovered, through the analysis of planetary history recorded in ice cores, sediments, and tree rings, that the Earth has experienced periods of drastic climatic change over the past 100,000 years. In some regions, scientists have observed temperature changes up to 16 degrees Celcius, or 28 degrees Fahrenheit, and these abrupt changes lasted for many decades. The collapse of the thermohaline flow in the Atlantic 8,200 years ago comprised one of these major disruptions.[12]

The National Academy of Sciences is now advocating a revision of how to research future climatic change scenarios to reflect the fact that Earth climate archives reveal evidence for drastic change. Scientists are arguing that novel, nonlinear mathematical models are needed to address the actual complexity of real-life ecological processes such as the climate. Whether technology can do this remains to be seen, for this itself rests upon the modernist assumption that technological fixes can bail us out of the problems that industrial technology has created. At least the scientific community is now recognizing that linear, predictable behavior encoded in the Earth is the exception rather the norm. Earth's history supports the claim that ecological processes are synergistic, holistic, and can spin out of control exponentially, not arithmetically. Goodstein, an eminent physicist, clearly states that scientists have no idea what the climate will do.

Ironically, the corporate-military elites that Mills warned us about sixty years ago are even beginning to consider future scenarios for sudden and rapid climatic change due to global warming. The field of environmental security involves research into how environmental degradation and disruption causes and leads to human conflict—social, economic, political, and military. The likelihood of sudden climatic change has now become a hot topic in the upper circles of the American corporate-defense structure.

Longtime Department of Defense planner Andrew Marshall sponsored a 2003 Pentagon report addressing the issue of how drastic climatic change circa 2020 might affect the national security of the United States. Since 1973, Marshall has headed a secretive defense think tank designed to warn the Pentagon of future threats to national security. This latest report, coming from the very people who have created the looming disaster by global warming through the profiteering of fossil fuels, paints a dire picture indeed, a "plausible scenario" where national security concerns are severely affected by environmental conflict and climatic change.[13] Marshall actually enlisted a former head of planning at Royal Dutch Shell, Peter Schwartz, to write the report. Schwartz has consulted organizations such as the CIA and DreamWorks (Steven Spielberg). His coauthor for the report, Doug Randall, works at the Monitor Group's Global Business Network, a scenario-planning think tank in California. This is a perfect example of the networking, overlapping power elites in the corporate-military-media complex working together to predict future scenarios that will likely affect their capital investments and profits. The corporations are hiring future studies planners to predict how the former might best protect their interests with the advent of major social, economic, and political conflict stemming from climatic change.

The report focuses upon one variable, the possible shutdown of the thermohaline flow in the Atlantic, circa 2020, speculatively leading to a rapid cooling in the Northern Hemisphere and longer, harsher winters in the United States and Europe. The colder temperatures would be accompanied by massive droughts and winds that are 15 percent stronger than they are now, turning agricultural regions into dust bowls. These droughts and winds would also cause widespread fires in forest areas, reducing them to ashes. By 2020, the authors speculate that the average temperature will fall by up to 5 degrees in some regions of North America and Asia and up to 6 degrees in Europe. The average temperature of the last ice age was 10 to 15 degrees lower than today. The average rainfall in northern Europe would drop by almost 30 percent, giving it a Siberian quality.

Of course, the droughts would be offset by violent storms as the thermohaline flow becomes increasingly unstable, verging on collapse. Severe storms could cause, for example, the levees in the Netherlands to break apart, making coastal cities such as the Hague uninhabitable. Storms could disrupt the flow of water south through the California aqueduct, as Sacramento River levees are breached.

Interestingly, the report addresses geopolitical points of conflict arising from the collapse of the thermohaline flow. The United States would be faced with severe security measures as masses of starving immigrants from Mexico, South America, and the Caribbean would make their way north: "Waves of boat people would pose especially grim problems." Confronted with the political and economic problems arising from increased energy demand, the United States would turn to nuclear fission power and further dependence on Middle East contracts. Perhaps the most dangerous development would involve the shift toward nuclear power by countries around the globe, as the decline in oil supplies picks up momentum: "Nuclear arms proliferation is inevitable. Oil supplies are stretched thin as climate cooling drives up demand. Many countries seek to shore up their energy supplies with nuclear energy, accelerating nuclear proliferation. Japan, South Korea, and Germany develop nuclear weapons capabilities, as do Iran, Egypt, and North Korea. Israel, China, India, and Pakistan also are poised to use the bomb."

In this scenario the Earth's ability to support the human population—carrying capacity—dramatically diminishes, and the "ancient pattern reemerges: the eruption of desperate, all-out wars over food, water, and energy supplies." Resource wars were commonplace up until approximately 300 years ago, according to Harvard archeologist Steven LeBlanc. During such wars, 25 percent of a population's adult males died. The Pentagon report predicts that sudden climatic change may well precipitate unprecedented violent competition over scarce water, food, and fossil fuel resources: "As the decade (following 2020) progresses, pressures to act become irresistible—history shows that whenever humans have faced a choice between starving and raiding, they raid." The starving Eastern European countries might invade a weakened Russia for its mineral and energy supplies, and an energy-starved Japan would look to Russian oil and gas reserves to power its desalination plants and energy-intensive farming. Nuclear-armed Pakistan, India, and China might "skirmish at their borders over refugees, access to shared rivers, and arable land."

The Pentagon report indicates that some people in the corporate-military complex have begun taking global warming and the likelihood of sudden climatic change very seriously. The field of environmental security and the subsequent study of how environmental change affects and will affect social, political, and economic processes promise to play a central role in the immediate future of interdisciplinary research.

THE NEW WAR OF WORLDVIEWS

The case of the ANWR may be used as a tool through which to view a matrix of worldviews from a variety of angles, all merging upon central themes of ecological sustainability or unsustainability, and social equality or inequality. The complicated debate over "corporate globalization" really addresses these latter two variables, which are hallmark themes in political ecology. The current push toward the corporate monopolization of human societies and natural environments is frightening in its arrogant and sociopathic disregard for the fundamental value of equality. I perceive equality to be conceived in political ecological terms as simultaneously social, economic, political, and "ecological." By ecological, I refer to an equality likened to a sense of equilibrium, or balance, achieved between humans and the rest of nature. This, I believe, is what the Gwich'in are arguing. Sustainability is an ecological equality or balance achieved to sustain a quality way of life, spiritually, biologically, and economically.

Corporate theology, in contrast, is proselytizing a type of dangerous sociopathy, an indifference to social ethics and environmental ethics: equality. Capitalism is currently declaring war upon the world's human poor and what is left of its natural environments. The upcoming decades may be remembered as the new great world war, a global civil war, waged between the competing worldviews or paradigms of rapacious economic growth and development versus sustainability and novel forms of socio-ecological democracy.

We may be witnessing, in the rise of this militant form of neoconservative corporate social Darwinism, an epochal backlash against the environmental thought and policy of the 1960s and 1970s. The "growth" ideology or belief system is coming to an end, is in its death throws, preceding a major historical paradigm shift. The growth adherents are clinging to their power wealth and using physical force to delay an inevitable epochal transition to a more equal and sustainable world. No industry better epitomizes this bunker mentality than the global oil people, refusing to give way to alternative values and ways of living in balance, of ecological and social justice and equality.

In terms of policy, common sense dictates that we must purge the state of money corruption and business influence: bribery. Immediate simple solutions would involve forcing corporations and wealthy individuals to pay their equal share of taxes, cutting all corporate subsidies paid at the expense of the common public citizen—especially to the fossil fuel corporations—and using these upper-class monies to pay for a broad social net of programs to help the poor and elderly while protecting the health of ecological systems. This is nothing original, as these are traditional democratic and progressive policy ideals. Make the rich pay their taxes, and do not subsidize them. Respect the law and the constitution, and revoke corporations' personhood (civil) rights that were given to them by the Supreme Court in 1886 while misinterpreting the Fourteenth Amendment.[14] Break up corporate monopolies and follow anti-trust law, and reimbed business within social institutions: government is accountable to the people, not to the elitist business community.

A legal theorist such as Bakan argues that regulatory government and law are capable of reviving control and oversight of corporate power. Nevertheless, it remains to be seen whether the chain of political-economic power can be broken at the national level now in the United States, in taking democracy back from the corporations and the private sector. While political reform is preferred to revolution, reform does not seem realistic in the imme- diate future, given the fact that the national politicians are bought and paid for by business lobbies and private interests. Institutional bribery is now the norm, and for Bakan's regulatory aims to take hold, it would appear that an entirely new set of representative officials will need to take over in Washing- ton, D.C., to serve public and environmental interests.

If a revolution against this plutocratic aristocracy becomes a future possi- bility, then this revolution will for the first time in history combine the tradi- tional revolt over social and economic injustice and inequality with a new consciousness and defense of our remaining global ecological systems. This will be a political ecological revolution, hopefully nonviolent, bringing together diverse forces under a common umbrella of progressive values. The inequality is going to get worse, just as the destruction of nature is going to accelerate under the current rapacious paradigm proselytized by the big-business worldview.

A critical mass of consciousness demanding alternative values and poli- cies to corporate globalization does not yet exist in the United States, though it is growing rapidly in the poorer countries, as in South America, where only 12 percent of the people throughout those countries see the United States in a favorable light. With the current direction of corporate neoconservative policy making in the United States, it is probable that masses of people will become poor, losing their jobs, losing social safety nets. Only then will a critical mass develop, and it will be crucial for the progressive leaders from the political, environmental, social justice, labor, academic, indigenous, and reli- gious sectors to unite to form a common value-policy platform, not merely resisting but providing firm alternatives and ideas to be placed into action.

Change will not occur until economic catastrophe affects the middle class and the average citizen and they are absorbed into poverty-stricken levels of class. Appeals and warnings by members of the intelligentsia will not change anything until stomachs are affected and people cannot feed their children—at that point, anger will erupt, and hopefully nonviolent solutions will be proposed. It is my sincere hope that political reform may purge money corruption from a theoretically sound system, and that public-spirited profes- sional statesmanship may prevail over a business worldview that coldly and without compassion has declared war upon nature and the world's poor, el- evating exploitation and rapacity of the weak to an art form, as revered values. If reform of a cancerous culture in moral decline is possible, then I am in full support of those able to effect fundamental change.

Nevertheless, my intuition and experience tell me that this is not likely, just as the Gwich'in are likely to lose the Arctic Refuge so Southern

Californians can fill up their gas tanks at the usual consumptive pace. Economic and ecological disaster likely waits upon the horizon, only because people refuse to look to the future, with an eye only for tomorrow's material well-being. When that well-being crashes, which alternatives will emerge from the ashes?

Notes

CHAPTER 1

1. For solid backgrounds on the ideological agendas of American corporate global capitalism, see Manfred Steger, *Globalism: The New Market Ideology* (Rowman & Littlefield, New York 2002); Immanuel Wallerstein, *The End of the World As We Know It* (Minneapolis: University of Minnesota Press, 1999); Noam Chomsky, *Profit over People: Neoliberalism and Global Order* (New York: Seven Stories Press, 1999).

2. John Gray, *False Dawn: The Delusions of Global Capitalism* (New York: The New Press, 1998).

3. See Peter W. Singer's *Corporate Warriors* (2003) for an analysis of the new privatized U.S. military, largely supported by transnational corporations such as Halliburton Brown and Root and Bechtel.

4. The August 25, 2003, report "Energy Task Force: Process Used to Develop the National Energy Policy," published by the U.S. General Accounting Office, the investigative arm of the U.S. Congress, outlines and describes the failure of the GAO in its effort to obtain information from Vice President Cheney's office concerning the actual participants and decision-making process of the Cheney-supervised National Energy Policy Development Group (NEPDG). The GAO notes that it filed suit in U.S. District Court for the refusal of the vice president's office to cooperate with the GAO's right to public information in obtaining factual information regarding the process of the NEPDG "governmental" meetings. This was the first time the GAO had ever filed suit against the U.S. executive branch. According to the report, page 1, the district court dismissed the suit "on jurisdictional grounds, without reaching the merits of GAO's right to audit and evaluate NEPDG activities or to obtain access to NEPDG records. For a variety of reasons, the GAO decided not to appeal the district court decision." The GAO was pressured by various powerful forces in Congress to drop the suit, one of whom was Senator Ted Stevens, chair of the Senate Appropriations Committee, who apparently threatened the GAO director with spending cuts to the GAO. Stevens will be a primary actor in this work, as he represents powerful oil interests in his state of Alaska.

5. See Richard Heinberg's *The Party's Over: Oil, War, and the Fate of Industrial Societies* (Gabriola Island, BC, Canada: New Society: 2003).

6. See Al Gedicks', *Resource Rebels: Native Challenges to Mining and Oil Corporations* (Cambridge, MA: South End Press, 2001) and his earlier *The New Resource Wars: Native and Environmental Struggles against Multinational Corporations* (Boston, MA: South End Press, 1993).

7. This is a reference to Amory Starr's original term used in her title *Naming the Enemy: Anti-Corporate Movements Confront Globalization* (New York: Zed Books, 2000).

8. David Harvey, *The Condition of Postmodernity: An Enquiry into the Origins of Cultural Change* (Oxford: Blackwell, 1990).

9. Steger, *Globalism*, 9.

10. Andrew J. Bacevich, *American Empire: The Realities and Consequences of U.S. Diplomacy* (Cambridge, MA: Harvard University Press, 2002).

11. Naom Chomsky, *Hegemony or Survival: America's Quest for Global Dominance* (New York: Metropolitan, 2003).

12. Christopher Doran's "Blood for Oil: How Oil and Corporate Profits Drove the U.S. Invasion of Iraq" is an incisive report summarizing the role of corporate oil-military activity in U.S. foreign policy, using Iraq as a case study, April 2004, http://www.pressurepoint.org. Also see the *Los Angeles Times* for its three-part investigative report "The Politics of Petroleum," May 12–16, 2004, for in-depth analyses on oil company activities in Angola, Kazakhstan, and Columbia.

13. Mills, *The Power Elite* (New York: Oxford University Press, 2000), 274.

14. Ibid., 275.

15. Chalmers Johnson, *The Sorrows of Empire: Militarism, Secrecy, and the End of the Republic* (New York: Metropolitan Books, 2004).

16. Wright Mills, *The Power Elite: New Edition*, New York: Oxford University Press, 2000, 276.

17. Ibid.

18. See Michael Kearney, *Worldview* (Novato, CA: Chandler and Sharp, 1984).

19. See Ralph Metzner, "The Transition to an Ecological Worldview," in his *Green Psychology: Transforming Our Relationship to the Earth* (Rochester, Vermont: Park Street Press, 1999).

20. The seminal theoretical work in political ecology is Raymond Bryant's and Bailey Sinead's *Third World Political Ecology* (London: Routledge, 1997).

21. Interview with Chanda Meek, San Francisco, June 15, 2002.

22. Warren Vieth, "Senate Passes Big Tax Breaks," Los Angeles Times, October 12, 2004.

23. See Joseph Stiglitz's *Globalization and Its Discontents* (New York: W.W. Norton, 2002) for a seminal explanation of the "Washington Consensus," a complex and largely secretive set of relationships constituted by American business, Wall Street,

the Treasury Department, and the Bretton Woods public institutions of the International Monetary Fund and its sibling, the World Bank.

24. See Robert Ayres, *Turning Point: The End of the Growth Paradigm* (New York: St. Martin's Press, 1998); Walden Bello, *The Future in the Balance: Essays on Globalization and Resistance* (Oakland, CA: Food First Books, 2001).

25. The term *social Darwinism*, according to *The Dictionary of Anthropology*, ed. Thomas Barfield (Malden, MA: Blackwell, 1997), 429, "can be applied more generally to any social theory that stresses the necessity of competition for social progress. The fact that such constructions stress competition rather than selection has led some historians to redefine social Darwinism as social 'Spencerism,' after Herbert Spencer, who coined the term 'struggle for existence'. . . . In the United States, social Darwinism was associated with the ideology of industrialists like John D. Rockefeller and Andrew Carnegie, who viewed success in business as proof that competition leads inevitably to progress (Hofstadter 1955)." The latter then coincides with my argument of the corporate state, the ascendance of the business worldview and the "survival of the richest." Steger notes that "perhaps the most influential formulation of classical liberalism appears in Herbert Spencer's justification of the dominance of Western laissez-faire capitalism over the rest of the world by drawing upon Charles Darwin's theory of evolution by natural selection. For Spencer, free-market economies constitute the most civilized form of human competition in which the 'fittest' would naturally rise to the top." (Steger, *Globalism,*10).

26. Possibly the best book written from an inside perspective on global politics and global warming is by international geophysicist and environmental activist Jeremy Leggett, in *The Carbon War: Global Warming and the End of the Oil Era* (New York: Routledge, 2001). According to the United Nations Environmental Program's *Global Environmental Outlook 3:* "Since the industrial revolution, the concentration of CO_2, one of the major greenhouse gases, in the atmosphere has increased significantly. This has contributed to the enhanced greenhouse effect known as 'global warming.' The CO_2 concentration in the atmosphere is currently 370 parts per million (ppm)—an increase of more than 30 percent since 1750. The increase is largely due to anthropogenic emissions of CO_2 from fossil fuel combustion and to a lesser extent land-use change, cement production, and biomass combustion. Although CO_2 accounts for more than 60 percent of the additional greenhouse effect since industrialization, the concentrations of other greenhouse gases such as methane (CH_4), nitrous oxide (N_2O), halocarbons, and halons have also increased" (London: Earthscan, 2002), 214.

CHAPTER 2

1. Throughout this book one theme will involve conflicting interests represented by the respective "preservationist" and "utilitarian or conservationist" positions within American environmental thought and politics. Preservationism, rooted in the philosophy and politics of John Muir, is a type of environmentalism that "seeks to preserve the natural environment from the effects (positive or negative) of human

intervention. Preservationism is often confused with conservationism, a term that denotes a utilitarian approach to the use of land and other natural resources rather than a desire to see them unaltered or not utilized by humans." See Ruth A. and William R. Eblen, eds., *The Encyclopedia of the Environment*, (New York: Houghton Mifflin, 1994), 577. The American debate between these two camps originated in the early twentieth-century environmental battle over whether to dam the Hetch hetchy river in Yosemite National Park. Gifford Pinchot and Theodore Roosevelt represented the conservationists who felt that San Francisco's need for water took precedence over the preservation of wilderness. Muir led the argument for preservationism.

2. Donald Craig Mitchell, *Take My Land, Take My Life: The Story of Congress's Historic Settlement of Alaska Native Land Claims, 1960–1971:* (Fairbanks: University of Alaska Press, 2001), 1.

3. Singer, *Corporate Warriors*; Klare, *Resource Wars* (New York: Metropolitan Books, 2001).

4. Ken Ross's *Environmental Conflict in Alaska* (Boulder: University Press of Colorado, 2000) is an excellent background account of post-World War II Alaska and the various resource conflicts that arose between developmental and environmental interests in the period preceding and succeeding statehood in 1959. As Ross details, Alaskan environmental battles have involved not only oil but issues ranging from resource management of wolves, migratory fowl, and bowhead whales to nuclear testing (Project Chariot), the Rampart Dam project, and, of course, continuing battles over the Tongass forest with logging interests.

5. Former President Jimmy Carter, in a speech in Anchorage in 2000, argued that the Arctic Refuge should be temporarily protected under National Monument status by presidential order and invocation of the 1906 Antiquities Act until passage of a congressional bill can afford it permanent wilderness protection.

6. Wilderness Society, "Alaska National Interest Lands Conservation Act" (Washington, D.C.: Wilderness Society, 2001), 16.

7. Mitchell, *Take My Land, Take My Life*, 4.

8. Ibid., 5.

9. John Bodley, *Victims of Progress* (Mountain View, CA: Mayfield, 1999), 30–46.

10. Alaska National Interest Lands Conservation Act, Jimmy Carter's forward based upon remarks delivered in Anchorage, Alaska, August 23, 2000.

11. Interview with Andrew Keller, Fairbanks, Alaska, July 21, 2003.

12. Alaska National Interest Lands Act, August 23, 2000.

CHAPTER 3

1. Michael Renner, "The New Oil Order" was accessed from Corporate watch, online, reproduced from Foreign Policy in Focus. No page listed http:// www.corpwatch.org/issues *Foreign Policy in Focus*. No page listed. http:// www.corpwater.org/issues. (January, 2003).

2. BP Exploration 2003 Charter Report to Governor of Alaska Murkowski from BP Exploration President Steve Marshall, http://www.alaska.bp.com/alaska/statereports/2003Report/presidentasp.

3. Interview with Richard Fineberg, Fairbanks, Alaska, July 15, 2003. Fineberg is a Ph.D. in government and the former oil advisor to the governor of Alaska, 1986–1989. He is now the principal advisor and consultant on oil and economics to the Alaska Wilderness League, based in Washington, D.C. Fineberg provided the chart for Figure 3.1.

4. Heinberg, *The Party's Over*, 81–123.

5. Ibid., 62.

6. Interview in Anchorage, Alaska, July 28, 2003.

7. Anthony Sampson, *The Seven Sisters: The Great Oil Companies and the World They Made* (London: Hodder and Stoughton, 1975).

8. Heinberg, *The Party's Over*, 62.

9. Daniel Yergin, *The Prize: The Epic Quest for Oil, Money, and Power* (New York: Simon & Shuster, 1992), 633–34.

10. See Michael T. Klare's discussion of present and future competition and war over oil in the Middle East in *Resource Wars*, 27–81. Chalmers Johnson provides evidence for the collusion of oil and military strategy in the invasion of Iraq in his important work, *The Sorrows of Empire*: "In the late 1990's, during the second Clinton Administration, the Pentagon began seriously to prepare for a renewed war with Iraq. The Joint Chiefs of Staff's *Strategic Assessment 1999* specifically said that an 'oil war' in the Persian Gulf was a serious contingency and that 'U.S. forces might be used to ensure adequate supplies' " (226). Johnson goes on to say: "The strongest evidence that oil was a prime motive was the behavior of the American troops in Baghdad after they entered the city on April 9, 2003. They very effectively protected the headquarters of Iraq's Ministry of Oil but were indifferent to looters who spent two days ransacking the National Museum of its priceless antiquities and burning the National Archives and the city's famed Quranic Library. The same thing happened to the National Museum in Mosul. While the marines defaced some of the world's most ancient walls at the site of the Sumerian city of Ur, near Nasiriya, the army was already busy building a permanent garrison at the adjacent Tallil Air Base to protect the southern oil fields" (234).

11. Klare, *Resource Wars*, 1–81.

12. Heinberg, *The Party's Over*, 193.

13. Renner, "The New Oil Order."

14. Lutz C. Kleveman, "The New Great Game," *The Ecologist*, 33:3 (April 2003): 29–33.

15. These were reserves as of 2000, cited in Klare's *Resource Wars*, 19. An excellent example of an oil consortium involving the current "big three" in Alaska is the Offshore Kazakhstan International Operating Co., a joint venture of ExxonMobil, BP Amoco, Phillips, Shell, and several other companies in control of a major oil find in

the Kashagan field in the northeastern corner of the Caspian Sea (*Resource Wars*, 85). The Caspian, second in oil reserves to the Middle East, has 30 to 50 billion barrels (source, Richard Fineberg).

16. "F.T.C. Staff Urges Rejection of Deal By Two Oil Giants," *New York Times*, December 1, 1999. (This copy was provided courtesy of Richard Fineberg.)

17. Pratap Chatterjee and Oula Farawati, "To the Victors Go the Spoils of War: British Petroleum, Shell, and Chevron Win Iraqi Oil Contracts," *Corporate Watch*, August 8, 2003, http://www.corpwatch.org/issues/PID.

18. See a report by the Public Interest Research Group, November 7, 2001. "The Arctic Refuge, the 'Filthy Four' and Organized Labor," to view the links between corporate elites. Donald Fikes, a member of the ExxonMobil board, also sits on AT&T's board. ExxonMobil Director Helene Kaplan is a member of the Verizon Board. ExxonMobil Director William Howell serves on Halliburton's board, Dick Cheney's company, and the former chairmen and CEOs of both ChevronTexaco and Phillips currently serve on Halliburton's board, as does the former president and CEO of the American Petroleum Institute. BP shares a director, R. L. Olver, with Reuters, a media giant, and another BP director, Charles Knight, serves on IBM's board. It does not stop there: another BP director, Sir Ian Prosser, sits on the board of pharmaceutical giant GlaxoSmithKline. ChevronTexaco shares two directors, former Senator Sam Nunn of Georgia, and Carl Ware with Coca-Cola. Nunn also sits on the board of General Electric, the mass-media giant. Phillips, the other oil transnational involved in Alaska, shares one director with media giant Knight Ridder. Another Phillips director sits on Proctor & Gamble's board. David Boren, a prominent Phillips Board member, is a former Democratic U.S. senator and governor from Oklahoma, and is now the president of the University of Oklahoma. Boren also serves on the board of AMR corporation, the parent of American Airlines. In other words, the oil companies are cross-fertilized with other corporate powers, reflecting the monopolization and merger mania of the 1990s and beyond.

19. Joshua Karliner, *The Corporate Planet: Ecology and Politics in the Age of Globalization* (San Francisco: Sierra Club Books, 1997), 1–30.

20. Leggett, *The Carbon War*, 1–75.

21. Stiglitz, *Globalization and Its Discontents*, preface.

22. Interview with Richard Fineberg, Fairbanks, Alaska, July 15, 2003.

23. Ibid.

24. Ibid.

25. President Steve Marshall, BP Exploration, Charter Report to Governor Murkowski, March 28, 2003.

26. Ibid.

27. See Nancy Lee Peluso and Michael Watts, *Violent Environments* (Ithaca, NY: Cornell Univeristy Press, 2001); Gedicks, *The New Resource Wars.*

28. Interview, July 10, 2003.

29. Letter from ExxonMobil, June 17, 2003.

30. Daniel Lashoff et al. *Kingpins of Carbon: How Fossil Fuel Producers Contribute to Global Warming* (New York: Natural Resource Defense Council, July 1999), 4.

31. Athan Manuel, "Green Words, Dirty Deeds: A U.S. PIRG Expose of BP Amoco's Greenwashing" (Washington, D.C.: October 1999).

32. "Historic Shareholder Vote against BP on Arctic Exploration Plans," April 13, 2000, Greenpeace, http://www.archive.greenpeace.org/pressreleases/arctic/2000.

33. Phone interview with Bill Strever, BP Alaska, Environmental Public Relations Department, June 15, 2003.

34. John Johnson, Episcopal News Service, "Victory for Arctic Drilling Opponents at BP General Meeting," April 15, 2004. Johnson paraphrased BP chairman of the Chairman's Committee for BP, Peter D. Sutherland.

35. "Extreme Oil," three-part documentary produced by the Public Broadcasting Station.

36. Justin Blum, "51–49 Senate Vote Backs Arctic Oil Drilling," *Washington Post*, March 17, 2005.

CHAPTER 4

1. See Amory Starr's excellent thesis, *Naming the Enemy*.

2. Kevin Phillips, *Wealth and Democracy: A Political History of the American Rich* (New York: Broadway Books, 2002.)

3. Interview with Richard Fineberg, Fairbanks, Alaska, July 15, 2003.

4. Interview with Mary Ellen Oman of the Sierra Club, June 8, 2003.

5. BP 2003 online report, "BP North America," http://www.bp.com.

6. Walter B. Parker, "Lower Pipeline Tariffs Deserve Look," *Anchorage Daily News*, January 3, 2003.

7. Interview with Alaska State Representative Beth Kertulla and former state Senator Jay Kertulla, July 28, 2003.

8. Parker, "Lower Pipeline Tariffs Deserve look."

9. E-mail from Fineberg, August 26, 2003.

10. Interview July 28, 2003.

11. As governor in 2002, Knowles hosted joint meetings with Russian officials to explore energy development in the Russian Far East, linking Alaskan and Russian oil interests. During the same month, an inaugural Energy Summit in Anchorage hosted by the state included representatives from BP, VECO Alaska, Flour, and high-level officials from the U.S. Interior Department and the Alaska state government.

The summit was designed to facilitate greater international investment in the Alaska energy sector and to explore possibilities for greater development. http://www.ibcenergy.com.

12. Mitchell, *Take My Land, Take My Life*, 235.

13. Figures cited from Athan Manuel, "No Refuge: The Oil Industry's Million Dollar Campaign to Open Up the Arctic" (Washington, D.C.: U.S. Public Interest Research Group, February 1999).

14. Center for Responsive Politics. http://www.opensecrets.org/politicians.

15. Ibid. http://www.opensecrets.org/races.

16. I have analyzed the language of numerous articles from past *Anchorage Times* editorials, and they regularly attack environmentalists, promote oil development in the refuge, and staunchly support Ted Stevens. Richard Fineberg wrote an editorial piece to the *Anchorage Daily News* on March 26, 2003, commenting on Stevens' use of misinformation while presenting the case before the Senate to open the ANWR. Stevens' March 19, 2003, tirade on the Senate floor has become legendary. He threatened senators who had voted against the refuge by declaring: "People who are voting against ANWR are voting against me, and I will not forget it." (This prompted a Pulitzer Prize-winning cartoonist to draw a screaming baby in a high chair, spitting out his pacifier and turning blue.) The Veco-owned *Times* retorted in its own editorial that Fineberg was a "bald-faced liar," and Fineberg is in the process of suing the *Times* for libel. Such are the travails of the ANWR "word wars."

17. Center for Responsive Politics. http://www.opensecrets.org/races.

18. Ibid.

19. Center for Responsive Politics, "Oil and Gas Long-Term Contribution Trends." http://www.opensecrets.org/industries.

20. Ibid.

21. Center for Public Integrity, "Trading in Favors: Soft Money Documents Imply Quid Pro Quo between Donors and Politicians" (Washington, D.C.: Center for Public Integrity, July 2, 2003).

22. Ibid.

23. "Tracking Arctic Oil: The Environmental Price of Drilling the Arctic National Wildlife Refuge" is an updated version of "Oil in the Arctic" by the Trustees of Alaska, the Natural Resources Defense Council, and the National Wildlife Federation. It includes findings of a "detailed, extensively referenced investigation based on a review of studies, reports, and other documents prepared by state and federal regulatory agencies, the oil industry, independent scientists" (Introduction, 10). Also see Pamela A. Miller, "Broken Promises: The Reality of Big Oil in America's Arctic" (Washington, D.C.: Wilderness Society, 2003). Another excellent report is Pete Morton's "Arctic Refuge Drilling or Clean Energy?" (Washington, D.C.: Wilderness Society, February, 2002), which challenges the misinformation portrayed by pro-drilling advocates such as Frank Murkowski, Ted Stevens, and Arctic Power, all mouthpieces for the oil industry.

24. Center for Responsive Politics, "Energy: Key Votes during the Debate of the Bush Energy Plan."

25. Liz Ruskin, "AFL-CIO's Biggest Union Opposes ANWR Drilling," *Anchorage Daily News*, October 31, 2001.

26. Liz Ruskin, "Gas Line Added to Energy Bill, No ANWR," *Anchorage Daily News*, March 27, 2003.

27. Liz Ruskin, "Narrow Vote Keeps ANWR Out of Senate's Budget Bill," *Anchorage Daily News*, March 20, 2003.

28. Ibid.

29. Mike Allen, "President Doesn't Emphasize 10-Year Price Tag," *Washington Post*, September 14, 2004.

30. Laurence J. Kotlikoff and Scott Burns, *The Coming Generational Storm: What You Need to Know about America's Economic Future*, Cambridge, MA: MIT Press, 2004, 65–67.

31. Danielle Knight, "USA: Documents Show Bush Energy Plan Fuelled By Industry," Inter Press Service, March 28, 2002, http://www.corpwatch.org.

32. Peter Brand and Alexander Bolton, "USA: GOP Threats Halt GAO Cheney Suit," *The Hill*, February 20, 2003, http://www.corpwatch.org.

33. Richard Simon, "Tribes Mine New Opportunities in Energy Projects," *Los Angeles Times*, October 16, 2003. I will return to this provision in the chapter on the Gwich'in.

34. Tom Curry, "Is Alaska Drilling a 'Smokescreen'? Debate Diverts Attention from Other Items That Aid Oil Industry," MSNBC, March 29, 2002.

35. Center for Responsive Politics, "Energy: Key Votes during the Debate of the Bush Energy Plan."

CHAPTER 5

1. Manfred Steger, *Globalism: The New Market Ideology*, Lanham, MD: Rowman & Littlefield, 2002, 5.

2. Steger, *Globalism*, 7–8.

3. Steger, *Globalism*, 7.

4. Ibid.

5. Steger, *Globalism*, 8.

6.. Leggett, *The Carbon War*.

7. Leggett explains: "Among the dozens of non-governmental organizations registering alongside Greenpeace International for the ICC plenary in Sweden were the Global Climate Coalition and the Global Climate Council. These sounded for all the world like scholarly and neutral Washington think tanks, but a scratch below the

surface revealed otherwise. The board membership of the Global Climate Coalition included representatives of the American Petroleum Institute, Amoco, Arco, Phillips, Texaco, Dupont, and Dow Hydrocarbons. Shell and BP were members. The major users of oil were there too, in the shape of the Association of International Automobile Manufacturers and the Motor Vehicle Manufacturers Association. Coal interests included the American Electric Power Service Corporation, the American Mining Congress, the Edison Electric Institute, and the National Coal Association." See *The Carbon War*, 10–11.

8. *The Carbon War*, 61.

9. Interview with Arctic Power, July 10, 2003.

10. Lou Dubose, Jan Reid, and Carl M. Cannon, *Boy Genius: Karl Rove, the Brains behind the Remarkable Political Triumph of George W. Bush* (New York: Public Affairs, 2003), 194.

11. Miller, "Broken Promises," 2.

12. Ibid.

13. Ibid.

14. Alaska Oil and Gas Working Group, "Hit First and Hit Hardest: Global Warming, the Oil Industry, and Alaska Natives," project of the Indigenous and Environmental Network and Project Underground, 2003, http://www.moles.org.

15. Morton, Ph.D., "Arctic Refuge Drilling or Clean Energy?" 1–37 (entire report).

16. It was prepared by the Wharton Economic Forecasting Association, an economic consulting firm.

17. Morton cites three studies that coincide with this assessment, one by the Tellus Institute (1993), E. B. Goodstein (1994), and D. Baker (2001). The three studies estimate job creation from 50,000 to a maximum of 70,000.

18. Cited in Ruskin, "AFL-CIO's Biggest Union Opposes ANWR Drilling."

19. Interview with state of Alaska Representative Sharon Cissna, June 10, 2003.

20. Interview with source who wished to remain anonymous. The information, while indirect, is viable from this source.

21. Simon, "Tribes Mine New Opportunities in Energy Projects," *Los Angeles Times*, October 16, 2003.

22. George Lakoff, "Framing the Dems: How Conservatives Control Political Debate and How Progressives Can Take It Back," *American Prospect* 14:8. (September 1, 2003).

23. Bakan, *The Corporation*. Bakan cites an interview with international psychologist Robert Hare.

24. Lakoff, "Framing the Dems," http://www.prospect.org.

25. Ibid.

CHAPTER 6

1. Interview with Chanda Meek.

2. There is a variety of literature concerned with the marriage of social justice and environmental elements in resource conflicts. See anthropologist Barbara Rose Johnston's *Life and Death Matters* (Walnut Creek, CA: AltaMira Press, 1997) and *Who Pays the Price* (Washington, D.C.: Island Press, 1994). Geographer Raymond Bryant's *Third World Political Ecology* frames resource conflict against a theoretical model of multiple actors: corporations, politicians and the state, international economic organizations (WTO, World Bank, IMF), environmentalists, human rights groups, and indigenous actors. Paul E. Little, 1999, "Environments and Environmentalisms in Anthropological Research: Facing a New Millennium," *Annual Review of Anthropology, volume 28,* 253–284 provides an excellent literature survey of the interdisciplinary fields of political ecology and environmental justice.

3. One Sierra Club activist in Anchorage informed me that the environmental community in Alaska has now switched to referring to themselves as "conservationists," because the pro-oil people have succeeded through negative public relations in denigrating the term "environmentalist," often trying to portray environmentalists as eco-terrorists. This has become a favorite public relations tool and misinformation ploy used by the corporate community ever since September 11, 2001, to associate environmentalists with terrorists.

4. Interview with Oman.

5. Interview with Kelly Hill Scanlon, July 15, 2003. Scanlon holds an M.A. in environmental politics and a B.A. in journalism, and she worked as a legislative aide in Washington, D.C. She served as an environmental policy analyst for the National Conference of Legislatures in Denver as well.

6. Interview with Sean McGuire, July 15, 2003. McGuire is a lifelong activist and once walked solo from Alaska to Florida to protest the loss of Alaskan public lands.

7. Oman, of the Sierra Club, referred me to her Presbyterian minister for an interview concerning spiritual ecology, politics, and the role of religious activists in working with other groups. This interview is included in chapter 7.

8. See Bron Taylor, ed., *Ecological Resistance Movements: The Global Emergence of Radical and Popular Environmentalism* (Albany: State University of New York Press, 1995).

9. Interview with Keller. Keller started working in grassroots environmental politics in the 1970s, mobilizing support for the ANILCA for the Sierra Club. He possesses an intimate knowledge of the refuge as a researcher and guide, having worked for the federal Fish and Wildlife Service in the "1002" area of the ANWR in the 1980s. He also has written a thesis on the ANWR. Keller is a perfect example of a local Alaskan activist who links up with the national activists on a continual basis. He travels to Washington, D.C., several times a year. He allowed me to listen to the

weekly Alaskan Coalition teleconference from his home in Fairbanks. The teleconference links D.C. activists to regional and local activists with weekly coordination and updates, in a remarkably organized "top-down" outreach.

10. http://www.alaskacoalition.org.

11. Interview with Scanlon, July 15, 2003.

12. Interview with McGuire, July 15, 2003.

13. Brian Tokar, *Earth for Sale: Reclaiming Ecology in the Age of Corporate Greenwash* (Boston: South End Press, 1997), 22–23.

14. Lakoff, "Framing the Dems."

15. Tyson Slocum, cited in "Is Alaska Drilling a 'Smokescreen'?" Tom Curry, MSN, March 29, 2002, http://www.msnbc.com/news.

16. Melinda Pierce, cited in ibid.

17. Interview with Sara Chapell, Anchorage, Alaska, July 28, 2003.

CHAPTER 7

1. See Gedicks, *Resource Rebels;* Peluso and Watts, *Violent Environments.*

2. Gwich'in Steering Committee protocol letter, provided in Fairbanks before the flight into Arctic Village.

3. Interview with Sean McGuire, July 15, 2003.

4. Interview with Bob Childers, Anchorage, July 29, 2003.

5. The Gwich'in will remain anonymous at their request. Already published comments by Gwich'in representatives may be quoted, and I do so in this chapter, citing the source. However, I paraphrase anonymous sources from my interviews with the Gwich'in during the two days in Arctic Village.

6. See Paul Ekins, ed. *The Living Economy: A New Economics in the Making* (London: Routledge, 1986) for a classic theoretical and interdisciplinary overview of sustainability.

7. Gwich'in Steering Committee protocol letter, distributed in Fairbanks prior to flight to Arctic Village.

8. Keynote address by Faith Gemmill, program director, Gwich'in Steering Committee, at the Alaska Native Health Consortium Annual Meeting, October 31, 2001, http://www.alaska.net/~gwich'in.

9. "Human Rights vs. Oil," a CorporateWatch interview with Sarah James, April 27, 2001.

10. In a note of irony, the office of the Alaska Oil and Gas Association in Anchorage displayed a picture of the Arctic Refuge on its wall, with the quote: "Save our heritage, the Arctic refuge." These were the same people who threw me out of their office when I merely asked for their views on the refuge.

11. "Alaska's Oil Melts Its Ice," BBC online, May 7, 2002. These claims are included in a film made by the Television Trust for the Environment, as part of its Earth Report series.

12. "Arctic's Loss of Sea Ice Linked to Warming Trend," *Los Angeles Times*, October 24, 2003. The study was conducted by NASA and was published in the *Journal of Climate*, November 1, 2003.

13. Chief Evon Peter, Arctic Village, "Oil and the Alaska Native Claims Settlement Act," the Alaska Oil and Gas Working Group, supported by Project Underground and the Indigenous Environmental Network, 2003, http://www.ienearth.org

14. Winona Duke, "Alaska: ANWR, Oil, and the Natives," April 7, 2003, http://www.yeoldconsciousnessshoppe.com.

15. "Oil and the Alaska Native Claims Settlement Act."

16. Dune Lanyard, Eyak Preservation Council, Eyak tribal member, "Oil and the Alaska Native Claims Settlement Act."

17. Alaska Oil and Gas Working Group, "Hit First and Hit Hardest."

18. "Alaska Natives Provide Personal Testimony of the Impacts of Global Warming, August 11, 1998, Greenpeace archive online, http://www.archive.greenpeace.org.

19. Rosemary Ahtuangaruak, "Oil Drilling Threatens Native Ways," *Anchorage Daily News*, April 1, 2003.

20. "Statement of Principles of the Native Oil and Gas Working Group," http://www.moles.org

21. E-mail from Evon Peter, March 2, 2004.

CHAPTER 8

1. Interview with anonymous source, July 14, 2003.

2. Murray Carpenter, "The Gwich'in and ANWR: The Most Anglican Group of People in the World Fight for the Right to Protect a Way of Life," *The Witness* archive (January–February, 2001), http://www.thewitness.org/archive.

3. Ibid.

4. Interview with Bob Childers, July 29, 2003.

5. Interview with Bishop Mark MacDonald, July 20, 2003.

6. Interview with Karen Lipinczyk, July 29, 2003. Lipinczyk holds a graduate degree in theology from the Graduate Theological Union at Berkeley and has been ordained for twenty-three years. She is a political activist as well and ran for the city council in Buffalo, New York. She has studied liberation theology, hermeneutics, feminism and women's spirituality, and animistic religions, and she has a background in anthropology.

CHAPTER 9

1. Margaret D. LeComte and Jean J. Schensul, *Designing and Conducting Ethnographic Research*, volumes 1 and 2 (Walnut Creek, CA: AltaMira Press, 1999).

2. Leggett, *The Carbon War*, 124.

3. The term "private governments" is taken from Peter Manicas's *The Death of the State* (New York, Capricorn Books, 1974), where he describes the ascendance of private governments in the evolution of the liberal state. The rhetoric of "public or civil liberties" is a conceptual smokescreen for the actual pursuit and accumulation of private property and wealth.

4. Bakan, *The Corporation*, 154.

5. Ibid, 155-6.

6. In a recent *Los Angeles Times* article, ExxonMobil is exposed for its funding of social science professors and academic studies designed to influence judicial decisions in favor of corporate defendants in punitive damage lawsuits. Corporate money—oil money—is infiltrating American academia: ExxonMobil has paid out an estimated $1 million, enough to fund 6,000 researchers, since 1994 when it was first ordered to pay out $5.3 billion in damages to Alaskan plaintiffs (an award it has still not paid due to ongoing appeals). It is literally bribing the judicial process, buying academicians along the way. See Alan Zarembo, "Funding Studies to Suit Need: In the 1990s, Exxon Began Paying for Research into Juries and the Damages They Award. The Findings Have Served the Firm Well in Court," *Los Angeles Times*, December 3, 2003.

7. Leggett, *The Carbon War*, 126.

8. David Goodstein, *Out of Gas: The End of the Age of Oil* (New York: W.W. Norton, 2004), 72–75.

9. Daniel Glick, "The Big Thaw," part of National Geographic's three-part series on global warming (September–November 2004).

10. Guy Gugliotta, "Study cites threat of global warming," *Washington Post*, January 8, 2004.

11. Goodstein, *Out of Gas*, 75.

12. Dr. David Jhirad, "Imagining the Unthinkable: Abrupt Climate Change," World Resources Institute, August 3, 2004. Jhirad is the vice president for science and research at the World Resources Institute.

13. David Stipp, "The Weather Nightmare," *Fortune* (February 9, 2004): According to Stipp, "The Pentagon agreed to share the results of its unclassified report with *Fortune*."

14. According to David Cobb, we need to "undo the legal fiction that corporations are 'persons' with Constitutional rights. A corporation is an artificial entity created by our state government to serve a public need, not an independent private entity with intrinsic 'rights.'" Quoted from "Corporate Power: The Perversion of the Promise of Democracy," the Program on Corporations, Law, and Democracy, http://www.poclad.org.

Bibliography

Ahtuangaruak, Rosemary. "Oil Drilling Threatens Native Ways." *Anchorage Daily News,* April 1, 2003.

Alaska Coalition. "National Members." http://www.alaskacoalition.org. November 4, 2003.

Alaska Conservation Foundation.. "Grants: Alpha List." http://www.akcf.org/grants. November 4, 2003.

Alaska Oil and Gas Working Group. "Hit First and Hit Hardest: Global Warming, the Oil Industry, and Alaska Natives." Project of the Indigenous and Environmental Network and Project Underground, 2003. http://www.moles.org. November 8, 2003.

Alaska Oil and Gas Working Group. "Oil and the Alaska Native Claims Settlement Act." Project of the Indigenous and Environmental Network and Project Underground, 2003. http://www.moles.org. November 8, 2003.

Alaska Oil and Gas Working Group. "Statement of Principles of the Native Oil and Gas Working Group." Project of the Indigenous and Environmental Network and Project Underground, 2003. http://www.moles.org. November 8, 2003.

Alaska Wilderness Coalition. "Senator Ted Stevens and Representative Don Young Biographies." Accessed October 15, 2003. http://www.capwiz.

Alaska Wilderness League. "Arctic National Wildlife Refuge: Boxer-Chafee Amendment." http://www.alaskawild.org. October 7, 2003.

Albo, Gregory, David Languille, and Leo Panitch, eds. *A Different Kind of State: Popular Power and Democratic Administration.* New York: Oxford University Press, 1993.

American Wilderness. "Votes on Arctic National Wildlife Refuge." http://www.americanwilderness.org. October 6, 2003.

Arctic Circle. University of Connecticut. http://www.arcticcircle.uconn.edu. October 8, 2003.

Arctic Power. http://www.anwr.org. May 10, 2003.

Arctic Power. "Top 10 Reasons to Support Development in ANWR." http://www.anwr.org. May 10, 2003.

Associated Press. "The Millionaires Club: Many Senators Worth at Least $1 Million." June 13, 2003. http://www.msnbc.com.

Atkinson, Adrian. *Principles of Political Ecology.* London: Belhaven Press, 1991.

Ayres, Ed. *God's Last Offer: Negotiating for a Sustainable Future.* New York: Four Walls Eight Windows, 1999.

Ayres, Robert U. *Turning Point: The End of the Growth Paradigm.* New York: St. Martin's Press, 1998.

Bacevich, Andrew J. *American Empire: The Realities and Consequences of U.S. Diplomacy.* Cambridge, MA: Harvard University Press, 2002.

Bakan, Joel. *The Corporation: The Pathological Pursuit of Profit and Power.* New York: Free Press, 2004.

Ballard, Chris, and Glenn Banks. "Resource Wars: The Anthropology of Mining." *Annual Review of Anthropology* 32: 287–313.

Banarjee, Neela. "BP Pulls Out of Campaign to Open Up Alaskan Area." Archive, New York Times, November 26, 2002. http://www.query.nytimes.com.

Barber, Benjamin R. *Jihad vs. McWorld: How Globalism and Tribalism Are Reshaping the World.* New York: Ballantine, 1995.

Barfield, Thomas, ed. *The Dictionary of Anthropology.* Malden, MA: Blackwell, 1997.

Barnett, Richard J., and John Cavanaugh. *Global Dreams: Imperial Corporations and the New World Order.* New York: Touchstone, 1995.

BBC online. "Alaska's Oil Melts Its Ice." May 7, 2002. http://news.bbc.co.uk.

Bell, Daniel A. *Communitarianism and Its Critics.* Oxford: Clarendon Press, 1993.

Bell, Daniel A. *East Meets West: Human Rights and Democracy in East Asia.* Princeton, NJ: Princeton University Press, 2000.

Bello, Walden. *The Future in the Balance: Essays on Globalization and Resistance.* Oakland, CA: Food First Books, 2001.

Berkes, Fikret. *Sacred Ecology: Traditional Ecological Knowledge and Resource Management.* Philadelphia: Taylor and Francis, 1999.

Bickel, Alexander. *The Morality of Consent.* New Haven, CT: Yale University Press, 1975.

Biersack, Aletta. "Introduction: From the 'New Ecology' to the New Ecologies." *American Anthropologist* 101: 1 (1999): 5–18.

Bird, Kenneth J. "Potential Oil and Gas Resources of the Arctic National Wildlife Refuge in Alaska: 1002 Area." *Polar Geography* 24: 1 (2000): 13–34.

Blum, Justin, "51–49 Senate Vote Backs Arctic Oil Drilling." Washington Post, March 17, 2005.

Bodley, John H. *Victims of Progress.* 4th ed. Mountain View, CA: Mayfield, 1999.

Boggs, Carl. *Imperial Delusions: American Militarism And Endless War.* Lanham, MD: Rowman & Littlefield, 2005.

Boggs, Carl. *The End of Politics: Corporate Power and the Decline of the Public Sphere.* New York: The Guilford Press, 2000.

Bolitho, Beth. "USA: Environmental Groups Look Ahead after Vote Against Oil Drilling in Arctic Reserve." *OneWorld US,* April 22, 2002. http://www.corpwatch.org.

Boulding, Kenneth E. *Three Faces of Power.* London: Sage, 1990.

Boxer, Senator Barbara. "Boxer Leads Bipartisan Fight to Save the Arctic Refuge." March 18, 2003. http://www.boxer.senate.gove.

Brand, Peter, and Alexander Bolton. "USA GOP Threats Halt GAO Cheney Suit." *The Hill.* February 20, 2003. http://www.corpwatch.org.

Brecher, Jeremy, and John Brown Childs eds. *Global Visions: Beyond the New World Order.* Boston: South End Press, 1993.

Brenner, Robert. "The Boom and the Bubble." *New Left Review* 6 (November–December 2000): 5–43.

Briody, Dan. *The Iron Triangle: Inside the Secret World of the Carlyle Group.* Hoboken, NJ: John Wiley & Sons, 2003.

British Petroleum. "BP North America." 2003 online report. http://www.bp.com.

British Petroleum. "Company Overview: Shocks and Successes." Accessed June 8, 2003. http://www.bp.com/company.

British Petroleum. "Investor Centre—Essential Investor Information—Executive Management." Accessed June 8, 2003. http://www.bp.com/investor_centre.

Brooks, Nancy Rivera. "Digging for Oil on Campus: ChevronTexaco Is Giving $5 million to USC to Develop New Technologies for Recovering Fossil Fuels. Is This the 'Corporatization' of Academia?" *Los Angeles Times,* December 14, 2003.

Brosius, J. Peter. "Local Knowledges, Global Claims: On the Significance of Indigenous Ecologies in Sarawak, East Malaysia." In *Indigenous Traditions and Ecology,* edited by J. Grimm and L. Sullivan, 125–57. Cambridge, MA: Harvard University Press and Center for the Study of World Religions, 2001.

Brosius, J. Peter. "The Politics of Ethnographic Presence: Sites and Topologies in the Study of Transnational Movements." In *New Directions in Anthropology and Environment,* edited by Carole L. Crumley, 150–77. Walnut Creek, CA: AltaMira Press, 2001.

Brosius, J. Peter. "Voices for the Borneo Rain Forest: Writing the History of an Environmental Campaign." In *Nature in the Global South: Environmental Projects in South and Southeast Asia,* edited by Paul R. Greennough and Anna Lowenhaupt Tsing, North Carolina: Duke University Press, 2003, 319–46.

Broswimmer, Franz J. *Ecocide: A Short History of the Mass Extinction of Species.* London: Pluto Press, 2002.

Brown, Lester R. "Crossing the Threshold: Early Signs of an Environmental Awakening." *World Watch* (March–April 1999): 12–22.

Bryant, Bunyan, ed. *Environmental Justice: Issues, Policies, and Solutions.* Washington, DC: Island Press, 1995.

Bryant, Raymond L. "Power, Knowledge, and Political Ecology in the Third World: A Review." *Progress in Physical Geography* 22:1 (1998): 79–94.

Bryant, Raymond L., and Sinead Bailey. 1992, "Political ecology: an Emerging Research Agenda in Third-World Studies," *Political Geography*, vol. 11, 12–36.

Bryant, Raymond L., and Sinead Bailey, eds. *Third World Political Ecology*. London: Routledge, 1997.

Bryson, George. "Unsuspecting Photographer's Arctic Explorations Spark Political Fire in Washington." Anchorage Daily News, May 25, 2003.

Carley, Michael, and Christie Ian. *Managing Sustainable Development*. Minneapolis: University of Minnesota Press, 1993.

Carpenter, Murray. "The Gwich'in and ANWR: The Most Anglican Group of People in the World Fight for the Right to Protect a Way of Life." *The Witness* archive (January–February 2001). http://www.thewitness.org.

Carrera, Alex. "Native Americans Speak against Arctic Refuge Drilling Plans." United Press International, February, 12, 2002.

Center for Public Integrity. "Trading in Favors: Soft Money Documents Imply Quid Pro Quo between Donors and Politicians." Washington DC: Center for Public Integrity, July 2, 2003.

Center for Responsive Politics. http://www.opensecrets.org.

Center for Responsive Politics. "Energy: Energy Bill." http://www.opensecrets.org.

Center for Responsive Politics. "Energy: Key Votes during the Debate of the Bush Energy Plan." www.opensecrets.org.

Center for Responsive Politics. "Frank H. Murkowski: 2002 Politician Profile." Accessed October 15, 2003. http://www.opensecrets.org.

Center for Responsive Politics. "High Mileage: The Auto Industry and Fuel Efficiency." March 5, 2002. http://www.opensecrets.org.

Center for Responsive Politics. "Oil and Gas Long-Term Contribution Trends." http://www.opensecrets.org.

Center for Responsive Politics. "Oil and Gas: Top Contributors 2004 Election Cycle." http://www.opensecrets.org/industries.

Center for Responsive Politics. "Oil and Gas: Top 20 Recipients." Accessed October 15, 2003. http://www.opensecrets.org.

Center for Responsive Politics. "Representative Don Young: 2004 Politician Profile." Accessed October 15, 2003. http://www.opensecrets.org/politicians/summary.

Center for Responsive Politics. "Senator Ted Stevens 2002 Election Cycle." http://www.opensecrets.org/politicians/summary.

Center for Responsive Politics. "Senator Ted Stevens: Top Industries Supporting Ted Stevens." Accessed October 15, 2003. http://www.opensecrets.org/politicians/industry.

Center for Responsive Politics. "Tracking the Payback. Energy: Key Votes during the Debate Of The Bush Energy Plan." Accessed October 19, 2003. http://www.opensecrets.org/industry.

Chatterjee, Pratap, and Oula Farawati. "To the Victors Go the Spoils of War: British Petroleum, Shell, and Chevron Win Iraqi Oil Contracts." *Corporate Watch*, August 8, 2003. http://www.corpwatch.org.

Chertow, Marion R., and Daniel C. Esty, eds. *Thinking Ecologically: The Next Generation of Environmental Policy*. New Haven, CT: Yale University Press, 1997.

Chomsky, Noam. *Hegemony or Survival: America's Quest for Global Dominance*. New York: Metropolitan, 2003.

Chomsky, Noam. *Manufacturing Consent: The Political Economy of the Mass Media*. New York: Pantheon, 1988.

Chomsky, Noam. *Profit over People: Neoliberalism and Global Order*. New York: Seven Stories Press, 1999.

Clark, Mary E. *Ariadne's Thread: The Search for New Modes of Thinking*. New York: St. Martin's Press, 1989.

Clark, Mary E. *In Search of Human Nature*. New York: Routledge, 2002.

Clay, Jason. "Armed Struggle and Indigenous People." *Cultural Survival Quarterly* 11 (4).

Clor, Harry M. "Forum on Public Morality: The Death of Public Morality." *The American Journal of Jurisprudence* 45 (2000): 33–49.

Cobb, David. "Corporate Power: The Perversion of the Promise of Democracy." The Program on Corporations, Law, and Democracy. http://www.poclad.org.

ConocoPhillips Petroleum. "ConocoPhillips Merger Completed." Newsroom 2002 News Release, August 30, 2002. http://www.phillips66.com.

ConocoPhillips Petroleum. "Worldwide Locations: North America-Alaska." Accessed June 10, 2003. http://www.phillips66.com.

Corporate Watch. "Campaigns: Climate Justice Initiative." May 9, 2002. http://www.corpwatch.org/campaigns.

Corporate Watch. "Climate Justice Initiative." December 10, 2001. http://www.corpwatch.org/campaigns.

Crumley, Carole L., ed. *New Directions in Anthropology and Environment*. Walnut Creek, CA: AltaMira Press, 2001.

Curry, Tom. "Is Alaska Drilling a 'Smokescreen'? Debate Diverts Attention from Other Items That Aid Oil Industry." MSN, March 29, 2002. http://www.msnbc.com/news.

Daly, Herman E., and, John B. Cobb Jr. *For the Common Good: Redirecting the Economy toward Community, the Environment, and a Sustainable Future*. Boston: Beacon, 1989.

De'Alessandro, Andres, and Hector Tobar. "Waves of Protests by the Poor Keep a Divided Bolivia on Edge." *Los Angeles Times*, October 7, 2003.

Defenders of Wildlife. "Arctic National Wildlife Refuge: Expert and Public Opinions, Scientific Opinions. United Nations Scientists Predict Arctic Ecosystem Impacts." Accessed May 23, 2003. http://www.defenders.org.

Defenders of Wildlife. "Issue in Detail: Saving the 'American Serengeti.'" Accessed May 23, 2003. http://www.defenders.org/wildlife/arctic.

Dobson, Andrew. *Green Political Thought.* 3d ed. New York: Routledge, 2000.

Doran, Christopher. "Blood for Oil: How Oil and Corporate Profits Drove the U.S. Invasion of Iraq." April 2004.

Douglass, Elizabeth. "Oil Supply Less Supple This Time." *Los Angeles Times,* April 7, 2003.

Dryzek, John S. *The Politics of the Earth: Environmental Discourses.* Oxford: Oxford University Press, 1997.

Dubose, Lou, Jan Reid, and Carl M. Cannon, *Boy Genius: Karl Rove, the Brains behind the Remarkable Political Triumph of George W. Bush.* New York: Public Affairs, 2003.

Earthjustice. "International Partnerships Program." Accessed June 24, 2003. http://www.earthjustice.org.

Eblen, Ruth A., and William R. Eblen, eds. *The Encyclopedia of the Environment.* New York: Houghton Mifflin, 1994.

Ecological Society of America. "Position Statement on the Arctic National Wildlife Refuge." Accessed May 23, 2002. http://www.esa.org/pao/arctic.

Economides, Michael, and Rodney Oligney. *The Color of Oil: The History, the Money, and the Politics of the World's Biggest Business.* Katy, TX: Round Oak Publishing, 2000.

Ehrlich, Paul and Anne. *One with Nineveh: Politics, Consumption, and the Human Future.* Washington, DC: Island Press, 2004.

Ekins, Paul. *A NEW World Order: Grassroots Movements for Global Change.* New York: Routledge, 1993.

Ekins, Paul, ed. *The Living Economy: A New Economics in the Making.* London: Routledge, 1986.

Ember, Melvin, ed. *Encyclopedia of World Cultures.* "Gwich'in." New York: Macmillan Reference USA, 2002.

Environment News Service. "USA: Against All Odds, Goldman Prize Winners Protect the Earth." April 23, 2002. http://www.ens-news.com.

Episcopal Diocese of Alaska. "The Bishop's Page." Accessed June 6, 2003. http://www.home.gci.net/~episcopalak.

Escobar, Arturo. "After Nature: Steps to an Antiessentialist Political Ecology." *Current Anthropology* 40:1 (February 1999).

Escobar, Arturo. *Encountering Development: The Making and Unmaking of the Third World.* Princeton, NJ: Princeton University Press, 1995.

Fineberg, Richard A. "Alaska Tax Structure and Charter for Alaska." E-mail to David Standlea, August 26, 2003.

Fineberg, Richard A. "The Arctic Refuge Coastal Plain: Pushing Development through a Litany of Lies." For Alaska Wilderness League and Northern Alaska Environmental Center, November 27, 1995.

Fineberg, Richard A. "Background on Randy Ruedrich and Doyon Drilling's North Slope Record." For Trustees for Alaska, February 19, 2003.

Fineberg, Richard A. *The Emperor's New Hose: How Big Oil Gets Rich Gambling with Alaska's Environment.* A status report on the Trans-Alaska Pipeline System, prepared for the Alaska Forum for Environmental Responsibility, June 2002.

Fineberg, Richard A. "Implications of BP's Failure at Badami for the Western Sector of the Arctic Refuge Coastal Plain." For Alaska Wilderness League, March 8, 2003.

Fineberg, Richard A. "Recent Articles Confirm Alaska North Slope Production Prospects without Arctic Refuge Exploration or Development." For Alaska Wilderness League, April 3, 2003.

Fineberg, Richard A. "Revenues from Proposed Leasing of the Arctic Refuge Coastal Plain." For Alaska Wilderness League, March 11, 2003.

Fineberg, Richard A. "Senator Mangles Arctic Refuge Facts." *Fairbanks Daily News-Miner,* March 30, 2003.

Fineberg, Richard A. "Setting the Record Straight on Interior Norton's Misleading Testimony before the House Resources Committee March 12." For Alaska Wilderness League, March 13, 2003.

Fineberg, Richard A. "Stevens Twists Facts in Pursuit of Arctic Refuge Oil." *Anchorage Daily News,* April 3, 2003.

Fineberg, Richard A. "Windfall Equal Sharing Tax: A Proposal by Oilwatch Alaska." Prepared for Oilwatch Alaska, February 11, 1999.

Forero, Juan. "Seeking Balance: Growth vs. Culture in Amazon." *New York Times,* December 10, 2003.

Fortune. "The 2002 Global 500: The World's Largest Corporations." http://www.fortune.com.

Gandhi, Ajay. "Indigenous Resistance to New Colonialism." *Cultural Survival.* Accessed April 28, 2002. http://www.cs.org/publications/CSQ/253/gandhi.

Gedicks, Al. *The New Resource Wars: Native and Environmental Struggles against Multinational Corporations.* Boston: South End Press, 1993.

Gedicks, Al. *Resource Rebels: Native Challenges to Mining and Oil Corporations.* Cambridge, MA: South End Press, 2001.

Gelbspan, Ross. *Boiling Point: How Politicians, Big Oil and Coal, Journalists, and Activists Have Fueled the Climate Crisis—and What We Can Do to Avert Disaster.* New York: Basic Books, 2004.

Gemmill, Faith, program director, Gwich'in Steering Committee. Keynote address at the Alaska Native Health Consortium Annual Meeting, October 31, 2001. http://www.alaska.net/~gwichin.

George, Robert P. "Forum on Public Morality: The Concept of Public Morality." *The American Journal of Jurisprudence* 45 (2000): 17–31.

Getter, Lisa. "Federal Worker Fired for Posting Refuge Map." *Los Angeles Times,* March 15, 2001.

Giddens, Anthony. *The Constitution of Society.* Berkeley: University of California Press, 1984.

Gills, Barry K., ed. *Globalization and the Politics of Resistance.* New York: Palgrave, 2001.

Gilman, Robert. "Design for a Sustainable Economics." *Context* 32: 52–59.

Glick, Daniel. "The Big Thaw." Part of National Geographic's, three-part series on global warming, September–November 2004.

Gonzales, George A. *Corporate Power and the Environment: The Political Economy of U.S. Environmental Policy.* New York: Rowman & Littlefield, 2001.

Goodstein, David. *Out of Gas: The End of the Age of Oil.* New York: W.W. Norton, 2004.

Gray, John. *False Dawn: The Delusions of Global Capitalism.* New York: The New Press, 1998.

Greenpeace Archive. "Alaska Natives Provide Personal Testimony of the Impacts of Global Warming." August 11, 1998. http://www.archive.greenpeace.org.

Greenpeace. "From Kiwis to Tigers—The Stop Exxon Campaign Spreads around the Globe." May 14, 2002. http://www.archive.greenpeace.org.

Greenpeace. "Greenpeace Activists Occupy BP's Control Centre En-Route to Controversial Arctic Oil Development." August 7, 2000. http://www.archive.greenpeace.org.

Greenpeace. "Greenpeace to Target U.S. Oil Companies." April 26, 2001. http://www.archive.greenpeace.org.

Greenpeace. "Historic Shareholder Vote against BP on Arctic Exploration Plans." April 13, 2000. http://www.archive.greenpeace.org.

Greenpeace. "Shareholders Vote against BP on Effect of Climate Change on Investments." April 19, 2001. http://www.archive.greenpeace.org.

Greenpeace. "Tactical Victory for U.S. and the Oil Industry: Greenpeace Calls on Scientific Community to Rise above Politics." April 22, 2002. http://www.archive.greenpeace.org.

Greider, William. *One World, Ready or Not: The Manic Logic of Global Capitalism.* New York: Simon & Schuster, 1997.

Grinde, Donald, and Bruce E Johansen. *Ecocide of Native America: Environmental Destruction of Indian Lands and Peoples.* Santa Fe, NM: Clear Light Publishers, 1995.

Gugliotta, Guy. "Study cites threat of global warming." *Washington Post*, January 8, 2004.

Gwich'in Steering Committee. Homepage. http://www.alaska.net/~gwichin.

Gwich'in Steering Committee. "Gwich'in Nation Calls Gathering in Alaska." May 23, 2001. http://www.corpwatch.org.

Gwich'in Steering Committee. Protocol letter. Fairbanks. July 15, 2003.

Handworker, W. Penn. *Quick Ethnography*. Walnut Creek, CA: AltaMira Press, 2001.

Hannum, Hurst. *Autonomy, Sovereignty, and Self-Determination: The Accommodation of Conflicting Rights*. Philadelphia: University of Pennsylvania Press, 1996.

Hartman, Thom. *The Last Hours of Ancient Sunlight: Waking Up to Personal and Global Transformation*. New York: Three Rivers Press, 1999.

Hartman, Thom. *Unequal Protection: The Rise of Corporate Dominance and the Theft of Human Rights*. Rodale, 2002.

Harvey, David. *The Condition of Postmodernity: An Enquiry into the Origins of Cultural Change*. Oxford: Blackwell, 1990.

Hebert, H. Josef. "Energy Dept.: Oil Imports Will Grow." Associated Press. November 20, 2002. http://www.anwr.org.

Heinberg, Richard. *The Party's Over: Oil, War, and the Fate of Industrial Societies*. Gabrida Island, BC, Canada: New Society, 2003.

Horta, Karinna. "Chad-Cameroon Oil Pipeline: ExxonMobil, Chevron, and the World Bank." *The Ecologist* archive. Accessed May 8, 2003. http://www.theecologist.org/archive.

Huffington, Arianna. *Pigs at the Trough: How Corporate Greed and Political Corruption Are Undermining America*. New York: Crown, 2003.

Indigenous Environmental Network and International Indian Treaty Council. "Stop Arctic Drilling, Support Native Rights." June 14, 2001. http://www.corpwatch.org.

Institute for Policy Studies. "New Database on World Bank Fossil Fuel Projects: First-of-Its-Kind Resource Catalogues $20 Billion in Dirty Energy Projects Since 1992." November 1, 2001. http://www.seen.org.

Institute of Social and Economic Research, University of Alaska, Anchorage. "Trends in Alaska's People and Economy." Anchorage: October 2001.

Inuit Circumpolar Conference. "Northern Contaminants and Global POP's Program." Archives. Accessed June 25, 2002. http://www.inuitcircumpolar.com.

James, Bernard J. *A Fourth World: An Anthropological-Ecological Look at the Twenty-first Century*. Lanham, MD: United Press of America, 1997.

James, Sarah. "Human Rights vs. Oil." A Corporate Watch Interview with Sarah James. April 27, 2001. http://www.corpwatch.org/campaigns.

Jhirad, Dr. David. "Imagining the Unthinkable: Abrupt Climate Change." World Resources Institute, August 3, 2004.

Johnson, Chalmers. *The Sorrows of Empire: Militarism, Secrecy, and the End of the Republic*. New York: Metropolitan Books, 2004.

Johnson, Huey D. *Green Plans: Greenprint for Sustainability*. Lincoln: University of Nebraska Press, 1995.

Johnson, John. "Victory for Arctic Drilling Opponents at BP General Meeting." Episcopal News Service, April 15, 2004.

Johnston, Barbara Rose, ed. *Life and Death Matters: Human Rights and the Environment at the End of the Millennium*. Walnut Creek, CA: AltaMira Press, 1997.

Johnston, Barbara Rose, ed. *Who Pays The Price? The Sociocultural Context of Environmental Crisis*. Washington, DC: Island Press, 1994.

Jones, Ken. *A Buddhist Political Ecology*. Oxford: Jon Carpenter, 1993.

Karliner, Joshua. *The Corporate Planet: Ecology and Politics in the Age of Globalization*. San Francisco: Sierra Club Books, 1997.

Kateb, George. *The Inner Ocean: Individualism and Democratic Culture*. Ithaca, NY: Cornell University Press, 1992.

Kauffman, John M. *Alaska's Brooks Range: The Ultimate Mountains*. Seattle: The Mountaineers, 1992.

Kearney, Michael. *Worldview*. Novato, CA: Chandler and Sharp, 1984.

Keck, Margaret E., and Kathryn Sikkink, eds. *Activists beyond Borders: Advocacy Networks in International Politics*. New York: Cornell University Press, 1998.

Kelly, Anne Keala. "Natives, Senators, and Oil: The Connection between Drilling in the Arctic National Wildlife Refuge and the Akaka Bill." *Hawaii Island Journal* (October 16–31, 2003).

Kennedy, Paul. *Preparing for the Twenty-first Century*. New York: Vintage, 1994.

Kennedy Jr., Robert F. "Crimes against Nature." *Rolling Stone*, December 11, 2003.

Kinsley, David. *Ecology and Religion: Ecological Spirituality in Cross-Cultural Perspective*. Englewood Cliffs, NJ: Prentice Hall, 1995.

Klare, Michael T. *Blood and Oil: The Dangers and Consequences of America's Growing Dependency on Imported Petroleum*. New York: Metropolitan Books, 2004.

Klare, Michael T. "Fighting for Oil—Still." The Nation, April 19, 2004.

Klare, Michael T. *Resource Wars: The New Landscape of Global Conflict*. New York: Metropolitan Books, 2001.

Kleveman, Lutz C. "The New Great Game: War on Iraq Is about a Lot More Than Boosting Oil Companies' Profits. It's the Latest Battle in the Ongoing War over Who Gets to Control the Earth's Remaining Energy Reserves." *The Ecologist* 33:3, (April 2003).

Knight, Danielle. "USA: Documents Show Bush Energy Plan Fuelled By Industry." Inter Press Service. March 28, 2002. http://www.corpwatch.org.

Kotlikoff, Laurence J., and Burns, Scott. *The Coming Generational Storm: What You Need to Know about America's Economic Future*. Cambridge, MA: MIT Press, 2004.

Krech III, Shepard. *The Ecological Indian: Myth and History*. New York: W.W. Norton, 1999.

Krugman, Paul. "Two Thousand Acres." Archive. *New York Times*, March 1, 2002. http://www.query.nytimes.com.

Kymlica, Will. *Multicultural Citizenship*. New York: Oxford University Press, 1996.

Labaton, Stephen. "F.T.C. Staff Urges Rejection of Deal By Two Oil Giants: BP Amoco and ARCO Merger Is Facing a Threat As Exxon and Mobil Join Forces." *New York Times*, December 1, 1999.

LaDuke, Winona. "Alaska: ANWR, Oil, and the Natives." April 7, 2003. http://www.yeoldconsciousnessshoppe.com.

LaDuke, Winona. "We Need a Seventh Generation Amendment." Detroit, MI: Southeast Michigan Coalition for Occupational Safety and Health SEMCOSH, 1997. http://www.semcosh.org.

Lakoff, George. "Framing the Dems: How Conservatives Control Political Debate and How Progressives Can Take It Back." *American Prospect* 14: 8. (September 1, 2003).

Lanyard, Dune. "Oil and the Alaska Native Claims Settlement Act." Indigenous Environmental Network and Project Underground. http://www.moles.org.

Lashoff, Daniel, et al. *Kingpins of Carbon: How Fossil Fuel Producers Contribute to Global Warming*. New York: Natural Resources Defense Council, 1999.

Lazaroff, Cat. "Bush's Reversal on Greenhouse Gas Cuts." Environment News Service, March 14, 2001.

Lazaroff, Cat. "Cheney Vows to Stick with Fossil Fuels." Environment News Service, May 1, 2001.

LeComte, Margaret D., and Jean J Schensul. *Designing and Conducting Ethnographic Research, vol. 1*. Walnut Creek, CA: AltaMira Press, 1999.

LeComte, Margaret D., and Jean J. Schensul. *Essential Ethnographic Methods: Observations, Interviews, and Questionnaires, vol. 2*. Walnut Creek, CA: AltaMira Press, 1999.

Leggett, Jeremy. *The Carbon War: Global Warming and the End of the Oil Era*. New York: Routledge, 2001.

Lewis, Charles, and the Center for Public Integrity. *The Buying of the President 2004: Who's Really Bankrolling Bush and His Democratic Challengers—and What They Expect in Return*. New York: Perennial, 2004.

Little, Paul E. "Environmentalists and Environmentalisms in Anthropological Research: Facing the New Millennium." *Annual Review of Anthropology*. Vol. 28, 253–284.

Los Angeles Times. "Energy's Pals in High Places." Editorial. September 15, 2003.

Loy, Wesley. "Oil Called Key to Budget Balance." *Anchorage Daily News*, February 13, 2003.

Lynas, Mark. "Oil Companies Wreak Destruction from Arctic Circle to Nigeria." Oneworld.net, November 19, 2000. http://www.corpwatch.org.

MacDonald, Mark. Statement to BP Shareholders, London, England: April, 2004.

Magin, Georgina, and Chanda Meek. "Forests of Fear: The Abuse of Human Rights in Forest Conflicts." London, England: Fern, 2001.

Mander, Jerry, and Edward Goldsmith, eds. *The Case against the Global Economy: And for a Turn toward the Local*. New York: Sierra Club Books, 1996.

Manicas, Peter. *The Death of the State*. New York: Capricorn Books, 1974.

Manning, Richard. "The Oil We Eat: Following the Food Chain Back to Iraq." *Harper's*, vol. 303, no. 1845 (February 2004).

Manuel, Athan. "The Arctic Refuge, the 'Filthy Four,' and Organized Labor." Washington, DC: U.S. Public Interest Research Group, November 7, 2001.

Manuel, Athan. "The Dirty Four: The Case against Letting BP Amoco, ExxonMobil, Chevron, and Phillips Petroleum Drill in the Arctic Refuge." Washington, DC: U.S. Public Interest Research Group, March 22, 2001.

Manuel, Athan. "Green Words, Dirty Deeds: A PIRG Expose of BP Amoco's Greenwashing." Washington, DC: U.S. Public Interest Research Group, October 1999. <http://www.prig.org>

Manuel, Athan. "No Refuge: The Oil Industry's Million Dollar Campaign to Open Up the Arctic." Washington, DC: U.S. Public Interest Research Group, February 1999.

Marshall, Steve, president, British Petroleum Exploration Alaska. "2003 Charter Report to Governor of Alaska Murkowski." http://www.alaska.bp.com/alaska/statereports/2003Report/presidentasp.

Martin, Calvin Luther. *In the Spirit of the Earth: Rethinking History and Time*. Baltimore, MD: Johns Hopkins University Press, 1992.

Martinez, Maria Elena, and Joshua Karliner. "Iraq and the Axis of Oil." Opinion. *Corporate Watch*, October, 23, 2002. http://www.corpwatch.org.

McCarthy, James. "First World Political Ecology: Lessons from the Wise Use Movement." *Environment and Planning* A 34 (2002): 1281–1302.

McCuen, Gary E. *Ecocide and Genocide in the Vanishing Forest: The Rainforest and Native People, Ideas in Conflict*. Hudson, WI: Gary E. McCuen Publications, 1993.

McDonough, William, and Michael Braungart. *Cradle to Cradle: Remaking the Way We Make Things*. New York: North Point Press, 2002.

McFarling, Usha Lee. "Arctic's Biggest Ice Shelf, a Sentinel of Climate Change, Cracks Apart." *Los Angeles Times*, September 23, 2003.

McFarling, Usha Lee. "Arctic's Loss of Sea Ice Linked to Warming Trend: NASA's New Satellite Data Show the Creation of More Open Water in the Region, Despite Inconsistencies in Heat around the Globe." *Los Angeles Times*, October 24, 2003.

McKibben, Bill. *The End of Nature*. New York, Anchor Books, 1999.

Merchant, Carolyn, ed. *Major Problems in American Environmental History*. Lexington, MA: Heath, 1993.

Metzner, Ralph. "The Transition to an Ecological Worldview," *Green Psychology: Transforming Our Relationship to the Earth*. Rochester, VT: Park Street Press, 1999.

Micklethwait, John, and Adrian Wooldridge. *The Right Nation: Conservative Power in America*. New York: Penguin, 2004.

Mikkelson, Randall. "USA: Bush Calls for More Coal, Oil, and Nukes." Reuters, May 17, 2001.

Miller, Debbie S. *Midnight Wilderness: Journeys in Alaska's Arctic National Wildlife Refuge*. Portland, OR: Alaska Northwest Books, 2000.

Miller, Pamela A. "Broken Promises: The Reality of Big Oil in America's Arctic." Washington, DC: Wilderness Society, 2003.

Miller, T. Christian. "Army Turns to Private Guards: The Military Is Criticized for Risking Security at Bases and for a Process That Awarded $1 billion in Contracts without Competitive Bidding." *Los Angeles*, Times August 12, 2004.

Miller, T. Christian. "ChevronTexaco Pollution Trial Begins: Ecuador Lawsuit Is a Test of Whether a Court Can Hold a Foreign Company Responsible for Damage to the Environment." *Los Angeles Times*, October 23, 2003.

Miller, T. Christian. "Contracts Take Alaska to Iraq: Native Firms Can Bypass Normal Bidding. Some Say It Speeds Rebuilding; Others Are Skeptical." *Los Angeles Times*, March 7, 2004.

Miller, T. Christian. "The Politics of Petroleum, Riding Shotgun on a Pipeline: Going Beyond the War on Drugs, the U.S. Backs Columbian Troops in a Campaign against Rebels That Protects an Oil Company's Operations." *Los Angeles Times*, May 16, 2004.

Mills, C. Wright. *The Power Elite: New Edition*. New York: Oxford University Press, 2000.

Milton, Kay, ed. *Environmentalism: The View from Anthropology*. New York: Routledge, 1995.

Mitchell, Donald Craig. *Take My Land, Take My Life: The Story of Congress's Historic Settlement of Alaska Native Land Claims, 1960–1971*. Fairbanks: University of Alaska Press, 2001.

Mokhiber, Russell, and Robert Weissman. "Wartime Opportunists." Focus on the Corporation, September 6, 2001. http://www.corpwatch.org.

Morton, Pete. "Arctic Refuge Drilling or Clean Energy?" Washington, DC: Wilderness Society, February 2002.

MSNBC Staff and Wire Reports. "Report: Arctic Refuge Drilling Risky: Interior Department Agencies Say Special Steps Would Be Necessary." March 29, 2002. http://www.msnbc.com/news/731219.

Murkowski, Senator Lisa. "Senator Lisa Murkowski Speech to the Alaska Legislature." April 25, 2003. Senate Web site. http://www.murkowski.senate.gov./legislaturesspeech4-25.

Murphy, Kim. "Jailed Tycoon Resigns from Oil Giant." *Los Angeles Times,* November 6, 2003.

Natural Resources Defense Council. "America's Western Arctic Is In Danger." Washington, DC: Natural Resources Defense Council, 2003.

Natural Resources Defense Council and Union of Concerned Scientists. "Kingpins of Carbon: How Fossil Fuel Producers Contribute to Global Warming." Washington, DC: Natural Resources Defense Council, 1999.

Neubauer, Chuck, and Richard T. Cooper. "Senator's Way to Wealth Was Paved with Favors: Ted Stevens Has Always Delivered for His Friends in Alaska. Now, with Their Help, He Has Become Part of 'the Millionaires' Club.' " *Los Angeles Times,* December 17, 2003.

Nietschmann, Bernard. "Militarization and Indigenous Peoples: The Third World War." *Cultural Survival Quarterly* 11 (3).

Oilwatch. "Statement on the occasion of the World Bank and IMF Meetings." April 15, 2000. http://www.corpwatch.org/issues.

Olukoya, Sam. "Environmental Justice from the Niger Delta to the World Conference against Racism." Special to Corporate Watch. August 30, 2001. http://www.corpwatch.org/issues.

Paehlke, Robert, ed. *Conservation and Environmentalism: An Encyclopedia.* New York: Garland, 1995.

Palast, Greg. *The Best Democracy Money Can Buy: The Truth about Corporate Cons, Globalization, and High-Finance Fraudsters.* New York: Plume, 2003.

Parker, Walter B. "Lower Pipeline Tariffs Deserve Look." Anchorage Daily News, January 3, 2003.

Peet, Richard, and Michael Watts, eds. *Liberation Ecologies: Environment, Development, Social Movements.* New York: Routledge, 1996.

Peluso, Nancy Lee, and Michael Watts, eds. *Violent Environments.* Ithaca, NY: Cornell University Press, 2001.

Phillips, Kevin. *Wealth and Democracy: A Political History of the American Rich.* New York: Broadway Books, 2002.

Pianin, Eric, and Helen Dewar. "New GOP Power May Spur Energy Industries." *Washington Post,* November 19, 2002. http://www.anwr.org.

Picchi, Debra. *The Bakairi Indians of Brazil: Politics, Ecology, and Change.* Long Grove: Waveland, 2000.

Planet Ark. "Equador Amazon Indians Appeal Texaco-Case Ruling." March 13, 2002. http://www.planetark.org.

Prial, Dunstan. "Merger Rumor Sends Shares of Chevron, Phillips Petroleum Higher." Associated Press, September 12, 2000.

Project Underground. http://www.moles.org.

Project Underground. "Former UNOCAL Consultant Appointed U.S. Special Envoy to Afghanistan." *Drillbits & Tailings* 7: 1 (January 31, 2002).

Project Underground. "Greasing the Machine: Bush, His Cabinet, and Their Oil Connections." *Drillbits & Tailings* 6: 5 (June 30, 2001).

Project Underground. "How Oil Interests Play Out in U.S. Bombing of Afghanistan." *Drillbits & Tailings* 6: 8 (October 31, 2001). http://www.moles.org/Project Underground/drillbits/6_08.

Project Underground. "Indigenous Communities at the Edge." Accessed May 11, 2002. http://www.moles.org.

Project Underground. "Militarization and Minerals Tour: Introduction." Accessed April 19, 2002. http://www.moles.org.

Project Underground. "Oil Campaign: Oil, the World Trade Organization, and Globalization." Accessed May 10, 2002. http://www.moles.org.

Renner, Michael. "The Anatomy of Resource Wars." *World Watch* Paper 162 (October 2002).

Renner, Michael. "Iraq Occupation Report: Control of Oil Revenues." *Foreign Policy in Focus* (September 2003).

Renner, Michael. "The New Oil Order: Washington's War on Iraq Is the Lynchpin to Controlling Persian Gulf Oil." *Foreign Policy in Focus* (February 14, 2003).

Reuters. "International Energy Agency: Energy Watchdog Sees Tight Crude Supplies This Winter." October 11, 2003. http://www.reuters.com.

Reuters. "Payments to Cheney Questioned: Deferred Compensation to Vice President from His Former Employer, Halliburton Co., Stirs Complaints from Senate Democrats." *Los Angeles Times,* September 17, 2003.

Rifkin, Jeremy. "Bush Plan for Hydrogen Is Just Hot Air." *Los Angeles Times,* November 9, 2003.

Roach, John. "By 2050 Warming to Doom Million Species." *National Geographic News* (July 12, 2004).

Roberts, Paul. *The End of Oil: On the Edge of a Perilous New World.* New York: Houghton Mifflin, 2004.

Roberts, Paul. "Running Out of Oil—and Time." *Los Angeles Times,* March 7, 2004.

Roche Jr., Walter F. "Private, Public Roles Overlap in Washington: Insiders Are Advising Officials and Working for Businesses That Profit from Government Contracts. It's a Growing Pattern of Networking." *Los Angeles Times,* August 8, 2004.

Rohmann, Chris. *A World of Ideas: A Dictionary of Important Theories, Concepts, Beliefs, and Thinkers.* New York: Ballantine Books, 1999.

Roodman, David Malin. "Reforming Subsidies." *State of the World 1997, World Watch.* New York: WW Norton.

Rosen,Yereth, Reuters. "USA: Pipeline Leaks Oil on Alaska Tundra." April, 17, 2001. http:www.corpwatch.org.

Ross, Ken. *Environmental Conflict in Alaska.* Boulder: University Press of Colorado, 2000.

Royce, Knut, and Nathaniel Heller. "Cheney Led Halliburton to Feast at Federal Trough: State Department Questioned Deal with Firm Linked to Russian Mob." An Investigative Report of the Center for Public Integrity. August 2, 2001. http://www.public-i.org.

Ruskin, Liz. "AFL-CIO's Biggest Union Opposes ANWR Drilling." *Anchorage Daily News,* October 31, 2001.

Ruskin, Liz. "ANWR to Stay in House Energy Bill." *Anchorage Daily News,* April 11, 2003.

Ruskin, Liz. "Gas Line Added to Energy Bill, No ANWR." *Anchorage Daily News,* March 27, 2003.

Ruskin, Liz. "Narrow Vote Keeps ANWR Out of Senate's Budget Bill." *Anchorage Daily News,* March 20, 2003.

Sachs, Aaron. "Upholding Human Rights and Environmental Justice." *State of the World 1996, World Watch.* New York: W.W. Norton.

Sachs, Jeffrey. "Jeffrey Sachs on Nature and Economic Development: Four Critiques." *CNS* 9: 2, (June 1998):113–23.

Sampson, Anthony. *The Seven Sisters: The Great Oil Companies and the World They Made.* London: Hodder and Stoughton, 1975.

Scherer, Glenn. "Religious Wrong: God's Role in the Republican Assault on the Environment." *Hartford Advocate,* May 8, 2003.

Sheasby, Walt Contreras. "The Coming Panic over the End of Oil—Coming to a Ballot Box Near You." July 4, 2003. Ecopolitics Online Discussion List.

Shklar, Judith. "The Liberalism of Fear." In *Liberalism and the Moral Life,* edited by Nancy Rosenblum. Cambridge, MA: Harvard University Press, 1989.

Shogan Cindy. "2004 Budget Resolution Passes with No Arctic Drilling Provisions." Alaska Wilderness League. Accessed June 24, 2003. http:www.alaskawild.org.

Sierra Club. "The Arctic National Wildlife Refuge: America's Natural Treasure in Peril." Washington, DC: Sierra Club 2003.

Sierra Club. "The Arctic National Wildlife Refuge: Drilling for Oil in the Arctic National Wildlife Refuge Won't Address National Security or Consumer Needs." Accessed May 9, 2002. http:www.sierraclub.org/wildlands/arctic/oilfactsheet.

Sierra Club. "Crude Behavior: Arctic National Wildlife Refuge." http://www.sierraclub.org.

Sierra Club. "Pick Your Poison: An Environmentalist's Guide to Gasoline." Accessed March 26, 2002. http://www.sierraclub.org/sierra/200109.

Silverstein, Ken. "Politics of Petroleum, Gusher to a Few, Trickle to the Rest: Courted By Oil Firms and the U.S., the Elite of Impoverished Angola Has Extracted Wealth in the Process." *Los Angeles Times,* May 13, 2004.

Silverstein, Ken. "The Politics of Petroleum, Oil Adds Sheen to Kazakh Regime: American Now Facing Federal Charges Directed a PR Effort Involving Former U.S. Officials." *Los Angeles Times,* May 12, 2004.

Silverstein, Ken. "With War, Africa Oil Beckons: The U.S. Trying to Cut Its Dependence on Mideast Crude, Hopes a Chad-Cameroon Pipeline Will Deliver." *Los Angeles Times,* March 21, 2003.

Simon, Richard. "Arctic Drilling Gets New Push by GOP." *Los Angeles Times,* September 23, 2003.

Simon, Richard. "Arctic Drilling Vote Looks Close." *Los Angeles Times,* March 17, 2003.

Simon, Richard. "Energy Bill Seen As a Gusher of Industry Breaks." *Los Angeles Times,* April 10, 2003.

Simon, Richard. "Tribes Mine New Opportunities in Energy Projects." *Los Angeles Times,* October 16, 2003.

Singer, Beth J. *Pragmatism, Rights, and Democracy.* New York: Fordham University Press, 1999.

Singer, Peter W. *Corporate Warriors: The Rise of the Privatized Military Industry.* Ithaca, NY: Cornell University Press, 2003.

Slack, Keith. "Poor vs. Profit in Bolivian Revolt." *Los Angeles Times,* October 19, 2003.

Smith, Eric Alden, and Joan McCarter, eds. *Contested Arctic: Indigenous Peoples, Industrial States, and the Circumpolar Environment.* Seattle: University of Washington Press, 1997.

Smith, Linda Tuhiwai. *Decolonizing Methodologies: Research and Indigenous Peoples.* New York: Zed Books, 1999.

Speer, Lisa. "Tracking Arctic Oil: The Environmental Price of Drilling the Arctic National Wildlife Refuge." Washington, DC: Natural Resources Defense Council.

Sponsel, Leslie E. "Do Anthropologists Need Religion, and Vice Versa? Adventures and Dangers in Spiritual Ecology." In *New Directions in Anthropology and Environment,* edited by Carole L. Crumley, 177–203. Walnut Creek, CA: Alta Mira, 2001.

Sponsel, Leslie E. "Excrement of the Devil: Oil Strikes in the Amazon." From Course Anthropology 435 Web site, University of Hawaii, November 26, 2003. http://mail.hawaii.edu.

Sponsel, Leslie E. "Human Impact on Biodiversity, Overview." *Encyclopedia of Biodiversity,* vol. 3. New York: Academic Press, 2001.

Starr, Amory. *Naming the Enemy: Anti-Corporate Movements Confront Globalization.* New York: Zed Books, 2000.

State of Alaska, Department of Community and Economic Development. "The Regulatory Commission of Alaska Rejects Rates for the 1997–2000 Intrastate Trans-Alaska Pipeline System, Sets Just and Reasonable Rates, and Requires Refunds and Filings By Carriers." Anchorage: November 27, 2002. http://www.dced.state.ak.us.

State of Alaska, Department of Natural Resources, Division of Oil and Gas. "Alaska's April 2003 Oil and Gas Production and May 2003 Revenue." Accessed June 23, 2003. http://www.dog.dnr.state.alc.us/oil.

State of Alaska, Department of Natural Resources, Division of Oil and Gas. 2001 Report: "North Slope Areawide 2001 Sale Results Summary." http://www.dog.dnr.state.alc.us/oil.

State of Alaska, Department of Natural Resources, Division of Oil and Gas. 2000 Report: "North Slope Areawide 2000 Sale Results Summary." Accessed May 21, 2003. http://www.dog.dnr.state.dlc.us/oil.

State of Alaska, Department of Natural Resources, Division of Oil and Gas. "North Slope Areawide 1999 Competitive Oil and Gas Lease Sale Results Summary." Accessed June 23, 2003. http://www.dog.dnr.state.ak/us/oil/products/publications/northslope.

State of Alaska, Governor's Office. *Charter for Development of the Alaskan North Slope*. June 30, 2003. http://www.gov.state.alc.us.

Steger, Manfred B. *Globalism: The New Market Ideology*. Lanham, MD: Rowman & Littlefield, 2002.

Stevens, Ted. http://www.stevens.senate.gov.

Stevis, Dimitris, and Valerie J. Assetto, eds. *The International Political Economy of the Environment*. Boulder, CO: Lynne Rienner, 2001.

Stiglitz, Joseph E. *Globalization and Its Discontents*. New York: W.W. Norton, 2002.

Stipp, David. "The Weather Nightmare." *Fortune* (February 9, 2004): 101–106.

Taylor, Bron Raymond, ed. *Ecological Resistance Movements: The Global Emergence of Radical and Popular Environmentalism*. Albany: State University of New York Press, 1995.

Taylor, Jerry, and Dan Becker. "A Complete Waste of Energy." *Los Angeles Times*, October 29, 2003.

The Ecologist. "Lee Raymond Is the Head of Oil Multinational Exxon, Known in the UK As Esso." Archive, May 22, 2001. http://www.theecologist.org/archive.

The Washington Post. "Halliburton Scores Big Off Iraq." MSN Online. August 28, 2003. http://www.msn.com/news.

Thomas, Chris D. "Extinction Risk from Climate Change." *Nature* 427, (January 8, 2004).

Tobar, Hector. "Protest Swelling in Bolivian Plaza." *Los Angeles Times*, October 16, 2003.

Tokar, Brian. *Earth for Sale: Reclaiming Ecology in the Age of Corporate Greenwash.* Boston: South End Press, 1997.

Townsend, Patricia K. *Environmental Anthropology: From Pigs to Policies.* Long Grove: Waveland, 2000.

Tribe, Laurence. *American Constitutional Law.* 3d ed. New York: Foundation Press, 2000.

Trustees for Alaska. "The Battle over Allowing Oil Development in the Arctic National Wildlife Refuge: Myths and Facts about the '2,000-acre Footprint.'" http://www.trustees.org.

Tucker, Mary Evelyn, and Duncan Ryuken Williams, eds. *Buddhism and Ecology: The Interconnection of Dharma and Deeds.* Cambridge, MA: Harvard University Press, 1997.

Turner, Tom. *Justice on Earth: Earthjustice and the People It Has Served.* White River Jct.: Chelsea Green, 2002.

United Nations Environment Program. *Global Environment Outlook 3.* London: Earthscan, 2002.

United States Fish and Wildlife Service. Arctic National Wildlife Refuge. "Conversations about Caribou: Caribou Migration." Accessed May 9, 2002. http://www.r7.fws.gov/nwr/arctic.

United States General Accounting Office Report GAO-03-894. "Energy Task Force: Process Used to Develop the National Energy Policy." Washington, DC: General Accounting Office August 2003.

United States Geological Survey. Biological Science Report: "Arctic Refuge Coastal Plain Terrestrial Wildlife Research Summaries." United States Department of Interior Geological Survey, Washington, DC, 2002.

United States Geological Survey. Department of the Interior. "Arctic National Wildlife Refuge, 1002 Area, Petroleum Assessment, including Economic Analysis." 2001. USGS, Washington, DC.

United States Geological Survey. "Guide to Alaska Geologic and Mineral Information." Information Circular 44. United States Geological Survey, Washington, DC, 2002.

United States Geological Survey. "U.S. Geological Survey 2002 Petroleum Resource Assessment of the National Petroleum Reserve in Alaska (NPRA)." United States Department of the Interior, U.S. Geological Survey, Washington, DC.

United States Public Interest Research Group. "BP Drops Out of Arctic Power, Stops Lobbying to Drill in Arctic Refuge: Company Responds to PIRG Campaign Urging BP to Stay Out of America's Arctic." November 25, 2002. http://www.savethearctic.com/arctic.

United States Public Interest Research Group. "False Profits: The Business Case against Drilling in the Arctic National Wildlife Refuge." Rev. ed., March 2003. http://www.savethearctic.com/arctic.

United States Public Interest Research Group. Save the Arctic Campaign. "Our Po-
    litical Campaign." September 17, 2003. http://www.pirg.org.

United States Public Interest Research Group. Save the Arctic Campaign. "Senate
    Rejects Arctic Refuge Drilling Amendment: Turns Back Attempt By Oil industry,
    Bush Administration to Allow Drilling in America's Arctic." April 18, 2002. http:/
    /www.pirg.org.

Vallette, Jim, and Pratap Chatterjee. "Guarding the Oil Underworld in Iraq." Special
    to Corporate Watch. September 5, 2003. http://www.corpwatch.org.

Vayda, Andrew P., and Bradley B. Walters. "Against Political Ecology." *Human Ecology*
    27: 1: 167–79.

Vayda, Andrew P. 1983. "Progressive Contextualization: Methods for Research in
    Human Ecology." *Human Ecology* 11: 265–81.

Vidal, Gore. *Dreaming War: Blood for Oil and the Cheney-Bush Junta*. New York: Nation
    Books, 2002.

Vidal, Gore. *Perpetual War for Perpetual Peace: How We Got to Be So Hated*. New York:
    Nation Press, 2002.

Vieth, Warren, and Elizabeth Douglass. "Gauging Promise of Iraqi Oil: Ousting
    Hussein Could Open the Door for U.S. and British Firms. French, and Russian,
    and Chinese Rivals Would Lose Their Edge." *Los Angeles Times*, March 12, 2003.

Voice of the Times: A Conservative Voice for Alaskans. "Perpetuating the Old ANWR
    Lies." *Anchorage Daily News*, April 4, 2003.

Wade, Robert. "Showdown at the World Bank." *New Left Review* 7 (January–Febru-
    ary 2001): 124-37.

Walker, Peter A. "Reconsidering 'Regional' Political Ecologies: Toward a Political
    Ecology of the American West." *Progress in Human Geography* 27: 1 (January 2003).

Wallerstein, Immanuel. *The End of the World As We Know It: Social Science for the
    Twenty-first Century*. Minneapolis: University of Minnesota Press, 1999.

Wallerstein, Immanuel. *Geopolitics and Geoculture*. New York: Press Syndicate of the
    University of Cambridge, 1994.

Watt-Cloutier, Sheila. "Local/Global Linkages for Sustainable Development." United
    Nations, New York City, February 6, 2002. Inuit Circumpolar Conference http://
    www.inuitcircumpolar.com.

Weart, Spencer R. *The Discovery of Global Warming*. London: Harvard University
    Press, 2003.

Wilderness Society. http://www.wilderness.org.

Wilderness Society. "Alaska National Interest Lands Conservation Act." Washington,
    DC: Wilderness Society, 2001. http://www.wilderness.org.

Wilson, Patricia. "USA: Bush Task Force to Recommend Alaska Drilling." Reuters,
    April 23, 2001.

Wolfe, Christopher. "Forum on Public Morality: Public Morality and the Modern Supreme Court." *The American Journal of Jurisprudence* 45 (2000): 65–92.

World Watch Institute. *State of the World 1999.* New York: W.W. Norton, 1999.

World Watch Institute. *State of the World 2002.* New York: W.W. Norton, 2002.

Worster, Donald. *Nature's Economy: A History of Ecological Ideas.* 2d ed. New York: Cambridge University Press, 1994.

Yergin, Daniel. *The Prize: The Epic Quest for Oil, Money, and Power.* New York: Simon and Schuster, 1992.

Zarembo, Alan. "Funding Studies to Suit Need: In the 1990s, Exxon Began Paying for Research into Juries and the Damages They Award. The Findings Have Served the Firm Well in Court." *Los Angeles Times,* December 3, 2003.

Index